Citizenship through Secondary History

Citizenship education is now a statutory part of the secondary school National Curriculum; and history is one of the key subjects through which citizenship must be taught. This is the first book available to lead professional and student teachers alike through this new and challenging development in the curriculum.

Citizenship through Secondary History reveals the potential of history to engage with citizenship education; it includes:

- a review of the links between citizenship education and the teaching and learning of history;
- an analysis of how citizenship education is characterised, raising key issues about what could and should be achieved;
- a critique of the discipline and the pitfalls to avoid in teaching citizenship through history;
- case studies, including one on slavery, offering practical teaching suggestions.

History teaching is at the vanguard of citizenship education; the past is the springboard from which citizens learn to think and act. This book offers positive and direct ways to get involved in the thinking that must underpin any worthwhile citizenship education, for all professional teachers, student teachers in history, heads of department, principals and policy makers.

James Arthur is Professor of Education at Canterbury Christ Church University College. **Ian Davies** is Senior Lecturer in Educational Studies at the University of York. **Andrew Wrenn** is Adviser for History and Citizenship at Cambridgeshire Education Authority. **Terry Haydn** is Senior Lecturer in Education at the University of East Anglia. **David Kerr** is Principal Research Fellow at the National Foundation for Educational Research.

Citizenship Education in Secondary Schools Series
Series Editor: John Moss
Canterbury Christ Church University College

Citizenship through Secondary Geography
Edited by David Lambert and Paul Machon

Citizenship through Secondary History
James Arthur, Ian Davies, Andrew Wrenn, Terry Haydn and David Kerr

Citizenship through Secondary English
John Moss

Citizenship through Secondary History

James Arthur, Ian Davies,
Andrew Wrenn, Terry Haydn
and David Kerr

London and New York

First published 2001
by RoutledgeFalmer
11 New Fetter Lane, London EC4P 4EE

Simultaneously published in the USA and Canada
by Routledge
29 West 35th Street, New York, NY 10001

RoutledgeFalmer is an imprint of the Taylor & Francis Group

© 2001 James Arthur, Ian Davies, Andrew Wrenn,
Terry Haydn and David Kerr

Typeset in Baskerville by
Keystroke, Jacaranda Lodge, Wolverhampton
Printed and bound in Great Britain by
St Edmundsbury Press, Bury St Edmunds, Suffolk

British Library Cataloguing in Publication Data
A catalogue record for this book is available from the British Library

Library of Congress Cataloging in Publication Data
A catalog record for this book has been requested

ISBN 0–415–24001–8

Contents

PART III
Conclusions **159**

Figures

Tables

Boxes

Authors

James Arthur is Professor of Education at Canterbury Christ Church University College and his work is located in the field of 'critical policy scholarship'. He has also developed a published record in the relationship between theory and practice in history teaching in schools. He has written widely on Church education policy and has also written on links between communitarianism, social virtues, citizenship and education. He has been a member of a number of national groups including the National Forum on Education and Values in the Community, the History Task Group and the DfEE Citizenship and Teacher Training Group. His publications include: *Schools and Community: the communitarian agenda in education* (Falmer), *Social Literacy and the National Curriculum* (Falmer), (edited) *Issues in Teaching History* (Routledge), *Teaching History in the Secondary School* (Routledge), *The Thomist Tradition in Education* (Gracewing) and *The Ebbing Tide* (Gracewing).

Ian Davies is a Senior Lecturer in Educational Studies at the University of York. His previous experience includes ten years as a teacher in comprehensive schools in England. At York he is Director of Undergraduate Studies in Education, leads the PGCE history and history citizenship courses, and supervises graduate research. He is the co-author of *Using Documents* (English Heritage), co-editor of *Developing European Citizens* (Sheffield Hallam University Press), co-author of *Good Citizenship and Educational Provision* (Falmer) and the editor of *Teaching the Holocaust* (Continuum). He is a member of the DfEE Citizenship and Teacher Training Group.

Andrew Wrenn is an Adviser for History and Citizenship in Cambridgeshire Education Authority. He was appointed to this role in 1997, following successive posts as head of history at comprehensive schools for 11–18-year-olds in Wiltshire and Gloucestershire. He leads training and professional devblepment courses at national and local level and is a member of the Historical Association Secondary Education Committee. Andrew has published teaching materials for Cambridge University Press, the BBC and Longmans, also contributing articles to the *Times Educational Supplement* and *History Teaching*.

Terry Haydn is a Senior Lecturer in Education at the University of East Anglia (UEA), where he is Curriculum Tutor for History. For several years he was Course Director of the Secondary PGCE course at UEA. Before working at UEA he worked in the Department of History, Humanities and Philosophy at the Institute of Education, University of London. He worked for many years as a history teacher in an inner city school in Manchester. He is co-author of *Learning to Teach History in the Secondary School* (2nd edition, RoutledgeFalmer), and has published several articles in the area of values and citizenship education.

David Kerr is Principal Research Fellow at the National Foundation for Educational Research (NFER). Prior to that he was a Lecturer in Education (History) at the University of Leicester and a history teacher. He has been closely involved in drawing up the proposals for the introduction of Citizenship into the revised National Curriculum in England. He was Professional Officer to the Citizenship Advisory Group and is a member of the Citizenship Education Working Party. His research interests include citizenship education, teacher education and cross-curricular areas. He is currently national research co-ordinator for the IEA Citizenship Education Study (Phases 1 and 2). His publications include *Citizenship Education Revisited: the case of England* (1999), *Citizenship Education: an international perspective* (1999), *Citizenship Education in Primary Schools* (1996) and *Developing Economic and Industrial Understanding in the Curriculum* (1994). He has also published articles in professional journals and contributed chapters in books.

Series editor's preface

The editors and authors of the books in this series share the conviction that all teachers who are concerned with the integrity of the education they provide need to take an interest in the relationships between citizenship education and the rest of the school curriculum. Citizenship and citizenship education are highly contested concepts. Historically, they have been appropriated by politicians and educators at every point in the political spectrum, to promote local, regional, national, international or global agendas, and social, cultural, political or commercial interests. The extent to which the citizen's role is constructed as active or passive, radical or conservative, communitarian or individualistic varies in every definition. Correspondingly, different versions of citizenship education place varying degrees of emphasis on civil rights and responsibilities, on compliance with and challenges to authority, and on participation in and critique of dominant practices in society. All citizenship education teachers need to consider where the curriculum and pedagogy they adopt places their teaching and their pupils' learning in this contested field. One aim of this series is to contribute to the development of teachers' awareness of how their citizenship education teaching is positioned.

In addition, the series is concerned with the fact that the version or versions of citizenship education taught in particular classrooms, schools, regions and nations will inevitably present pupils with messages which are held in tension with those they learn from other curriculum subjects, from the hidden curriculum, and from their broader social and cultural education in and beyond school. Where citizenship education is taught entirely as a discrete subject, unless (and perhaps even if) it is completely trivialised, its explicit presence in the curriculum will still influence pupils' perceptions of subjects which purport to explore any aspect of the social contexts of the knowledge, understandings, skills and experience with which they are concerned. Moreover, what is taught and learned in these subjects, and indeed what is not taught and learned, will influence pupils' experience of citizenship education. The books in this series consequently invite an assessment of the tensions that will exist in the curriculum in schools which choose to teach citizenship education discretely. However, they are also concerned, more ambitiously, to encourage schools, departments and individual teachers to seek out the ways in which citizenship education can be productively integrated with other parts of the curriculum, to redefine and enrich pupils' experience of both citizenship education and those other subjects.

The immediate context of the series is the statutory introduction of citizenship education into the National Curriculum in England, which makes it necessary for schools to make decisions about how and where to place it in the curriculum. The series is intended to help teachers and schools to inform these practical decisions with an understanding of the issues outlined above. Most of the individual books in the series focus on the relationship between citizenship education and one other subject in the secondary curriculum, because the authors and editors believe that secondary teachers will want and need to focus on the implications and possibilities of citizenship education for the subject they teach most. Because primary teachers tend to teach across the curriculum, a single book will be included in the series with a whole-school primary perspective.

In this volume, the authors acknowledge that they can explore only some of the diversity of approaches to citizenship education which are available to history teachers. While retaining distinctive viewpoints, they share a belief in the value to both history and citizenship education of maximal engagement in the classroom with the implications of the truism that history education benefits when past and present inform each other.

The National Curriculum for citizenship education has been developed in the context of a complex, ongoing debate about English society and the role of education in it, which has had to take account of postmodernism, globalisation and both Thatcherite and Blairite politics. In this light, Kerr's opening chapter challenges teachers to use Crick's national initiatives as a stimulus for further development of: the definition of citizenship education; the relative roles of schools and the wider community in providing it; and a pedagogy to support both citizenship knowledge and participation. In Chapter 2, Davies proposes history's potential as a vehicle for much of this development work, demonstrating its capacity to teach concepts such as power and ideology, and skills such as enquiry and reasoned argument, as well as to draw out the effects of various forms of social participation through the study of historical events.

Two of Arthur's chapters explore longstanding relationships between history and citizenship education which are sometimes not made explicit. In Chapters 4 and 6, he exposes the fact that all history teaching is consciously or unconsciously politically positioned and value laden. He calls on teachers to acknowledge the effect of history teaching on pupils' moral understanding and suggests that a consciously adopted liberal communitarian stance in citizenship education teaching might best promote social cohesion while respecting difference.

Three chapters suggest various ways in which history teachers can begin to plan to make contributions to citizenship education. In Chapter 3, Arthur shows how history departments can audit the curriculum to identify opportunities to include citizenship education topics, and argues for the extension of participative child-centred teaching approaches which allow pupils to experience citizenship in the classroom. This anticipates Wrenn's contrast between a dull lesson on the State Opening of Parliament, which teaches minimally *about* citizenship education, and a curriculum-enriching Democracy Day, which, by drawing out legitimate analogies between past and present, offers pupils a maximal approach to learning *through* and *for* citizenship, while enriching their experience of history. In Chapter 7, Haydn outlines principles through which the shared aims of citizenship education and history can be addressed. These include pupils' need to learn how to analyse national history critically, to use the language of political discourse, and to explore historical evidence, seeking out motives and treating dubious claims and limited openness with caution.

A shared perception of the book's authors is that both the interpretation of evidence as a combination of fact, fiction, imagination and point of view, and the interrogation of historical events from multiple perspectives, can help teaching to avoid the kind of monolithic nationalism which fails to reflect pupils' experience of multiple identities and belonging in contemporary Britain. They find a strong correlation between the rigorous questioning of historical events, investigative approaches to history and the development of the skills needed for active citizenship. In Chapter 8, Davies describes how pupils were engaged in this way by questions about post-1945 Europe in a European History and Citizenship project. In Chapter 9, he identifies a need for a post-national, global history education to focus on: world perspectives on national histories, historical and regional diversity, and multiple perspectives on historical events. In the final and most practical chapter in the book, Wrenn demonstrates how an investigative approach in a scheme of work on the British slave trade supported coverage of both citizenship education and history curriculum objectives.

This book will challenge the history teachers who read it to acknowledge that all history teaching influences pupils' understanding of citizenship, and urge them to accept that maximal engagement with citizenship education will reinvigorate history, and contribute to the strengthening of its place in the curriculum.

John Moss
Head of Secondary Education
Canterbury Christ Church University College

Foreword

This book could not possibly be timelier. The new citizenship order comes into force in August 2002. Planning in some schools is well ahead (and plenty of time, for once, was given); in some others, it has scarcely begun; but in most it is still – as senior officials would say – 'under active discussion'. How it is to be done and who is to do it may not yet be finally decided. So it is very important for History to stake its claim, both intellectually and to play a leading role in the needed reorganization sometimes of timetables and always of cross-curricular co-operation of different areas of the curriculum. I am delighted that this book makes the claim so strongly and clearly.

The Citizenship order is in several ways peculiar. As the first two chapters make clear, the order itself is what David Blunkett has called 'light-touch' and I glossed as 'strong bare bones'. It is less prescriptive than the other subjects. Four pages are enough to set it out in broad headings in the revised National Curriculum. More freedom of interpretation is left to teachers than in the other subjects. There is a strong intellectual reason for this: it would be not merely paradoxical but self-contradictory if a subject meant to enhance active and informed citizenship, in other words the understanding and use of freedom, was to be too prescriptive. I suspect that there was a sensible political reason too, that ministers would not have wanted argument about detail – leave that to the good sense of teachers, and, of course, of the inspectorate – indeed, in difficult cases, of governors. This deliberate lack of detailed prescription allows the order to be wide – if we look at the knowledge side alone; it covers national and local political and social institutions, as well as demanding some awareness of international institutions and of global problems. It goes wider than some of us advocated in the Hansard Society report of 1978, 'Political Education and Political Literacy', for it now includes knowledge of the social services, the main NGOs, the voluntary sector and of the institutions of business. Good citizenship is more than political activity alone. The subject order may look impossibly wide, but it is a wide general knowledge that is looked for and needed as a preparation for full citizenship (and some participative practice of it, indeed, as the order enjoins, both in school and in the local communities). To get relationships right is more important than in-depth knowledge of this and that. This means that it has to be flexible as well as light-touch. So long as pupils understand the significance of all the items in the order and the effect they can have on each other, equal weight need not be attached to each line nor equal coverage either. The QCA Citizenship at Key Stages 3 and 4: Initial

Guidance makes this clear, as do the admirable OfSTED notes to inspectors (which followed the fall of the Great Cardinal). Flexibility allows variations in concentration to suit the needs of a school's existing coverage and its teachers' talents, specialisms and interests.

The Report which I chaired that led to the order saw this width as of the essence and also knew that teaching would have to be begun (and continue for some time, indeed) by teachers not trained in Citizenship, therefore it explicitly envisaged delivery of parts of the order through other subjects; and this was clearly implicit in the actual order and was explicit again in QCA's Initial Guidance.

History and Geography were mentioned, of course. Geography for a long time has been concerned with political and social issues of environmental policy – local, national and international – and has found that the best way to motivate learning of the necessary facts is to discover and discuss the evidence for the issues. English can make a contribution too, already involved in discussing critically books or plays that raise issues of loyalty, freedom, responsibility, the nature and limits of tolerance, all of which figure in the conceptual base of citizenships. A close reading and discussion of *Animal Farm* is often the beginning of 'political literacy', and *The Lord of the Flies* still neatly divides opinion as to whether all power corrupts or whether democratic habits and organisation are appropriate to survival in extreme circumstances. The multiplicity of electoral systems now present in the United Kingdom may have been invented so that Maths teachers can inject a little citizenship, and ask the reason why for each different system (both justification and history, presumably). Even many Science teachers are now either struggling with or seizing the enlivening opportunity to discuss the controversial moral, social and political issues raised by scientific advance – especially now in biology and medicine; and the same issues can confront Citizenship teachers who must discuss 'issues, problems and events'. Co-operation and mutual guidance is plainly called for, indeed is being called for quite happily. Religious Education commonly touches on several specific parts of the new curriculum (quite apart from the general question of 'values' as raised in a comparative approach to religions) – most obviously in KS4: 'That pupils should be taught about: "the origins and implications of the diverse national, regional, religious and ethnic identities in the United Kingdom and the need for mutual respect and understanding".'

In many schools, however, it is teachers of PSHE who find themselves made citizenship coordinator or team leader. Sometimes that person may have been longing for years to be able to teach something like Citizenship (I have met a good few such in my recent wanderings through schools, conferences and training sessions). But more often, I fancy, not; or if so, then wanting to do something far more limited in scope than the new subject order, especially having in mind the third vital strand of political literacy, building on social and moral responsibility and community involvement. A union of PSHE and Citizenship is wholly appropriate to primary school (indeed that is the name of the new Advisory Framework), but it is not appropriate to deliver a full and new National Curriculum subject. There is overlap, certainly, useful overlap; but possibly no wider than for History and Geography. A clear decision on good grounds was made for PSHE to be advisory and Citizenship to be statutory. To put it gently, schools will be in difficulty with assessment, inspection and preparation for the coming GCSEs, etc. in Citizenship Studies if their headteachers, whether by a misunderstanding, inertia or desperation amid so many other demands, take a line of least resistance and think that PSHE, with a wee bit of padding and pulling, can do the trick.

My personal view, that I have had to be a little bit discreet about at times, is that of all the other subjects History may have (should have) overall the greatest role to play. This may not always be possible. But the intellectual case is very strong. Seeley long ago said that politics without history has no root, and that history without politics has no fruit – and I take it even then he meant both the disciplines and the activities. The most common reason why something happens is that some antecedent thing or things occurred in the proximate past, and so on back as far as one needs to understand. In trying to understand the working of any institution it is, after all, somewhat rationalistic to inquire only about its professed purposes, or nowadays its 'mission statement'; one also inquires about its performance, track record or history (just as in considering applications for grants or jobs). A democratic socialist can agree with the late Michael Oakeshott that one understands a society by knowing its traditions (even if they are not always of one kind) rather than its laws or official doctrines. And I think the professional case is strong also. Historians in discussing alternative interpretations of complex events, say of the English Civil War (or is it better seen as 'The Wars in the Three Kingdoms'?), the growth of the franchise (the cry for rights but also the necessities of rule in an industrialising society), political and social change, are developing the kind of skills of informed discussion and concern for evidence that are at the heart of the Citizenship order and, indeed, the practice of citizenship.

I could say a lot more, but the contributors to this book have said it more fully. Repetition blunts the edge of even intellectual pleasure – such as I have had in reading this book. I think all those involved in the delivery of the order should read it because on one level it states the intellectually obvious, but in another it challenges the common assumption that PSHE is necessarily the best way into delivering Citizenship. To end on an even more personal note. When the Advisory Group reported unanimously in favour of a new statutory subject, I could not be sure that the government as a whole, despite the known support of the then Secretary of State, would welcome such prominence and possible adverse publicity; and there was also the open opposition of the then Chief Inspector to consider and, at that time, the somewhat equivocal position of QCA. Therefore, I had in the back of my mind a fallback position to propose as a best possible second-best: a Key Stage 4 statutory subject in Modern History and Citizenship. I think I might have had Lord Baker's support on this who served most helpfully on the advisory group; for one of my compensating pleasures among some inevitable tedium was to hear him, quite informally of course, express his views on Kenneth Clarke for having removed History from Key Stage 4 and producing his foolish twenty year exclusion zone.

Bernard Crick

Acknowledgements

We would like to thank a number of publishers for permission to reproduce material in this book. Figure 8.1 produced by A. Osler and H. Starkey, appeared in *Oxford Review of Education* 25, (1&2) (1999), published by Taylor & Francis Ltd. Figures 5.3 and 5.5 by Andrew Wrenn were published in *Teaching History*, published by the Historical Association. Figures 9.1 and 9.2, by Derek Heater, were published in I. Davies and A. Sobisch (eds) (1997) *Developing European Citizens*, Sheffield, Sheffield Hallam University Press. Figure 10.1 by Derek Heater, first appeared in D. Heater (1998) *The Elements of Citizenship*, London, Citizenship Foundation. Table 9.1 by Mary Rauner, appeared in M. Rauner (1997) 'Citizenship in the curriculum: the globalization of civics education in anglophone Africa: 1955–1995', in C. McNeely (ed.) *Public Rights, Public Rules: constituting citizens in the world polity and national policy*, New York, Garland Publishing. Figures 3.1 and 3.2 were first published in Qualifications and Curriculum Authority (1998) *Education for Citizenship and the Teaching of Democracy in Schools*, London: Qualifications and Curriculum Authority. Table 5.1 appeared in T. McAleavy (1993) 'Using the attainment targets in Key Stage 3: AT 2 Interpretations of History', *Teaching History*, 72, pp. 14–17.

The authors are greatly indebted to administrative staff, students, teachers and colleagues who have helped with the preparation of the text, discussed ideas and suggested ways forward. Particular mention can be made of Daniel Wright and Mary Yates. Lynn Davies as well as Rachael, Hannah and Matthew Davies deserve grateful thanks.

The authors are grateful to Professor Bernard Crick for agreeing to write a Foreword to the book and to Rosamund Howe for her careful and thorough work on the manuscript.

Introduction

Issues in citizenship and history

This book has been written by authors who have a strong background in history education and a clear, longstanding professional interest in citizenship education. Citizenship is now a key national and international issue. Politicians, educationalists and, indeed, all in public life refer repeatedly to the significance of citizenship. And yet much of the debate surrounding citizenship can be described as being characterised by extreme diversity. The authors of this book, while being convinced of the significance of the issues and the need for positive professional action, do not pretend that a simple, uniform view of citizenship is either possible or desirable. Thus, although a measure of discussion and debate has taken place about the writing, the chapters are to some extent free standing and each is the responsibility of an individual author. This certainly does not mean that citizenship education lacks coherence. Rather, it is important to identify a number of ways of thinking about and practising citizenship education. This book responds to this difficult challenge by making use of a structure that allows for a number of strands to be examined and woven together. We did not want to produce an edited collection in which the separate chapters were so different from each other that citizenship appeared to lack central, defining features. Neither did we wish to leave the work to a single author who would lack the expertise or necessary breadth of perspective to do justice to citizenship, an issue that can seem at times to take the form of a many-headed educational monster.

The overarching structure of the book has three parts: 'Contexts', 'Curriculum issues', 'Conclusions'. The first sketches the background to change; the last makes some comments about where we are now in relation to the development of citizenship education and what needs to be done in future. Part 2 ('Curriculum issues') is by far the longest of the book. It has not been the intention of the authors to provide some sort of 'how to' book. The authors have produced very practical guides for teachers in other sorts of publications but are prompted in this collaborative project more by the need to recognise at least part of the diversity of perspectives and the need to encourage professional initiative. Guidance for citizenship education must not become a straitjacket, and we seek in this book to achieve a scattering of professionally based 'hits' on the spectrum that veers perilously between actionless thought and thoughtless action. It is hoped that teachers and others will see in our discussions of issues and the provision of practical classroom examples ideas that will make their own work meaningful and suggestions that will encourage professional experimentation. This stimulus will, hopefully, be provided within the main body of the chapters but also at the end of each piece with the use of key questions and recommended reading.

In Part 1, two chapters are presented which focus on what we have called contexts. In Chapter 1 David Kerr examines the policy background, including legislation and the variety of preparatory committees which have considered citizenship education within the context of history teaching. This is an insider's account of the key debates within the working groups but it has been written in such a way as to raise issues and suggest possible ways forward rather than merely to describe what happened. There has for too long been a worrying gap between the rhetoric of politicians and the development of practical strategies. David Kerr's chapter is an account of what is probably the best chance ever to implement citizenship education in secondary schools in an explicit and professional way. Moreover, the processes of implementation within citizenship education are of particular importance. It would be rather incongruous if government were to proceed by diktat in this field, and the efforts made by policy makers and advisers need to be considered carefully.

In Chapter 2 by Ian Davies the key issues that relate to citizens and citizenship are outlined in general terms. This chapter also examines the key debates and perspectives within citizenship education and how they are applied.

The second, and main, part of the book discusses curriculum issues. The general intention is to allow history teachers the opportunity to see how they can interpret the meaning of citizenship for their professional work, but within that general framework curriculum issues are targeted in three main ways. Firstly, in Chapter 3, James Arthur emphasises the current significance of citizenship education and, by means of examining a variety of 'official' documentation as well as exploring other issues, shows how citizenship education can be secured within the history department. This is to some extent a structural matter. The history teacher should know both that she is not alone in pursuing work that focuses on citizenship and that there are important, useful and straightforward ways in which the legitimate development of citizenship education can take place within the 'home' department. Secondly, the key aspects of citizenship education (communitarianism, morality, political literacy and diversity) are discussed in Chapters 4–7. James Arthur, in his chapters on communitarianism (Chapter 4) and moral education (Chapter 6), provides a critical perspective on the links and disjunctions between citizenship history teaching. In Chapter 5 Andrew Wrenn writes about the concept of 'political literacy' and its relationship to history teaching. A number of practical classroom strategies are suggested, and some comments are made about certain aspects of political literacy. Terry Haydn in Chapter 7 discusses social, cultural and ethnic diversity. Thus, it is hoped that by this point in Part 2 an overarching account of the links between citizenship and history has been given, together with a full exploration of the main elements of citizenship as identified by the Crick Committee (social and moral responsibility, community involvement and political literacy).

Towards the end of Part 2 we present three chapters that are designed to illuminate particular areas of citizenship education and to give further practical suggestions for what could happen in history classrooms. This has been attempted in two specific ways. Firstly, there are two chapters that tackle a separate context for citizenship education. In

Chapter 8 Ian Davies writes about European citizenship and in Chapter 9 he looks at global citizenship. In Chapter 10 a slightly different approach is taken: Andrew Wrenn shows that simple dividing lines between the local, national, European and global should not be allowed to obscure positive ways forward. By drawing attention to certain key theoretical issues, but mainly through the provision of practical classroom strategies, he shows that a 'global' topic such as slavery is also of obvious significance in other ways. Slavery was also a local, national and European matter. By using such vital concepts as identity and by developing skills and understanding in areas such as interpretations, it is perhaps more possible in practical classroom work to make citizenship meaningful than it would be if developed as an isolated academic discourse of the kind that often seems to suppose a delineation of issues that is too clear cut. Slavery is a sensitive and controversial topic. But an examination of slavery is perhaps one of the key ways in which history lessons can relate to citizenship education in its capacity to raise fundamentally important matters such as justice. A brief conclusion has been provided which attempts to summarise some of the main issues raised in the book and to suggest some avenues for further work.

James Arthur, Ian Davies, Andrew Wrenn,
Terry Haydn and David Kerr
March 2001

Part 1

Contexts

Chapter 1

Citizenship education and educational policy making

Introduction

Citizenship education has never been far from the top of the political and educational agenda in England. This chapter concentrates on the latest policy review of citizenship education, that undertaken by the Advisory Group on Education for Citizenship and the Teaching of Democracy in Schools (QCA, 1998). This review has led to a historic shift in educational policy making in this area. As a result of the work of the Advisory Group, citizenship is to be included, for the first time ever, as an explicit part of the school curriculum. It is a new foundation subject for pupils aged 11 to 16, from August 2002, and part of a non-statutory framework alongside personal, social and health education (PSHE) for pupils age 5 to 11 from August 2000 (DfEE/QCA, 1999a, 1999b). This chapter sets out to explain how this historic shift has come about. It begins by outlining a number of lessons from past policy approaches to citizenship education in England. These were absorbed by the Citizenship Advisory Group and had a major influence on the shape of its terms of reference, membership and working practices. The chapter goes on to explore the main debates about citizenship education within the Advisory Group and their impact on its definition of and recommendations for citizenship education. It then sets the work of the group within the wider frame of current educational policy. Finally, key challenges are identified which need to be tackled if the latest policy proposals for citizenship education are to lead to effective practice in schools and elsewhere. A number of these challenges raise questions about the potential for stronger links between history and citizenship education.

Citizenship education: lessons from past policy approaches

The history of approaches by policy makers to educating for citizenship in England is well documented (Batho, 1990; Brown, 1991; Heater, 1990, 1991; Kerr, 1999, 1999a; Oliver and Heater, 1994; Annette, 1997). There are a number of lessons that emerge from these past approaches, and it is important to understand them because they have had a major influence on the latest attempt by policy makers to review citizenship education. That attempt has been made by the Advisory Group on Education for Citizenship and the Teaching of Democracy in Schools (hereafter referred to as the Citizenship Advisory

Group) (QCA, 1998). The legacy of past approaches weighed heavily on the Advisory Group, particularly the inability to set out a clear definition of citizenship education as a necessary precondition to establishing a consensus on how to approach the subject. It influenced not only the group's terms of reference and membership, but also its working practices and the nature of its recommendations. The Citizenship Advisory Group absorbed the lessons from the failure of past policy approaches in its attempt to lay down stronger foundations for citizenship education in schools.

The first lesson to emerge from past policy approaches in the context of England is that there is no great tradition of explicit teaching of citizenship education in English schools or of voluntary and community service for young people. As a result, there is no consistent framework in which to posit discussion of this area and no solid research base on which to make judgements about the effectiveness of practice. Indeed, Rowe (1997) has identified at least eight approaches to citizenship education, which he asserts are competing for primacy in democratic societies such as England. They are the constitutional knowledge, the patriotic, the parental, the religious, the value conflict or pluralist, the empathetic, the school ethos and the community action approaches. There is no space to outline these approaches here, but they serve as a useful reminder of the disparate thinking and practice in citizenship education which are present in England. A major task for the Citizenship Advisory Group was to blend elements of these approaches into an acceptable working definition of citizenship education. It was vital to achieve such consensus, firstly within the Advisory Group, and then outside, among politicians, those in education, parents and those promoting particular approaches. Consensus was necessary in order to develop a strong framework for citizenship education in schools.

Many of the past approaches of policy makers have foundered because of a lack of consensus on definition and approach. This is despite general agreement that the development of citizenship education in English schools is important. All too often, the noble intentions of policy makers have been watered down into general pronounce-ments that, in turn, have become minimal, and largely ineffectual, guidance for schools. It explains why, when citizenship education has periodically come to the fore in the English education system, it has been located, primarily, in the implicit or hidden curriculum rather than in the explicit or formal curriculum. Indeed, what passes as citizenship education has been characterised more by an emphasis on indirect trans-mission through school values, ethos and participation in school rituals than by direct delivery through subjects. Transmission has been weighted towards pupil exposure to good role models and sound habits rather than towards direction through specified subject content. The intention has been to mould character and behaviour rather than to develop civic awareness. As such, citizenship education in England has been traditionally insular and largely devoid both of political concerns about contemporary society and of awareness of developments in other countries.

The Citizenship Advisory Group was determined, from the start, to ensure that its efforts would not fail in the same way. Accordingly, the definition of citizenship education put forward in the group's initial report was purposely concise but broad based, and the accompanying recommendations for future action short and to the point. The intention was to produce a report that achieved maximum exposure, within and outside education, and brought a swift answer as to the degree of consensus on the proposed definition of citizenship education.

The second lesson to emerge from past policy approaches is that there is a complex relationship between citizenship and education for citizenship. Citizenship is a contested concept. At the heart of the contest are differing views about the function and organisation of society. Because education is accepted as central to society, it follows that attitudes to education, and by default to citizenship education, are dependent on the particular conception of citizenship put forward. It is important to understand this connection. The periodic redefinition of citizenship education is a by-product of a much larger, wide-ranging debate concerning the nature of English society and the role of education within that society.

Attempts to redefine citizenship and, concomitantly, citizenship education, as emphasised in Chapter 2, are often born out of perceived crises in society at large. The latest attempt to redefine citizenship education, undertaken by the Citizenship Advisory Group, is no exception to this rule. The current debate about society has been triggered by the rapid pace of change in the modern world and its detrimental impact on social, political and economic structures. This has led intellectuals to ask whether a watershed has been reached, namely the end of modern, liberal democratic society and the onset of a less certain postmodern world. They have begun to redefine the concept of citizenship in this postmodern world. Indeed, citizenship has been a continuous topic of discussion in the past two decades in intellectual and political circles, cutting across party and class divides (Heater, 1990; Turner, 1990; Wexler, 1990; Andrews, 1991; Roche, 1992; Demaine and Entwistle, 1997; Callan, 1997; Beck, 2000).

These attempts to redefine citizenship have had an impact on recent debates about the nature of citizenship education in schools. The discussion in the late 1980s and early 1990s was dominated by the implications for schools of the then Conservative government's championing of civic obligation or 'active citizenship' (Hurd, 1988; MacGregor, 1990; Oliver, 1991; Abrams, 1993). Since the mid-1990s the focus has broadened to take in concern about the seemingly pervasive erosion of the social, political, economic and moral fabric of society in England, in the face of rapid economic and social change, what some have termed 'globalisation' (Bentley, 1999; Beck, 2000). This concern has led to increasing discussion of citizenship education in relation to: values education and pupils' spiritual, moral, social and cultural (SMSC) development; pupils' experiences of personal, social and health education (PSHE) and their preparedness for life in modern society, as citizens, parents, consumers, employers and employees (Pearce and Hallgarten, 2000).

The Citizenship Advisory Group was keenly aware of this broader debate and made a point of addressing it directly. The proposed definition of citizenship education, though set within the political tradition from Greek and Roman times, very much addressed the needs of modern democratic society. This was reflected in its broad-based approach and scope. It applied not just to schools but across society, and tackled political, social, economic and moral aspects of pupils' development and understanding of local, national, European and global dimensions. The framework also had a modern focus. Its main aim, as in history, was to develop an understanding of the past and present to help pupils become better prepared for the challenges in their current and future lives. Indeed, it could be argued that citizenship education, as defined by the Advisory Group, provides the opportunity for pupils to address their understanding and experiences of modern society and to think critically about the values which underpin it, as an explicit part of their learning in schools. This opportunity can be missing from pupils' studies in history. History teaching often does not go much beyond the 1960s, thereby sending out an implicit message to pupils that the past and present are separate entities. It is no coincidence that citizenship concerns in Scotland are addressed largely through a subject deliberately titled 'modern studies'.

The third lesson to emerge from past policy approaches is how far definitions of citizenship are a product of the spirit and concerns of the age. As is made clear in other chapters, citizenship education has been ascribed various purposes in the past. The focus is often dependent on the views of the whatever social or political group is dominant, and the underlying philosophy that shapes those views. This has been very much the case over the past two decades. It is no coincidence that the focus in the late 1980s and early 1990s, on the rights, obligations and allegiances of the individual citizen, was influenced by the rhetoric and policies of the prevailing Conservative government. It was encapsulated in the then Prime Minister Margaret Thatcher's famous remark in the mid-1980s that 'there is no such thing as "society". There are men. And there are women. And there are families.'

The Conservative government championed the individualism of the free market and placed an emphasis on the importance of civic obligation or 'active citizenship'. The term 'active citizenship' was part of a wider Conservative philosophy centred on the primacy of the rights and responsibilities of the individual over those of the state. The philosophy was based on a 'liberal-individualist' concept of citizenship. The Conservative government urged individuals to take up actively their civic responsibilities rather than leave it to the government to carry them out. It backed up the call with policies that encouraged greater private ownership and the primacy of consumer rights in all areas of life, including education.

The New Labour government which came to power in May 1997 has championed a different philosophical approach to citizenship. It is one centred on the 'communitarian' concept of citizenship. The communitarian concept focuses on the meaning and role of community, with a particular emphasis on 'civic morality'. This is part of the wider philosophy of 'New Labour', as the Prime Minister Tony Blair has termed his party and its policies, based on the civic responsibilities of the individual in partnership with the state. The Labour government is urging individuals to act as caring people, aware of the needs and views of others and motivated to contribute positively to wider society. This is part of what is commonly referred to as 'third way' politics (Giddens, 1998). The emphasis on 'civic morality' is heralded publicly as a much-needed antidote to counter the harmful effects of the rampant individualism which underpinned the previous government's stress on 'active citizenship'.

The shifting emphases in approaches to citizenship over the past two decades had an influence on how the Advisory Group was formed and viewed its work. The group was deliberately set up with all-party backing. This was to avoid accusations that it was a creature of the Labour government and therefore biased in its approach. That spirit of cross-party co-operation and consensus was carried over into the definition of citizenship education. There was a conscious effort to forge a definition of citizenship education that was acceptable to all parties and also met the pressing needs of modern democratic society. The working definition had to achieve a balance between the 'active citizenship' approach, based on the 'liberal-individualist' concept of citizenship, and the 'civic morality' approach, based on the 'communitarian' concept. The Advisory Group achieved the balance through a 'civic participation' approach, based on the 'civic republican' concept of citizenship and neatly combining elements of the other two approaches. Nowhere was this successful combination more apparent than in the essential elements to be developed in pupils through an education for citizenship. These included pupil understanding of the paired key concepts of 'individual and community', 'rights and responsibilities' and 'freedom and order', among others.

The final lesson to emerge from past policy approaches is the renewed interest in citizenship education over the past two decades. This lesson was the one most keenly absorbed by the Citizenship Advisory Group. The renewed interest was instrumental in establishing the conditions for the group's existence and the parameters of its work. It helped: to fuel the calls, within and across parties and groups in society, for citizenship education to be reconsidered as part of the review of the National Curriculum; to provide a clear indication of the major concerns in society that a redefined citizenship education must address; and to pave the way for the favourable reception of the group's recommendations.

The renewed interest was sparked in the late 1980s with the then Conservative government's concept of 'active citizenship' and the debate about its implications for education and young people (Hurd, 1988; MacGregor, 1990; Abrams, 1993). It led, in 1989, to the renaissance of citizenship education as a cross-curricular theme, 'Education for Citizenship', in the National Curriculum (England). The debate was further fuelled by the publication of two documents that attempted to define citizenship education: firstly, *Encouraging Citizenship* (Commission on Citizenship, 1990), which made recommendations as to ways of encouraging social citizenship through education, public services and the voluntary sector; and secondly, *Education for Citizenship* (National Curriculum Council, 1990) which offered guidance for schools from the National Curriculum Council (NCC) on how to develop essential components of education for citizenship. The latter offered considerable advice on the major contribution that history could make to citizenship education.

The early 1990s approach failed to encourage the development of consistent and coherent citizenship education in schools (Saunders *et al.*, 1995; Whitty *et al.*, 1994). This failure had a number of causes. These included the lack of consensus about the specific purposes, approaches and outcomes of educating for 'active citizenship' in schools; the ineffectiveness of the chosen non-statutory, cross-curricular policy route; the general nature of the official advice given to schools, as embodied in NCC (1990), and the distrust, in schools and elsewhere, of anything associated with attempts to introduce overt political education into the curriculum. The failure of the cross-curricular policy route for citizenship education in schools, particularly through subjects such as history, weighed heavily on the Citizenship Advisory Group. It was a constant reminder of the folly of following a similar policy route.

Despite this failure, the interest in citizenship education has continued to grow apace from the mid-1990s, bringing with it increasingly urgent calls for its review. These calls have been brought to a head by a number of developments in the public domain. Firstly, the social, political and moral fabric of society in England has seemingly been eroded by the impact of rapid economic and social change. This has resulted in increasing disquiet, in many quarters, at the apparent breakdown of the institutions and values that have traditionally underpinned society and encouraged social cohesion and stability, such as marriage, family and respect for the law. There has been particular concern about growing apathy towards public life and participation, as evidenced at the formal level by the decline in the number of people voting at national, local and European elections. Secondly, such developments have had an apparently damaging effect on contemporary English society. A number of research studies, both national and comparative, have concluded that there is a perceptible decline in civic culture in English society, in contrast to other countries, and a marked absence of a political and moral discourse in public life (Crewe *et al.*, 1996; Phillips, 1997; Arnot *et al.*, 1996).

Thirdly, such developments have had an increasingly negative impact on young people. A number of studies have focused on the attitudes and behaviour of the 18 to 34 age group. The findings have prompted concerns about the following generation of school-aged children (Cannon, 1994; Wilkinson and Mulgan, 1995; Park, 1995; Roberts and Sachdev, 1996). There has been increasing anxiety at the rising levels of anti-social behaviour by school-aged children and at the sharp rise in the number of pupil exclusions from schools. These developments have, in turn, been translated into growing anxiety about the lack of a coherent framework for moral, spiritual and social education both inside and outside schools in England (White, 1994; Tate, 1996a, 1996b).

This anxiety prompted action both from within the education system and from without. A series of national and grassroots initiatives were launched, aimed primarily at influencing the behaviour and attitudes of pupils and enabling them to voice their feelings and concerns (Willow, 1997; CRE, 1996; BYC, 1997). The most prominent of these initiatives was the establishment of the National Forum for Values in Education and in the Community by the School Curriculum and Assessment Authority (SCAA) in 1996 (now replaced by the Qualifications and Curriculum Authority (QCA)). The National Forum, with strong backing from Dr Nick Tate, SCAA's Chief Executive, set out to identify and gain public agreement on a number of core values vital to the functioning of modern English society (National Forum, 1996).

These lessons from past policy approaches are important. They help to explain why the Citizenship Advisory Group was set up, and why, ultimately, it proved to be more successful in its outcomes than previous policy attempts in this area. The explanation of why the group was set up lies in a complex interplay of factors, some deep-seated and others more immediate, with the usual mixture of good fortune, opportunity, personalities and planning thrown in for good measure. Perhaps, above all, the main reason for the group's establishment was that by the late 1990s there was broad support, from within and outside the education system, for a comprehensive review of this area. The time was right. The conditions necessary to sustain a review were in place. There was growing concern, in particular, about the rapidly changing relationships between the individual and the government and the decline in traditional forms of civic cohesion: what has been termed a 'democratic deficit'. This concern resulted in increasing calls for action to address the worrying signs of alienation and cynicism among young people about public life and participation, leading to their possible disconnection and disengagement from it. Such signs are apparent in a number of industrialised nations across the world, though there is debate as to whether they are a natural feature of the life cycle – engagement increasing with age – or a more permanent phenomenon (Jowell and Park, 1998; Wilkinson and Mulgan, 1995; Putnam, 2000).

The final catalyst for action was the existence of a strong political will. This had not always been present in past policy approaches, particularly in the early 1990s, which goes some way to explain their failure. The political will came not just from the new Secretary of State for Education and Employment, David Blunkett, a long-time advocate of political and citizenship education, but also from the new Labour government, supported by the other major parties. The political will, combined with growing public and professional calls for action, paved the way for the establishment of the Citizenship Advisory Group. How the group was set up and went about its work is explored in the next section of this chapter.

The Citizenship Advisory Group: terms of reference and membership

The latest review of citizenship education was heralded in the new Labour government's first education White Paper, *Excellence in Schools*, early in 1997 (House of Commons, 1997). David Blunkett pledged in the White Paper 'to strengthen education for citizenship and the teaching of democracy in schools'. Later that same year he announced the setting up of the Advisory Group on Education for Citizenship and the Teaching of Democracy in Schools with the remit 'to provide advice on effective education for citizenship in schools – to include the nature and practices of participation in democracy, the duties, responsibilities and rights of individuals as citizens; and the value to individuals and society of community activity'. It is worth setting out the group's title in full. It is a reminder that the group was concerned not just about education for citizenship but also about the promotion of democratic processes in schools.

The Secretary of State also made clear that he expected the main outcomes of the group's work to be:

A statement of the aims and purposes of citizenship education in schools;

A broad framework for what good citizenship education in schools might look like, and how it can be successfully delivered – covering opportunities for teaching about citizenship within and outside the formal curriculum and the development of personal and social skills through projects linking schools and the community, volunteering and the involvement of pupils in the development of school rules and policies.

The group's title, terms of reference and outcomes were carefully crafted. They reflected a keen understanding both of the lessons learnt from past policy approaches and of the underlying calls for the review of this area. The wording conveyed a number of important indicators about how the group would approach its work. Firstly, the term 'strengthen' underlined the fact that citizenship education was not something new in schools but rather an area that required clearer definition and greater rigour in its delivery. This was an important message, given the pressures on schools in managing the existing National Curriculum. Citizenship education was not something to be 'bolted on' to the National Curriculum. Many of its facets were present already in schools.

Secondly, the terms 'participation', 'community activity' and 'pupil involvement' signalled the intention to take what philosophers have termed a 'maximal' rather than a 'minimal' approach to citizenship education (McLaughlin, 1992). The approach signalled was not the narrow education *about* citizenship, with its emphasis on pupils' acquisition of knowledge and understanding of national history and the structures and processes of government and political life (the old-style civics courses of the 1950s and 1960s), nor the particular education *through* citizenship, with its emphasis on pupils learning by doing through active experiences in the school or local community (what in the USA is termed 'service learning'), but, as stated in the group's title, the broader education *for* citizenship (Kerr, 1999b). Education *for* citizenship combines elements from the *about* and *through* approaches, and focuses on equipping pupils with a set of tools (knowledge and understanding, skills and aptitudes, values and dispositions, and key concepts) which prepare them for active and informed participation in their roles, responsibilities and duties in adult life.

The terms of reference also stressed the need to strike a balance between duties, responsibilities and rights, and between the primacy of individuals, communities and societies. This signalled a strong desire to construct a definition of citizenship education which encompassed competing concepts of citizenship, most notably the 'liberal-individualist' and 'communitarian' concepts. Finally, the group was to produce two very clear outcomes: firstly, a definition of and rationale for citizenship education in schools; and secondly, a broad framework for what it might look like in practice. This was very deliberate. Without a consensus on definition it would be very difficult to proceed with the broad framework.

To deliver these outcomes, the group had a carefully chosen, balanced membership. The members were a mixture of practitioners with a track record in citizenship education, from schools and link organisations, and those offering political and wider professional expertise. The latter included well-known public figures such as Kenneth Baker, ex-Secretary of State for Education and Home Secretary, Michael Brunson, political editor at ITN, and Sir Stephen Tumim, former HM Chief Inspector of Prisons in England and Wales, as well as church and thinktank representatives. The former included representatives of citizenship and community organisations, such as Jan Newton, Chief Executive of the Citizenship Foundation, and Elisabeth Hoodless, Chief Executive of Community Service Volunteers (CSV), as well as those drawn from primary and secondary schools and post-16 institutions. Marianne Talbot represented the work of the SCAA-sponsored National Forum for Values in Education and in the Community. This balance gave the group the necessary credibility and clout within and outside education circles. Interestingly, a closer examination of the membership reveals that it contained advocates of most of the differing approaches to citizenship education identified by Rowe (1997), and referred to earlier in this chapter. This created the potential for consensus to be reached within the group on the definition and framework. However, there was no guarantee that this would happen in practice or that the definition arrived at would be accepted beyond the confines of the group.

The group's chairman, Professor Bernard Crick, was also carefully chosen. He had a proven track record in this area and thus the necessary gravitas to lead the review. He wrote the classic *In Defence of Politics* in the 1960s and spearheaded the push for political education in schools in the 1970s (Crick and Porter, 1978). He also possessed a keen understanding of what would be needed, in professional and public circles, to achieve a consensus on what citizenship education is about. This acute political acumen proved invaluable both within and outside the group. The group also had considerable representation of those with experience of and a keen interest in history education. Kenneth Baker remained a strong advocate of the subject while the OfSTED observer, Scott Harrison, was the Chief Inspector for History. This had an influence on the nature of the group's recommendations, particularly in relation to the framework for schools. It meant that from the start the group had a very clear view of the strong links between teaching and learning in history and citizenship education.

It is worth emphasising that, though set up under the New Labour government, the group was deliberately non-partisan, as evidenced by the presence of the Speaker of the House of Commons, Betty Boothroyd, as its patron and Lord Baker as one of its members. Indeed, the Speaker could only participate with the consent of the leaders of both the Conservative and Liberal Democrat parties. This non-partisan approach was and is vital. If citizenship education is to be truly effective it must not only address the issue of party politics but also stand above it. It must command the support and respect of all parties rather than being seen as the creature of one.

The group worked to a very tight time scale in order to dovetail with QCA's timetable for providing advice on the overall review of the National Curriculum. The work was divided into two phases. The group first convened in November 1997 and produced an initial report in March 1998 stating the case for citizenship education. This included a working definition, a statement of need and a plan of action. The group then consulted on the initial report and produced a final report in September 1998, once more in line with QCA's timetable. This reiterated the main points from the initial report, amended in the light of the consultation, and contained detailed proposals for a framework for citizenship education in schools based on learning outcomes (QCA, 1998).

Citizenship Advisory Group: key debates, definition and recommendations

The nature of the tasks and fierce time scale forced the group to find answers to a number of key debates concerning citizenship education in a very short space of time. It is to the credit of the group's members that they attacked the challenge with enthusiasm and gusto from the very first meeting. The key debates are listed below.

Definition

How best to accommodate the disparate, competing approaches to citizenship education that exist in a coherent definition, which also meets the needs of modern society? How best to accommodate the eight approaches identified by Rowe (1997), such as the values, the community action, the political knowledge, the identity, race and human rights approaches, alongside the broader philosophical conceptions of citizenship such as the 'liberal-individualist' and 'communitarian'?

Scope/involvement

What is the scope of citizenship education? Is it to focus just on schools or more broadly on society at large? How far should it address the concerns of contemporary English society as well as those in other countries across the world? Who is to be involved, whether pupils, parents, teachers, local communities, or those in the public eye?

Status/location

Should citizenship education be a statutory or non-statutory part of the curriculum? Is it best located in the school curriculum or in the community, or in a mixture of the two? If in school, is it best as a separate subject, or as a cross-curricular component, or in particular subjects such as history or personal and social education (PSE), or in whole-school activities? What percentage of curriculum time is it to occupy? What is the role for community-based activities?

Approach

Is it a body of knowledge, or about developing skills and attitudes and inculcating values, or all of these? Is it also experiential, encouraging learning through participation and action? How far should central government prescribe the approach, in laying down the knowledge, understanding and skills to be developed, as in other curriculum subjects such as history? How, if at all, can pupil progression be assessed and measured?

Support

What are the support needs of pupils, teachers, parents and community representatives in citizenship education? Who will teach citizenship in schools? What are the training and resource needs for teachers, particularly those in training and newly qualified? How can these needs best be met? How can the longstanding fear of teachers about the dangers of bias and pupil indoctrination in this area be overcome? What needs to be done to develop a solid research base to underpin judgements about citizenship education?

This is a sizeable list of debates, many of which are longstanding. It was not possible for the Advisory Group to answer them all in the limited time available. Indeed, a number remain as considerable challenges for the development of effective citizenship education and are touched on again in the final two sections of this chapter. However, the Advisory Group went some way to agreeing a way forward on the majority of them. This is evident in the production of a unanimous final report. Thankfully, given the emphasis on democratic processes, there was no call for an embarrassing minority report from dissenters. The members were helped towards unanimity, in particular, by the group's terms of reference and working practices in meetings. The careful wording of the terms of reference set the parameters for some of the debates, notably those on *scope/involvement* and *approach*.

Meanwhile, the primary working practice of, firstly, general discussion and agreement on the main thrust of each report, carefully minuted, followed by in-depth discussion and debate of draft sections of the report, encouraged a spirit of frankness and co-operation between members and observers alike during meetings. The draft sections were pre-prepared by the chairman and professional officer, taking into account the minuted results of the general discussion. Though there were differences of opinion on some of the debates, sometimes marked in the initial general discussion, the process of detailed discussion and debate of draft sections invariably crystallised the main concerns. Once they were crystallised it was easier to consider, as a group, how differences in opinion might best be resolved and/or accommodated in the final text of the reports.

Three debates in particular generated discussion within the group, which, though sometimes heated, was always constructive. The first debate was that concerned with *definition*. There was strong lobbying from some members for their particular interests. They claimed that on-going work in their area of interest provided ready-made answers on definition. This was particularly so concerning the relative emphasis that should be given to the community action, values and constitutional knowledge approaches in any definition. The second was *status* and the curriculum time implications of citizenship education. Kenneth Baker was especially concerned that citizenship education should not threaten the time given to other curriculum subjects, particularly history. With history a statutory subject only up to the end of Key Stage 3, there was considerable debate as to whether citizenship education posed a threat or an opportunity. In the main, the group believed the potential links between the two areas, and the chances to tap the knowledge and skills of history teachers in delivering citizenship education, offered considerable opportunities rather than threats. The third debate was about *approach* and what were appropriate assessment and inspection arrangements for citizenship education, particularly those concerning the active component – the involvement of pupils in project work, volunteering and democratic processes in school. Interestingly, the internal focus on these debates was mirrored in the external reaction of the press and public to the group's two reports.

Reviewing the Advisory Group's definition and recommendations for citizenship education in schools highlights how the debates were resolved within the group.

Definition

The working definition was deliberately founded on elements of past approaches, updated to meet the particular needs of modern democratic society. The definition was centred on 'civic participation' and based on the 'civic republican' concept of citizenship. Above all, it picked up and strengthened elements of other approaches, providing a workable 'third way' between the competing 'liberal-individualist' and 'communitarian' concepts of citizenship. It revisited the three elements of citizenship – namely, *the civil, the political* and *the social* – contained in T.H. Marshall's classic definition (Marshall, 1963). The definition re-emphasised the importance of the second element, *the political*. This had been strangely absent from the Conservative government's 'active citizenship' in the early 1990s and remained limited in scope in communitarian approaches in the mid- to late 1990s. It also placed considerable emphasis on the values and community action approaches, in line with the thrust of 'civic morality'. The group agreed that 'effective education for citizenship' consists of three strands, interrelated but also distinct.

1   *Social and moral responsibility*: children should learn from the very beginning self-confidence and socially and morally responsible behaviour both in and beyond the classroom, both towards those in authority and towards each other. It is essentially a precondition for the other two strands.
2   *Community involvement*: children should learn about, and become helpfully involved in, the life and concerns of their communities, including learning through community involvement and service to the community. This, of course, like the other two strands, is by no means limited to children's time in school.
3   *Political literacy*: pupils should learn how to make themselves effective in public life through knowledge, skills and values. This strand updates the 1970s definition of political education and seeks a term that is wider than political knowledge alone. 'Public life' is used in its broadest sense to encompass realistic knowledge of and preparation for conflict resolution and decision-making, whether involving issues at local, national, European or global level.

The group believed that there was considerable scope for history to provide a vital underpinning to the third strand through its focus on the development of British society and its political, social and economic systems and institutions. There are numerous opportunities to link past developments with present-day arrangements at community, local, national, European and international levels.

The group also placed considerable stress on what effective citizenship education should lead to, namely active and responsible participation. Interestingly, this is in line with what some commentators have called the 'missing element' in Marshall's trilogy, namely *the participative* (Janoski, 1998). They argue that Marshall's definition takes participation as a given, but that this is no longer sufficient in modern society. The combined effects of the rapid pace of modern life, the spread of the suburbs and the increasing domination of global companies have contributed to the sharp decline in civic culture since the 1950s. People have less time and motivation to contribute to community and democratic processes. Given this, there is an urgent need to make explicit statements about the rights and responsibilities of participation if democratic traditions are to survive.

Scope/involvement

The scope of citizenship education was broad based. The group stated that the teaching of citizenship and democracy is so important for schools and for society that it must be an entitlement for all pupils. However, schools cannot fulfil this entitlement alone but require the active support of parents, community representatives and those in the public eye. Citizenship teaching was declared to be:

> The knowledge, skills and values relevant to the nature and practices of participative democracy; the duties, responsibilities, rights and development of pupils into citizens; and the value to individuals, schools and society of improvement in the local and wider community . . . both national and local and an awareness of world affairs and global issues, and of the economic realities of adult life.
>
> (QCA, 1998)

Status/location

The group decided after considerable discussion, based on the failure of past policy approaches and knowledge of existing educational policy, that the best way to guarantee that pupils received their entitlement was to make it statutory. This decision was not taken lightly. The group was unanimous in its resolve that citizenship education should be established in schools by means of a statutory Order and that all schools should be required to show they are fulfilling the obligation that this places upon them. The group believed that previous attempts at non-statutory, cross-curricular guidance in this area, particularly in secondary schools, had inherent difficulties. In order to guarantee flexibility in how schools approached citizenship education, the entitlement and statutory Order should be set out by means of a framework of learning outcomes for each key stage.

The group recommended that the learning outcomes should be based on what can take no more than 5 per cent of curriculum time across the key stages. This was a marker rather than an absolute figure, to be further debated when citizenship education was considered as part of the overall review of the National Curriculum. The group believed that it was disingenuous to say that effective citizenship education did not require real curriculum time. However, the time issue was clouded by the fact that aspects of citizenship education were already given in many schools and therefore the time required included a mixture of existing and additional provision. This distinction was conveniently ignored in press reporting of the curriculum time issue (Cassidy, 1999).

How this time is distributed was left as a matter for schools themselves to decide in the interests of local conditions and opportunities and existing good practice in each school. Schools could combine elements of citizenship education with other subjects (such as history and geography), so long as the statutory requirement for all pupils was met. The final report contained a section on how part of the statutory citizenship education curriculum could be fulfilled in combination with other subjects. It was no surprise that the subject first mentioned in this section was history. This reflected the group's strong belief that it was the subject, along with geography, that could make the strongest contribution to citizenship education because it was the closest in terms of content, contexts and teaching and learning approaches. Schools would also need to consider discrete time for some citizenship elements as well as whole-school activities. It was recognised that, because of existing practice, the best way to approach citizenship education in primary schools might be in combination with PSHE.

Approach

What is often forgotten in the reporting of the Citizenship Advisory Group's work is that the actual detail of the approach was determined largely by practitioners and then endorsed by the group. The group had neither the time nor sufficient expertise to draw up the detailed framework for citizenship education in schools. Instead, the work was delegated to two sub-groups of teachers and experts in the area, one for primary schools and one for secondary. It was the privilege of the author of this chapter, David Kerr, as the Advisory Group's professional officer, to chair both sub-groups. The sub-groups took as their starting point the best existing good practice in England in this area, the most effective aspects of past approaches, notably NCC (1990), and the best of practice in other countries, notably in the Republic of Ireland, Australia, Scotland and some US states.

This explains the considerable overlap between developments in teaching and learning in history over the past twenty years, as detailed in Chapter 2, and the approach of the framework for citizenship education in schools. A number of those involved with the sub-groups had a background in history and the humanities, which influenced their approach. The framework had a considerable emphasis on the use of evidence, processes of enquiry, the making of judgements and development of communication skills in order to take informed action. These are the lifeblood of history as well as of citizenship education.

The framework of learning outcomes was based on key concepts, values and dispositions, skills and aptitudes, and knowledge and understanding. It was deliberately set out in this way, with the knowledge and understanding component last, so as to encourage pupils' growing understanding, development and application of the key concepts, values and skills which underpin education for citizenship. The knowledge and understanding element was seen as providing the contexts and content to support learning in the other elements. This approach is very familiar to those brought up on the 'new history' developments of the past twenty years. The emphasis in knowledge and understanding was on topical and contemporary issues, events and activities. The learning outcomes were to be supported by a broad range of teaching and learning approaches. The mainstay of these approaches was structured opportunities for pupils to be involved in discussion and debate on topical and contemporary issues. There were also opportunities for pupils to learn through action in case studies, projects and activities in school and in the local community. As the final report stated, 'It is difficult to conceive of pupils as active citizens if their experience of learning in citizenship education has been predominantly passive' (QCA, 1998).

As stated above, the approach to teaching and learning in citizenship education, advocated by the Citizenship Advisory Group, is one that is very familiar to history teachers. The group left the question of the assessment and inspection of citizenship education largely open for further consideration.

Support

The group argued that there should be a phased introduction and implementation of the statutory Order for citizenship education over a number of years. This was in recognition of the time needed to prepare sufficient quality support structures in terms of initial and pre-service training for teachers and the provision of new and revised materials. A phased introduction would minimise disruption for schools in their existing curriculum arrangements. The group placed considerable store on the ability of history teachers to be in the vanguard of those promoting citizenship education in schools in the first few years. This confidence was based on evidence of the involvement of history teachers in existing citizenship education activities in some schools. Such involvement could also include assistance with teacher training both for new and existing teachers in this area. The final report also contained a guidance paper on 'The teaching of controversial issues'. This was felt to be important in order to assuage fears among teachers and others about the dangers of indoctrination and bias in this area.

How far the Advisory Group's vision for the strengthening of citizenship education in schools would be taken forward as a blueprint for real change was dependent on the wider context of educational policy making. This wider context is considered in the next section of this chapter.

Citizenship education within the wider context of educational policy making

Making recommendations is easy, as demonstrated by past policy approaches. However, getting them accepted and acted upon is far more difficult. Despite the groundswell of support for a review of citizenship education, both within and outside the teaching world, and the political will for change, there was no guarantee that the outcomes from the Citizenship Advisory Group's work – namely the definition and framework for schools – would be endorsed. Their fate was dependent on what happened to them at four interrelated levels of policy making: the specific, the particular, the collective and the broad.

The first level of policy making was the reaction to the outcomes as a specific, or stand-alone, set of proposals. How far had the group succeeded in achieving a consensus on the definition of citizenship education and meeting the expectations of those who supported a review of this area? The second level was the status of the outcomes within the particular context of the review of the National Curriculum. How would the proposals for strengthening citizenship education rank alongside other areas and aspects competing for inclusion in the revised National Curriculum? The third level of policy making was the degree of fit of the outcomes with the collective detail of educational policy in schools. If the outcomes were accepted for inclusion in the revised National Curriculum, how far would they have to be remodelled to conform with, for example, the format of subject Orders and the nature of supporting advice and guidance? How would the outcomes be affected by the national priority areas of literacy, numeracy and information and communications technologies (ICT)? The fourth and final level of policy making was the degree of congruence of the outcomes with broad government policy. How far did the outcomes dovetail with the tenor of the government's social, economic and political policies and, therefore, encourage connectivity across government as well as between schools and their communities? The fate of the Citizenship Advisory Group's proposals at each of these four levels of policy making is explored in turn.

The general reaction to the Advisory Group's proposals can be classified into three broad categories: pro, anti and ambivalent. These categories were and continue to be present across all four levels of policy making. The reaction to the outcomes at the first level was positive. The Advisory Group's initial and final reports were warmly welcomed by the Secretary of State for Education and Employment and by the other political parties. Most importantly, there was general consensus, both within and outside the world of education, on the definition of citizenship education and on the need for a statutory entitlement. There was also little public or professional concern expressed about the dangers of political indoctrination of pupils, a factor which has dogged discussion of citizenship education in the past.

Those in favour welcomed most aspects of the proposals. This was the position of those representing history. The Historical Association was invited by the group to take part in the consultation process. A number of history teachers and advisers also contributed. The majority gave the proposals a warm welcome, picking up on the considerable overlap between history and citizenship education, in terms of content, contexts and teaching and learning approaches, as emphasised in the final report. However, beyond the history representatives, there were concerted calls from certain interest groups for greater stress on particular aspects and approaches. The most common demands were for more emphasis on human rights legislation, on identity and diversity, on values, on the global and economic dimensions and on making school councils compulsory. The human rights lobby pressed for greater recognition of the government's signing of major international conventions on children's and human rights. Those calling for strengthening identity and diversity in the reports wanted greater synergy with the recommendations of the MacPherson Committee. Following the consultation process on the initial report, a number of adjustments were made to the text and framework in the final report to meet some of these concerns.

Those opposed to the proposals can be divided into two camps: firstly, those opposed to citizenship education in principle (Phillips, 1999); and secondly, those opposed to the proposals because of their impact on the school curriculum. The former were remarkably small in number, underlining the change in public mood which had enabled the Citizenship Advisory Group to undertake its work. The latter consisted of those, such as the teacher unions, concerned about the curriculum time and implementation implications of the proposals, and those who supported other areas competing for inclusion in the school curriculum. The ambivalent reaction was from those preoccupied with what they saw as more pressing priorities for schools and society, such as the focus on basic skills, standards and pupil transfer and progression. To them, the proposals for citizenship education were an unnecessary distraction. Such ambivalence remains a considerable challenge to be overcome in developing effective citizenship education in all schools and all communities. The generally positive welcome of the proposals enabled them to be considered at the second level.

Getting the proposals accepted at the second level of policy making, as part of the revised National Curriculum, was much more difficult to accomplish. It was this level which was to decide ultimately whether the efforts of the Citizenship Advisory Group would mark a historic shift in policy making in this area, or be consigned to the fate of past policy approaches, that of failure. The outcome was dependent on three interrelated decisions. The first was how the proposals for citizenship education compared to other areas that were also seeking inclusion in the revised National Curriculum. The second was which of these areas, if any, should be put forward for inclusion in the revised National Curriculum. The third was how far any such proposals would prove acceptable to those both inside and outside education.

At the same time as the Citizenship Advisory Group was established the government also set up national advisory groups on PSHE, education for sustainable development, and creative and cultural education. The remit of the groups was similar. Each group was asked to produce a report on its particular area, to be considered as part of the review of the National Curriculum. In addition, following the work of the National Forum for Values in Education and in the Community, QCA had begun piloting guidance on pupils' spiritual, moral, social and cultural development (SMSC). These initiatives were collectively referred to, in the review process, as the 'new agenda'. The task of considering how these initiatives might be included in the revised National Curriculum was undertaken by QCA, which set up a co-ordinating committee for this purpose, the cumbersomely titled Preparation for Adult Life (PAL) group. The group comprised representatives from each of the advisory groups and the SMSC initiative, plus a representative selection of headteachers from primary and secondary schools.

The PAL group was assisted in its work by two aspects of how these initiatives had been taken forward. The first was the nature of the recommendations. Each advisory group argued for different emphases within the curriculum. It was relatively easy to incorporate these into existing arrangements, along with a statement about the aims and values of the school curriculum. The draft report of the PSHE Advisory Group proposed that this subject be clearly highlighted in the aims and purposes of the school curriculum; it recommended the publication of a non-statutory code of practice and a national framework. The Panel for Education for Sustainable Development recommended incorporating sustainable development into the aims and purposes of the school curriculum and increasing its statutory basis through existing National Curriculum subjects, notably geography and science (CEE/DEA, 1998). The draft report of National Advisory Committee for Creative and Cultural Education (NACCCE) recommended a greater emphasis on breadth, balance and relevance across existing subject areas in the

National Curriculum and more explicit reference to the area in the aims and purposes of the school curriculum (NACCCE, 1999). The SMSC pilot looked to strengthen these aspects through the whole-school approaches and greater emphasis across the curriculum. The exception to this rule was the Citizenship Advisory Group, with its call for new statutory provision for the area. This was primarily because citizenship education was less well established in the school curriculum than the other areas and therefore less easily accommodated within existing arrangements.

One crucial decision therefore facing the PAL group was whether the call for statutory provision for citizenship education could be accommodated in a revised National Curriculum alongside the recommendations from the other groups. The answer was aided by the degree of co-operation between the groups during their deliberations. Especially close links were forged between the Citizenship Advisory Group and the PSHE Advisory Group. As professional officer to the Citizenship Advisory Group, David Kerr, the author of this chapter, was invited to become a member of the PSHE Advisory Group to improve dialogue and communication between the two groups. The first two strands of the definition of citizenship education – *social and moral responsibility and community involvement* – offered the potential for considerable co-operation with PSHE work in schools. This was reflected in the assertion in the final report that the learning outcomes for citizenship education at Key Stages 1 and 2 could be best achieved as part of PSE or PSHE programmes in primary schools. However, the advisory group made clear that citizenship education should be separate and distinct at Key Stages 3 and 4 because of the emphasis on the third strand in the definition – *political literacy*.

The links were not restricted to PSHE. The Citizenship Advisory Group also stressed the considerable potential to cover environmental and sustainable development, as well as social and health issues, through the emphasis in the framework for schools on topical and contemporary issues. The values dimension in citizenship education also had close links with the SMSC initiative. This cooperation between the advisory groups and SMSC initiative meant that the issue of accommodation was not a straight either or. It was not either citizenship education or the rest. The connections between the groups enabled them to be considered as both distinct and linked areas in the curriculum. This was particularly the case in the close relationship between citizenship and PSHE in the first two strands of the definition of citizenship education – *social and moral responsibility* and *community involvement*.

The PAL group was thus able to draw up a number of options for how to include these areas within the national framework for the school curriculum. These options ranged from statutory to non-statutory provision for distinct as well as linked areas. The statutory entitlement to citizenship education with links to PSHE was one of these options. The PAL group's report constituted part of QCA's advice to the Secretary of State on the revision of the National Curriculum. After reviewing each option against the general aims of the National Curriculum review and in the light of further expert advice from OfSTED, the Teacher Training Agency (TTA) and others, the Secretary of State announced that the option of statutory citizenship education with close links to PSHE should be pursued. It was therefore proposed that citizenship education should be introduced as a new statutory foundation subject in secondary schools and as part of a non-statutory framework alongside PSHE in primary schools. Both decisions were strongly influenced by the failure of past policy approaches in citizenship education, combined with a keen understanding of existing policy and practice. For example, the proposal for non-statutory provision in primary schools was determined by how schools currently approached the area and by the pressures associated with the existing national initiatives in literacy, numeracy and ICT.

This did not mean that citizenship education had won out over the other areas under consideration in the revised national framework for schools. It was proposed that in the revised framework sustainable development could be strengthened through existing links with geography and science, and creativity and culture education likewise in the arts and across the curriculum as a whole. Strong links would be made between the areas represented by the various advisory groups and the aims and values statement for the school curriculum, which was to be included for the first time. This statement was influenced by the outcomes of the SMSC initiative. The proposal for statutory citizenship education in secondary schools and non-statutory citizenship education alongside PSHE in primary schools was considered within the public and professional consultation on the shape of the revised National Curriculum. The consultation resulted in the same level of general support for the proposal as had met the advisory group's final report. The way was therefore clear for citizenship to become part of the statutory school curriculum for the first time ever in schools in England. The Citizenship Advisory Group had achieved a historic breakthrough in policy making.

With the second level of policy making successfully cleared, the third level, ensuring that citizenship fitted into the National Curriculum framework, should have been relatively straightforward to negotiate. However, in reality, considerable changes had to be made to the Citizenship Advisory Group's definition and framework for schools, and their presentation in the final report, in order to conform with the requirements for statutory and non-statutory provision. The statutory requirement necessitated the drawing up of a subject Order, with programmes of study and an attainment target, at Key Stages 3 and 4. The non-statutory provision meant negotiating with the PSHE Advisory Group over the nature of the combined PSHE and citizenship framework at Key Stages 1 and 2. The opportunity for continuity and pupil progression between the non-statutory and statutory elements also had to be built in. These revisions had to be undertaken in a very short space of time in order to fit with the timetable for the publication of the revised National Curriculum framework.

The required changes, though understandable within the overall context of the revised National Curriculum, have presented a new range of problems in attempts to strengthen citizenship education in schools. Above all, they have weakened considerably the holistic impact of the Citizenship Advisory Group's final report (QCA, 1998). In particular, a number of key messages from the report have had to be detached from the wording of the new Citizenship Order at Key Stages 3 and 4, and of the PSHE and citizenship framework at Key Stages 1 and 2. These include the rationale for citizenship education in schools and beyond, the clear three-pronged definition, an explanation of the main teaching and learning approaches and the links to other curriculum areas. What has been presented to schools is the bare bones of what pupils should be taught in citizenship without the connecting history, in terms of content, contexts and teaching and learning approaches, are no longer stated as explicitly as they were in the final report. They are assumed rather than directly spelt out.

The new 'light touch' Order at Key Stages 3 and 4 has programmes of study for citizenship and an attainment target based on three elements:

- knowledge and understanding about becoming informed citizens
- developing skills of enquiry and approach
- developing skills of participation and responsible action

The non-statutory framework for Key Stages 1 and 2 has the citizenship element, defined as 'Preparing to play an active role as citizens', as one of four strands.

There are suggested opportunities for links to other subjects in both the Order and the framework. However, there is a danger that, because citizenship and PSHE were introduced into the revised National Curriculum framework at the same time, the underlying message is that the major link is between citizenship and PSHE, with weaker links to other subjects such as history and geography. This is potentially very damaging in secondary schools. If it gained currency it could distort approaches in schools, leading to an overemphasis on citizenships relationship with PSHE and an underdevelopment of its links with closely allied subjects such as history. This was never the intention of the Citizenship Advisory Group.

Policy makers have recognised that the Order and framework, by themselves, are not sufficient to encourage the development of effective citizenship education in schools and beyond, and that more needs to be done to take forward the Advisory Group's work. Accordingly, a new Citizenship Education Working Party has been set up by DfEE to consider the issues of implementation. The working party was chaired by the Education Minister Jacqui Smith. The membership was drawn mainly from those within education – from schools, LEAs, churches and link agencies – in line with the focus on implementation. A number of members were closely associated with the original Advisory Group, notably Professor Bernard Crick, Jan Newton, Scott Harrison and Phil Snell. David Kerr, this author, is also a member. The working party has set up sub-groups to consider the pressing issues of assessment, teacher training, community involvement and the sharing of resources and good practice. The latter encompasses a focus on the links between citizenship education and ICT, including the web. QCA has also produced initial advice and guidance for citizenship at Key Stages 3 and 4 and for PSHE and citizenship at Key Stages 1 and 2 (QCA/DfEE, 2000a, 2000b). This guidance goes some way to restoring some of the important central messages from the final report, for example its explanation of the links between what pupils should be taught and the rationale for, definition of and approach to citizenship education as put forward by the Advisory Group. However, there is still a considerable understatement of the links that can be made between citizenship and subjects such as history.

The fourth level of policy making, that of broad government policy, at first glance has a less obvious influence on the fate of the proposals for citizenship education than the other three policy levels. However, the impact of this level should not be underestimated. It has influenced the scope and nature of the Advisory Group's recommendations and continues to shape the content and contexts for citizenship education. The Advisory Group was concerned to ensure that the definition and framework for schools were compatible with the focus in citizenship education on pupil discussion of topical and contemporary issues and events. This meant making certain that the main thrusts of government policy were included in the framework, alongside broader developments in society. The essential elements in the framework – the concepts, values, skills, knowledge and understanding – were deliberately drawn up so as to offer opportunities to explore many key government policy areas, including the economy, human rights, identity and diversity, Europe, international relations and the reform of government within the United Kingdom. These opportunities have been carried over into the programmes of study in the new Citizenship Order and framework. They present a myriad content elements and contexts for linking past developments with current arrangements.

However, concern is a two-way process. The government, despite all-party support for the work of the Citizenship Advisory Group, also needed to be comfortable with the tenor of the proposals for citizenship education. In particular, the definition and approach to citizenship education had to be acceptable, and so they proved to be. The proposed definition and approach, with the emphasis on 'civic participation', was sufficiently broad-based to be in tune with much of the New Labour philosophy of 'civic morality', particularly the emphasis on community. This acceptance has been confirmed by active government efforts to ensure that the broad implications of citizenship education, strengthening the links between schools and their communities, are well understood in official circles. There has been a concerted effort to raise awareness about citizenship education across government. This has resulted in attempts to bring greater connectivity in the work of departments in the areas of identity and diversity, social exclusion, health, human rights and international relations.

The main tenets of the Citizenship Advisory Group's recommendations have successfully negotiated the various levels of wider policy making, though not without considerable change in their detail and presentation along the way. However, a series of challenges, both practical and philosophical, remain to be overcome if the latest policy proposals for citizenship, as part of the revised National Curriculum, are indeed to lead to effective citizenship education practice in schools and beyond. These challenges are considered in the final section of this chapter.

Challenges

The Citizenship Advisory Group's final report contained a bold statement that the central aim of strengthening citizenship education is to effect

> no less than a change in the political culture of this country both nationally and locally: for people to think of themselves as active citizens, willing, able and equipped to have an influence in public life and with the critical capacities to weigh evidence before speaking and acting; to build on and to extend radically to young people the

best in existing traditions of community involvement and public service, and to make them individually confident in finding new forms of involvement and action among themselves.

(QCA, 1998)

If this expectation of the group is to be realised, it is essential that citizenship education becomes a strong, evolving and lasting feature of the curriculum experience of all pupils in the twenty-first century. The challenges in accomplishing this are considerable. They were not underestimated by the Citizenship Advisory Group. As the chairman, Bernard Crick, was so fond of reminding members, 'the devil is in the detail'. The work of the policy makers, with considerable support from practitioners, in drawing up the new Citizenship Order and framework marks the beginning rather than the end of the process of strengthening citizenship education in schools. Privately, the Advisory Group envisaged that this strengthening, bringing with it a change in the political culture of the country, would take at least ten years to achieve in practice.

If the vision of citizenship education becoming firmly established in schools and radiating out into communities and society is to become a reality, then a number of challenges have to be faced in the coming years. These are both deep-seated and practical. Many of them have been touched on in the preceding sections of this chapter. There are four challenges in particular which must be faced. These are the *curriculum, community, global* and *individual* challenges. They apply not just to England but to wherever attempts are made to review and strengthen citizenship education (Torney-Purta *et al.*, 1999; Kennedy, 1997; Hahn, 1998).

The first is the *curriculum* challenge: this is essentially an issue of *definition* linked to status/location and approach. It is centred on the question of how and where citizenship education is best located in schools. It is inextricably tied up with the process of teaching and learning and the range of approaches, experiences and activities that make up citizenship education. This challenge is uppermost as schools prepare to deliver the new Citizenship Order and framework. The efforts of the Citizenship Education Working Party in tackling some of the key implementation issues will provide considerable help to schools attempting to meet this challenge. How it is met has implications not only for how effective citizenship education is in schools and beyond, but also, and more specifically, for how strongly links are made between history and citizenship.

The *curriculum* challenge can be met by setting out a clear definition of citizenship education and of its benefits to pupils, teachers, schools and society. This is vital in order to underline the distinctiveness of the area and to enable stronger links to be made to other curriculum aspects and areas, such as history. The Advisory Group realised the importance of a clear and concise definition. The group's final report went a long way to providing such clarity and distinctiveness, and to encouraging connectivity, particularly with subjects such as history as well as with PSHE. Unfortunately, much of this clarity and connectivity has been lost in the drafting of the new Order and framework for citizenship in schools. There is an urgent need to reaffirm the central messages in the final report, particularly those concerning the rationale for citizenship education to overcome the 'democratic deficit' in modern society, the three-pronged definition of *social and moral responsibility, community involvement* and *political literacy*, and the approach based on a mixture of active learning through discussion and debate, political knowledge and critical thinking. The relative absence of these central messages weakens the potential to achieve agreement among teachers and other groups in society on what citizenship education is, how it is best approached and how they can contribute. There is a considerable danger that such absence weakens the potential for history to contribute to citizenship as fully as envisaged by the Advisory Group.

The central messages are important because they convey the Advisory Group's belief that history and history teachers can make a lasting contribution to citizenship education and how they can do so. For example, the definition underlines the contribution that history teachers can make to the *political literacy* strand, particularly in secondary schools. This is the new element of citizenship education for most schools and potentially the most important in terms of how effectively it is delivered. It is therefore vital that the content, contexts and approaches in history are used to their full potential in making links to citizenship. History teachers, in particular, could use their knowledge, understanding and skills to help dispel the continued distrust in schools and elsewhere of anything political. They are also very adept at dealing with sensitive and controversial issues in a balanced and professional way.

Understanding the definition, in turn, has a knock-on effect on understanding the contribution that history teachers can make to the scope, status/location, approach to and support needs for citizenship education in schools. The scope of citizenship education is broader than just schools, encompassing contemporary British society and its links to other countries across the world. As such, it provides a myriad of opportunities to link the past contexts of history to contemporary events and institutions. This scope has an impact on the status/location of citizenship in schools. Seen in this way, citizenship education is more than just an adjunct of PSE or PSHE; it offers an ideal opportunity to establish links with whole-school issues as well as with other closely related subjects such as history. It is therefore vital that history teachers are actively involved in decisions in schools as to how citizenship is approached.

History teachers can also make a significant contribution to the approach to and support needs for citizenship education. The teaching and learning approaches in citizenship, particularly those based on discussion and debate of contemporary issues and events, are already very familiar to history teachers, who are skilled in developing them with pupils. History teachers can therefore make a considerable contribution to the delivery of effective citizenship education in schools, particularly in emphasising the active component of learning. Such skills and expertise suggest that history teachers should also be heavily involved in the training of teachers for citizenship, through in-service and pre-service programmes. The sooner these central messages are conveyed to history teachers the better able they will be to decide the extent of their contribution to citizenship education in their schools.

There is also a need in the *curriculum* challenge to address the issue of the knowledge and research base to underpin this area. Currently we know far too little about approaches to and outcomes of citizenship education. The work of the Advisory Group provides an ideal opportunity to begin to establish a much more coherent research and information base upon which to build future practice. Once again, some of the research on teaching and learning in history can be helpful in this respect.

The second challenge is that of *community*. This is essentially an issue of *involvement*. Schools can only do so much. They could do more, and must be helped so to do. However, pupils' attitudes to active citizenship are influenced quite as much by schools as by many factors other than schooling: family, the immediate environment, the media and the example of those in public life. The challenge is how to involve parents, governors, community representatives and support agencies in citizenship education in meaningful partnership with schools. This entails getting them to understand what citizenship education is about and how they can actively contribute to it through careful dialogue with schools. Community involvement should not be merely a box which is ticked without due regard to how it contributes to pupils' curriculum experiences; it should be natural and not forced. History, in linking current developments in society with what has happened in the past, offers a natural means for providing depth and meaning to community experiences. Links between schools and their immediate communities can be strengthened through the vehicle of local history.

The third challenge is the *global*. This is an issue of *preparation*. We are citizens of individual countries and it is through these countries that we can best affect global issues. Global citizenship revolves around the challenge facing all nations of how to prepare and equip people, particularly young people, for the incredible pace of change in modern society and its impact on aspects of their lives. We must constantly guard against the feeling of a lack of meaning, direction and control in people's lives, which would lead to alienation and cynicism. An important part of overcoming this challenge is to learn from the experience of others who are facing similar issues and problems. There is much that we can learn from citizenship education in other countries (Kerr, 1999b).

Finally, there is the *individual* challenge. This is an issue of *participation* that some commentators have termed the 'missing element' in previous conceptions of citizenship. Surprisingly, behind all activities of governments and big corporations, the world is still composed of individual human beings. The challenge here is two-fold: to understand our roles and responsibilities as individual citizens in a modern democratic society, but also to think about the consequences of our actions. It entails treating young people with respect and giving them meaningful fora in which their views can be aired and considered as part of the democratic process, whether in schools, in local communities or at national level. After all, it is the actions of the next generation of pupils that will be the acid test of whether the group's recommendations have had any lasting impact. The aims and purposes of history and citizenship, within the revised National Curriculum framework, are very similar in this respect. Both are concerned with equipping young people with the necessary knowledge, understanding, skills, attitudes, values and experiences for life in modern society.

Conclusion

The Citizenship Advisory Group has worked hard to develop a definition, framework and approach to citizenship education which offer consensus, and to get citizenship education as an entitlement for all pupils in the revised National Curriculum. However, policy can only ever provide opportunities for change. Such opportunities must then be grasped and acted upon. However, as the growing literature on models of policy change and on the process of change in schools highlights, grasping such opportunities in education can be a slow and painful process. It is therefore premature to speculate as to whether the advisory group's efforts to strengthen citizenship education and change the political culture of this country will prove successful. It is also difficult to tell the extent of the contribution that history and history teachers will make to the process. A historic and promising start has been made but we are entering new and largely unchartered territory.

How citizenship education fares will rest on how well the challenges of *definition, involvement, preparation* and *participation* are met over the coming years. However, revisiting past approaches suggests that two conclusions may be drawn with certainty: firstly, citizenship education will remain on the political and educational agenda in the twenty-first century in England; and secondly, that there will be continuing debate about what is meant by 'effective education for citizenship and the teaching of democracy in schools'. Hopefully this debate will involve not only policy makers but also teachers, schools, pupils, parents, local communities and all those with an active interest in citizenship education. If this happens, citizenship will have gone a long way to reinvigorating the *participative* element in modern society. It will also have met the vision of the Citizenship Advisory Group about the nature and practices of educating for citizenship. An integral part of that vision is stronger links between history and citizenship education.

Key questions

What would your response have been to the debates undertaken within the Advisory Group?

1 Definition: what is citizenship?

2 Scope/involvement: what is the scope of citizenship education?

3 Status/location: who should teach and learn citizenship and for how long?

4 Approach: what should be the focus for teachers and learners and how can progression be evaluated or assessed?

5 Support: how can those who will teach and learn citizenship be supported?

Recommended reading

B. Crick (2000) *Essays on Citizenship*. London, Continuum.
This is a collection of essays written over a period of time by the key adviser on citizenship education.

D. Heater (1999) *What is Citizenship?* Cambridge, Polity Press.
A very clearly written, intelligent account of the key issues in citizenship.

Chapter 2

Citizenship education and the teaching and learning of history

> History is a priceless preparation for citizenship.
>
> (DES 1990)

Introduction

This chapter discusses the meaning of citizenship and citizenship education and how they relate to the teaching and learning of history. The intentions of the policy makers (discussed in Chapter 1) are explored in terms of the particular challenges that will be faced by history teachers. This does not mean that a simple transmission model will be used to implement the policies. Rather, an exploration of some of the fundamental issues will help history teachers clarify the nature of the choices that they can make.

The question 'what is citizenship?' is not answered easily (see Heater 1999) but an attempt is made here to draw attention to the traditions and ideas within some of the principal debates. Some comments are made about the status of both citizenship education and the teaching and learning of history. A more explicit consideration of the links between citizenship and the teaching and learning of history is then provided. Issues are raised that relate more immediately to the implementation of citizenship education through the teaching and learning of history. It is argued that the full benefits that could arise from securing links between the teaching and learning of history and citizenship education are not being achieved. Finally, a number of practical suggestions are made for the realisation of citizenship education through history.

What is citizenship?

It is necessary at the outset to make clear in general terms my preferred meaning of citizenship. According to Oliver and Heater (1994, p. 8):

> Individuals are citizens when they practise civic virtue and good citizenship, enjoy but do not exploit their civil and political rights, contribute to and receive social and economic benefits, do not allow any sense of national identity to justify discrimination or stereotyping of others, experience senses of non-exclusive multiple citizenship, and by their example, teach citizenship to others.

In considering what the above means for the work of teachers and pupils, Heater (1990, p. 336) has explained that: 'a citizen is a person furnished with *knowledge* of public affairs, instilled with *attitudes of civic virtue*, and equipped with *skills to participate* in the political arena' (italics added).

The two quotations above can, however, tend to hide a number of significant difficulties. It is important to identify at least some of the conceptual problems associated with citizenship. Unless there is a reasonable degree of clarity about the nature of citizenship, then there is little chance of effective implementation. Much contemporary thinking about citizenship is linked with the ideas of Marshall (1963), but this should not be taken to mean that there is a single and straightforward characterisation. Part of the difficulty of discussing citizenship is that it needs to be 'understood and studied as a mosaic of identities, duties and rights rather than a unitary concept' (Heater 1999, p. 114).

An appreciation of citizenship requires some sort of accommodation between two distinct traditions. Civic republicanism, generally, has insisted on the primacy of public over private life. According to the ideology of civic republicanism, individuals should search for ways to serve the community. Liberal citizenship, on the other hand, simply stated, emphasises the importance of rights over duties. Part of Heater's (1999, p. 117) answer to this dilemma of seemingly contradictory ideologies is to assert that 'by being a virtuous, community conscious participant in civic affairs (a republican requirement), a citizen benefits by enhancing his or her own individual development (a liberal objective). Citizenship does not involve an either/or choice.' This sort of accommodation between seemingly opposed ideologies makes it possible for some sort of coherence to be developed for citizenship education. However, it does need to be recognised that the nature of the synthesis that individual teachers favour when dealing with the civic republican and liberal traditions within citizenship education will vary. It should also be recognised that the nature of the various elements implied within these traditions is not always straightforward. The nature of, for example, what can be included in an understanding of citizenship can vary as to whether cognitive or affective outcomes are stressed. Teachers will choose to give different emphases to elements within citizenship such as social and moral responsibility, political literacy and community involvement. Within and between each of these areas are a number of issues that require careful conceptual consideration which in turn demands the development of an appropriate pedagogical process. The fundamental question is whether a broad-brush approach to citizenship education, which recognises the essential nature of morality, communities, identity and many other issues, can retain its intellectual coherence. If the citizenship net is cast very wide, the knowledge, skills and dispositions aimed at in citizenship education could be extended *ad infinitum*. Or, perhaps a slightly different way of saying the same thing, the key terms are so ambiguous and contested that meaning risks being lost. Audigier (1998, p. 13) notes that:

> Since the citizen is an informed and responsible person, capable of taking part in public debate and making choices, nothing of what is human should be unfamiliar to him [*sic*], nothing of what is experienced in society should be foreign to democratic citizenship.

Unless we hold on to central features of citizenship (a few key substantive concepts that are principally related to power, explorations of identity, and investigations into the nature of practising citizenship by promoting action), it will be about everything and so it will be about nothing of any coherent worth. Perhaps even worse, it will be 'paradoxically reduced to the teaching of collective behaviours that conform to our cultural habits' (Audigier 1998, p. 13). If we do not have a clear sense of what it is and if we allow the continuation of a situation in which teachers and 'experts' seem to talk a different language in citizenship debates, there will simply be confusion.

The connections between teaching and learning history and citizenship education

The meanings and purposes ascribed to the teaching and learning of citizenship and history are very similar. Dewey (1966, p. 93), in his key work *Democracy and Education*, believed that education utilises 'the past for a resource in a developing future'. Many relate citizenship to politics particularly, and there are some commentators who have stressed the importance of seeing, consequently, a particular link with history. Oakshott (1956, p. 16) defined political education as 'knowledge as profound as we can make it of our tradition of political behaviour'. Seeley (quoted by Heater 1974, p. 1) argued that: 'Politics are vulgar when they are not liberalised by history and history fades into mere literature when it loses sight of its relation to practical politics.' Heater (1974, p. 1) himself even went so far as to say that history and politics are 'virtually identical subjects'.

Complementary trends can also be seen in the way the areas of history and citizenship have been characterised. For citizenship education prior to the 1960s, if anything was done explicitly, it was in the form of factual knowledge about institutions transmitted to high-status students. By the end of the 1970s political literacy (Crick and Porter 1978) was gaining support from key figures (e.g. Slater and Hennessey 1978). Political education, they suggested, should be issue-focused. A broad concept of politics was to be used that emerged, at least partly, from everyday contexts such as trade unions and youth clubs as well as from Whitehall and town hall. In other words, Politics was being replaced by *p*olitics. Procedural values were regarded as more significant than substantive values. Those procedural values would include such elements as toleration, respect for truth and reasoning, and justice, and they were valued more by teachers than the delivery of the 'right' answer. Finally, there was a concern with skills and not just knowledge or attitudes. Global education came to the fore during the 1980s and is perhaps an umbrella heading for a long list of adjectival educations: peace education, gender education, human rights education, development education. Often these various 'educations' are concerned with the development of various types of consciousness (such as planet awareness), and are described by their supporters as being holistic (e.g. Pike and Selby 1988). Ideas for citizenship education were initially associated at the end of the 1980s with Home Office ministers. It is perhaps no coincidence that a junior Home Office Minister, John Patten (who later became Secretary of State for Education), stressed that citizenship was more about obligations than rights. At the end of the 1980s the concept of citizenship developed from a concern about a crisis in the provision of welfare, a rising crime rate and a concentration on economics and consumerism rather than politics. The shortfall in services that had hitherto been provided by the state was to be made up by young people realising their obligations to the local and wider communities. Since the late 1990s, the possibility has emerged that citizenship education could become rather more professionally based. The influence of Bernard Crick, who was the principal figure in the political education movement of the 1970s, has been significant. The DfEE committee that Crick chaired established a three-pronged approach to citizenship education: social and moral responsibility, community involvement and political literacy. This brief summary should not be taken as a complete outline of the nature of citizenship education. It focuses on a particular understanding of citizenship (emphasising politics, for example, and, less explicitly, moral behaviour). It does not give a full account of the many different models that exist. Rauner (1997) has concentrated on post-national conceptions of citizenship; McLaughlin (1992) gives a model related to four key aspects of identity, virtue, political involvement and social prerequisites; and Sears (1996) gives activist and elitist conceptions. But it does give a brief account of the shifting characterisations of citizenship education. The main argument being made here is that those shifts are mirrored in developments in the teaching and learning of history.

There are, at least, five similarities between the fields of teaching and learning history and citizenship education. Firstly, there has been in both a shift in knowledge from institutions and Politics with a capital 'P' to a concern with issue-based politics in everyday life and a wider-lens approach, through a focus on political, economic, social and cultural matters in history. Secondly, there are ongoing debates in both areas concerning appropriate contexts which see work taking place on local, regional, national and global citizenships and histories. Thirdly, the debate on skills in both areas shifts from a narrow concentration on remembering information to a recognition of the importance of critical thinking. Fourthly, preferred dispositions of pupils who have studied history and citizenship are discussed in terms of the promotion of a commitment to a tolerant, pluralistic, democratic society, and so there are the same debates about the limits to that pluralism within a more or less relativist or universalist context. Finally, there is the resonance of the 'real world' as debates occur over the extent to which pupils can be involved in practical activities either in the classroom or in the wider community. The fear of the bias of teachers and even of the potential threat of indoctrination has had an impact on how citizenship education was discussed. For history teachers, the debate was made explicit when Kenneth Clarke was Secretary of State for Education. He put into place a 'twenty-year rule' which disallowed discussion of recent historical events. In citizenship education it is not hard to find inappropriate and unfair allegations concerning young people who are said to be exploited by teachers who are attempting to indoctrinate them (Scruton 1985). In these circumstances the lack of evidence is less important than the significance of the accusations that could be brought against teachers.

Implementing citizenship education through history: the challenges

Some of the ideas discussed above are obviously relevant to the potential for implementing citizenship education. Certainly, the essentially contested nature of citizenship referred to at the start of this chapter is very relevant. It is now intended, however, to give more explicit consideration to the difficulties associated with actually getting something worthwhile done in classrooms.

The amount of work to be undertaken by teachers needs to be considered. Experience of the disastrous early stages of implementing the National Curriculum suggests that any reform that overburdens teachers will simply not work. It is refreshing that citizenship in the National Curriculum has a relatively long lead-in time (statutory force does not become operative until August 2002). It is helpful that 'It is for schools to choose how they organise their school curriculum to include the programmes of study for citizenship' (DfEE/QCA 1999b, p. 6). However, in such a fiercely contested and conceptually difficult area as citizenship it is possible that the output model chosen will not be sufficiently strong, despite the expressed intention to generate a more rigorous inspection programme for citizenship education than has previously been seen.

The nature of teachers' thinking and knowledge needs to be explored. It is a very worrying sign that there is a huge chasm between the thinking of the theorists and that of teachers when the nature of citizenship is discussed. The models referred to above, which have been produced by academics, mean little to classroom teachers (Davies *et al.* 1997, 1999). This is not to argue that either the authors of the models or the teachers are in some way 'wrong'. Rather, theorists and teachers need, obviously, to talk to each other. It would be rather ridiculous if the value of subject knowledge was stressed for the purposes of teaching history (Baker *et al.* 1999) and a similar message was not given in relation to citizenship. But, of course, any attempts at implementation through diktat would surely fail. The benefits of citizenship education, being fashionable, will be lost if flesh is not put on the skeleton of worthy goals. This does not mean that there should be very detailed control of citizenship education by the DfES. The positive potential of the flexible approach adopted by the Crick Report (QCA 1998) has been referred to above. Rather, there is a need for greater understanding of what citizenship education is supposed to do. The plethora of high-minded goals are given instead of a more useful understanding of the relevant content, process and preferred outcomes.

The sensitive nature of citizenship needs to be explored, so those conceptual and practical obstacles that give rise to pedagogical difficulties can be countered. An example is the opposition that has been generated to political learning. Four arguments have in the past been presented to maintain a low level of political understanding among young people.

1   Politics is an adult activity. This position arises from a negative view of children, who are seen as being unable to understand politics, and/or from a negative view of institutions within which children work – largely schools – as being incapable of providing sufficient opportunities for *genuine* political understanding.

2   Pupils will be open to the possibility of indoctrination. This position arises from a negative view of teachers and/or a negative view of the nature of all political activity which seeks to control and would use education as a means of gaining power.

3   There is a lack of an explicit tradition of political education in the United Kingdom. This point recognises that whereas other countries used a nationalist form of education as a unifying force, this was not possible in a United Kingdom made up of England, Wales, Ireland and Scotland. If anything was done, it was more to strengthen imperialist sentiment and general obedience to authority.

4   Teachers are not trained to give political education and are not interested in it. This recognises the difficulties of conceptualising the area, and also relates to the ways in which schools have institutionalised 'traditional' knowledge forms, such as history and geography – with associated career paths – rather than issue-based approaches.

All four of the above arguments can be countered. However, as the fourth point shows, citizenship education also suffers from low status, teachers not seeing strong reasons why they should engage with its contested nature. The combination of conceptually difficult and controversial content, a lack of structural support and the absence of adequate reward for teaching citizenship suggests that implementation will not be easy.

Given the outpourings of rhetoric about citizenship from high-profile politicians and others, the point about low status needs a little further elaboration. It is true that there is a good deal of international research and writing on citizenship (Torney-Purta 1996; IBE 1997; Ichilov 1998; Torney-Purta et al. 1999). There is a plethora of projects on education for European citizenship (Osler et al. 1996; Davies and Sobisch 1997). Action has been taken by national governments, with various initiatives emerging within the UK (e.g. NCC 1990; Commission on Citizenship 1990; QCA 1998). A large number of organisations are playing an active role in citizenship education (e.g. Citizenship Foundation; Council for Education in World Citizenship; the Values Education Council; Politics Association). This interest is itself a sign of the increased importance in which citizenship education is held. However, there is, in fact, more heat than light in these debates, and more talk by academics and politicians than action in classrooms. Citizenship education has usually been promoted only when there has been a perceived sense of crisis (Stradling 1987). In recent decades citizenship education (in various guises) has been called upon as a weapon against particular problems. During the 1970s senior politicians such as Shirley Williams and Keith Joseph looked for a way to distance young people from right- and left-wing extremist groups. In the 1980s economic inefficiency was targeted, as the New Right strove to introduce economic diversity and an entre-preneurial spirit within a substantive moral framework. In the 1990s citizenship education was seen as a means of tackling moral decline, fragmented communities and rising crime, particularly among young people. In contradiction to this high-profile hand wringing, little was actually achieved in terms of classroom action and therefore the real status of the subject remained low.

Although there are departments with the title 'history' in almost all secondary schools, the status of history is probably little better than that of citizenship. Although the rhetoric is highly charged as participants dispute the 'big prize' of controlling the past (Crawford

1995; Phillips 1998a, 1998b), the battle, perhaps, is vicious in practice (as Henry Kissinger once said about university politics) precisely because there is so little at stake. History has for some considerable time been 'in danger' (Price 1968) of disappearing from the curriculum. The Dearing Review saw no reason why history should be compulsory for pupils beyond the age of 14; and the announcement in early 1998 by the Labour government that primary schools were required to spend more time on numeracy and literacy clearly meant that history would not, at least for a temporary period, be a compulsory element in Key Stages 1 and 2 (for pupils aged 5–11). The campaign launched by the Historical Association in 2000 to save history seems very necessary, well timed and depressingly familiar. The grand rhetoric associated with both teaching and learning history and citizenship education is not matched by action by most teachers. There seems little chance of an unproblematic implementation of citizenship education with all its ambitious aims if it is to be infused through the traditional subject of history that is itself of relatively low status.

The particular form of implementation under discussion here is the infusion of citizenship education through a traditional subject. Currently we know very little, beyond what is described by philosophers, curriculum theorists and others, about the way in which history and citizenship interact in classrooms. Generally, however, some signs are apparent of at least the difficulties (if not necessarily their solutions) to be encountered in attempts to infuse citizenship into the curriculum effectively through history. Whitty *et al.* (1994) have argued that:

- some teachers feel that the themes to be infused get in the way of their real work
- pupils at times do not know what their teachers are trying to do
- talk is often an important feature of PSE work but is generally seen as a low-status, non-work activity; also there are very different types of talk in lessons, and pupils cannot easily distinguish the sort that PSE teachers want
- so-called 'real' examples are often not genuinely from pupils' experience
- some subjects use 'hooks' as a preparation for understanding key concepts, but pupils cannot distinguish between 'hook' and 'substance'
- the relationship between PSE knowledge and subject knowledge is not clear
- in PSE there is little or no scaffolding such as examinations or recognisable and widely understood limits to discourse

When history teachers are asked to tackle citizenship education the above problems are immediately recognisable (Davies 1997). The establishment of different groups working on history and on guidance on citizenship education in the National Curriculum indicates the lack of any co-ordinated effort to present the knowledge in an integrated and positive way. The quotation which began this chapter ('History is a priceless preparation for citizenship') is a good example of this gap between the characterisations of the two areas. At times citizenship is characterised as a political goal rather than an educational process. Recent research seems to suggest that some history teachers may misunderstand key aspects of political learning and even those who talk initially about the centrality of teaching citizenship through history are in fact most concerned to teach aspects of the past or to explore the nature of being human, and see citizenship as only one relatively small part of their role (Bousted and Davies 1996). For some, or probably most, history teachers, work on, for example, human rights as a key citizenship issue is seen as less important than the development of knowledge about the past and the development of skills for understanding the past. In explaining the reluctance to include such an approach, one teacher involved in a project to promote citizenship through history explained (Davies 1995b, p. 156): 'You see that would have led me too far away from the history really. . . . There is potential . . . but is not history really . . . I mean it's not building up kind of raw ideas of historical change or causation or attitudes.'

History teachers must do more than provide an academic narrative. It is true that history teaching now explores very many vitally important issues. The teaching of, for example, aspects of causation is, of course, necessary. However, there may exist a desire to understand a particular sort of narrative which avoids posing important questions. It is important to make more explicit links between history and citizenship. It would be possible, for example, for work in history classrooms to explore education for European citizenship. This could be done by focusing on such issues as the existence of core European values at different points; or the degree to which Europe has become more or less integrated; or issues arising from the cases that have come before the European Court of Justice. But these questions and methods tend not to be used because they are deemed by some not to be 'proper' history. There is a significant problem relating to the perceived sensitivity of citizenship education that needs to be overcome if implementation is to be achieved. Many history teachers talk about the importance of rights but there is some limited evidence that they may be more concerned than teachers of some other subjects to stress the importance of responsibilities over rights and to misunderstand the nature of politics and political learning (Bousted and Davies 1996). History teachers can seem at times overly concerned about possible accusations of indoctrination. The reality of history teaching is that there is no real evidence of moral relativism or an explicit insistence that pupils accept particular ideas. Rather, there is a potential danger that the lack of an explicit focus on citizenship will either remove the opportunity for political learning or inadvertently stress a particular form of politics. History teachers already recognise that their work is intensely political. They need to be able to to ask pupils to consider explicitly the nature of power in historical situations.

Finally, in considering the challenges of implementation, there is a pressing need to recognise that teachers are perfectly capable of providing activities for pupils at an appropriate level of complexity. This rather obvious point needs to be emphasised as there is some slight evidence to suggest that new material, unless based directly on a teacher's own academic discipline and constructed in such a way as to show congruence with existing practice, will be rejected as being too difficult for pupils. Citizenship is not intrinsically more difficult than any other topic. Why should the hugely complex Roman Empire be seen as undeniably suitable for 11-year-olds whereas the philosophical issues of the Enlightenment (which encourage people to think about the meaning of right and wrong) are perceived only as accessible for the very able and work on dinosaurs (hardly a topic within concrete everyday experience) as largely for pupils aged below 9? We need not be bound by the simplistic thinking which has led to these accepted ways of working, and we should develop a way of teaching and learning about citizenship which is appropriate for pupils.

Implementing citizenship education through history: a way forward?

There are a number of general ways forward which could be worked on by policy makers, for example: giving citizenship education high status; increasing the focus on citizenship during initial and in-service teacher education; co-ordinating the various relevant committees and advisory bodies; commissioning research which would tell us more than the very little we currently know about the way pupils think about the key issues related to citizenship. There are also examples of action that can be taken generally in schools which may not necessarily or directly involve the history staff (e.g. ensuring that the personal and social education programme does not show an imbalance towards the interpersonal and neglect the other necessary elements). It would be possible to clarify the ways in which citizenship education can be assessed. David Blunkett's period of office as Secretary of State for Education and Employment has seen a dramatic increase in the emphasis placed on the importance of citizenship education, and recent work by Bernard Crick, for example, is positive and to be welcomed. However, in aiming 'at no less than a change in the political culture of this country both nationally and locally' (QCA 1998, p. 4), the scale of the task must not be underestimated.

Specifically, there are a number of very straightforward ways in which the history teacher can take a strong lead in the development of citizenship education. The most obvious (and very limited) step is perhaps merely to ensure that appropriate content is being offered and – very important – that pupils are made aware, in an appropriate manner, of the purpose of this content. This purpose can be explored at first in terms of the framework(s) that a teacher chooses to work within (or the framework that is insisted upon by a government agency). When working within such a framework, teachers need to be able to see the ways in which relationships can be established with citizenship education.

Generally, there are five main types of curriculum framework used by Ministries of Education (Stradling 1995). Teachers should consider the approach they are using and explicitly identify the potential within that approach for citizenship education.

1   An outline survey provides a chronological framework which covers an extended period of time. Such an overview may provide pupils with a mental map for considering significant issues, although there is always a risk of teaching and learning being conducted in rather superficial ways as the class moves in haste through the centuries in order to complete the outline.

2   A thematic framework is preferred by some, so as to allow for the inclusion of a limited number of case studies for particular and often comparative purposes. Supporters of this approach often claim that it is a useful way of teaching pupils historical skills and of explicitly exploring a connection with contemporary society. Critics argue that it provides a fragmented agenda that is driven by a perception of

what is important today as opposed to a more rounded attempt to explore the past.

3   The patch approach involves the selection of a limited number of historical periods (or patches) and a range of perspectives for their study. There is a good deal of overlap between the patch and the thematic approaches.

4   A dimensional framework concentrates singly or in combination on the political, social, economic and cultural. The benefits of such an approach are usually stated in terms of the potential either to understand one dimension in the context of others, or to ensure that one dimension is not being taught exclusively and to the neglect of other important aspects. Some feel that it is an approach which is very demanding for pupils and which is built on uncertain grounds, as the meaning of each dimension is potentially so varied (what, for example, is meant by 'political'?)

5   Finally, some argue for an inter-disciplinary framework which allows for a valuable focus on methods and skills while at the same time issues are properly placed in the context of 'real life' and not separated artificially by arbitrary academic dividing lines. Of course, those who see something genuinely distinct about historical method and the purposes of teaching and learning history are very wary of such efforts and would prefer to make links or infuse important matters with and through history as opposed to establishing a framework which would not necessarily be titled history.

It is possible when using any one of the five frameworks outlined above to show explicit links with citizenship education. The type of history that is being taught and the potential outcomes will depend at least in part on the decisions both to choose a particular framework and to develop it in certain ways by highlighting some of its features and purposes.

Examples already exist of how links can be made between history and citizenship (e.g. Davies and John 1995). It is relatively straightforward to suggest ways in which explicit links can be made, using the ideas and suggestions contained within the Crick Report. Social and moral responsibility could, for example, be illustrated through a case study of the life of Anne Frank, with questions being posed about the actions that were taken, could have been taken and should have been taken in particular historical circumstances. Community involvement could be illustrated through a local history project that required, for example, the gathering of evidence about the changing purpose and function of a local site which may be deemed to be worthy of redevelopment or preservation. The views of local people today could be used as a means of developing insight into the changing value (sentimental, financial and other) we place on the remains of the past. Political literacy could be illustrated very easily through an examination of the growth of political rights at particular periods of history. A study of the French and Russian revolutions is already very common in schools and would need little or no alteration for developing an understanding of, for example, rights and responsibilities within a democratic society. Again, it is unlikely to be helpful for one part of Crick's three-pronged approach to be seen as necessarily more related to teaching and learning history than another. Nor is it necessary to insist that all three elements are the exclusive responsibility of the history teacher. However, it would be valuable for teachers in an individual school to consider which aspects of the Crick Report belong particularly within their remit, and then perhaps decide to go beyond the minimal requirement.

Now that the Crick Report has been developed into detailed statutory and non-statutory guidance, the links between history and citizenship education can be made clearly. There are three areas that need to be taught: knowledge and understanding about becoming informed citizens; developing skills of enquiry and communication; developing skills of participation and responsible action.

Knowledge and understanding about becoming informed citizens

So much of the knowledge and understanding that are promoted in history lessons is absolutely central to citizenship education. The focus on this part of the recommendations on topical and contemporary issues is very important and can allow for the good work of history teachers to be recognised. Said (1993, p. 2) comments:

> Even as we must fully comprehend the pastness of the past, there is no just way in which the past can be quarantined from the present. Past and present inform each other, each implies the other, and in the totally ideal sense implied by Eliot, each coexists with the other.

The key characteristics of parliamentary government, together with the electoral system and the importance of voting, are already commonly explored in teaching about Reform Acts generally and the suffragettes in particular. The importance of resolving conflict fairly could be the theme of an investigation into the Treaties of Versailles. The significance of the media in society lends itself to lessons on the use of propaganda and perhaps a case study of the impact on the US government of the television coverage of the war in Vietnam. The diversity of national and regional religious and ethnic identities in the UK and the need for mutual respect and understanding describe much of the work that is done in history classrooms. These themes can be seen in the gradual development of the UK which is already a central feature of National Curriculum history. The Reformation and its impact on religious and other communities form an essential part of pre-examination history, as well as still being popular at 'A' level. The role of the EU (see Chapter 8) or the Commonwealth is not often taught but the nature of international politics, whether in the context of aspects of the British Empire or the establishment and actions of the United Nations, is already common. Another example that could be given in this section relates to human rights with, perhaps, reference to the particular case of slavery (although care would need to be taken to ensure that positive role models are developed rather than particular groups being preserved in stereotypical fashion as victims).

Of course, in all the above examples it would not be sufficient to teach knowledge as if it were somehow isolated from understanding. For understanding to be achieved, it is necessary for pupils to be encouraged to explore the conceptual aspects of historical issues. In general, four types of key concepts can be outlined. Firstly, general political concepts (as outlined by Crick 1978) can be successfully understood through a study of history. In the medicine part of the Schools History Project GCSE syllabus, for example, power can be explored through the Roman ability to provide public health facilities; welfare by a study of the modern National Health Service; order through an understanding of the development of the relatively stable Egyptian civilisation. Secondly, pupils can gain a greater understanding of the concepts that underpin democratic machinery through a study of history. The introduction and impact of factory legislation is an important part of the National Curriculum. The impact of the Reform Acts of 1832, 1867, 1884 and 1918 is similarly regarded as basic ground to cover. Of course, historical study will always automatically teach pupils about the democratic institutions of today, but it seems obvious that the examination of historical issues encourages the establishment of an increasing conceptual awareness which may be transferred between different periods of the past and the present, and deepened as study continues. Thirdly, particular political beliefs and ideologies can be understood in a more sophisticated way through history. It would not be difficult to teach a series of lessons around the themes of communism, fascism and totalitarianism. The First World War can be used to develop debates around the issue of conscientious objectors. The life of Gandhi is a useful way into debates about state power and passive resistance. Fourthly, and perhaps most importantly, pupils need to know more about what could be termed the procedural concepts of history, and again political material provides a very useful motivating influence. There is a need, for example, to show interlocking factors in webs of causation and pupils must show that they have considered the nature of unintended and intended consequences, as well as the difference between short-term and long-term issues. Work on interpretations of history seems to hold particular potential for developing insights relating to citizenship education. If pupils can come to understand that different judgements have been developed at particular points in history, then it may be possible not only to develop greater tolerance but also to recognise the forces that act upon citizens as they create specific forms of society. Many of these features are commonly included in assessment schemes for GCSE and other history courses as well as within the National Curriculum. Furthermore, it would be a major step forward if there could be an elaboration of the procedural, or second-order, concepts of citizenship. The issues involved in such a suggestion cannot be explored in depth here but guidance does exist for how further work might be undertaken (Cloonan and Davies 1998). Whereas first-order concepts such as monarchy and revolution are obviously linked to historical events, procedural concepts relate more obviously to the process of 'doing' history. To do well at history, students need to develop an understanding of such procedural concepts as evidence, empathy, cause and change. If a better understanding existed of the nature of procedural concepts of citizenship it would be possible to focus more explicitly on an exploration of the meaning of being a citizen.

Developing skills of enquiry and communication

One of the main purposes of the work of history teachers is to encourage pupils to adopt a critical approach to evidence, an aim so absolutely central that there is no need to develop an elaborate justification for it. There is, however, a need to go further to ensure that politics is perceived more broadly as something which affects pupils' everyday lives and allows them to begin to develop the active skills necessary for the full enjoyment of their democratic capabilities. The skills and aptitudes noted by the Crick Report cover both cognitive and active aspects of citizenship. There is currently no research evidence available which would demonstrate that there is a simple link between active political skills and history teaching. But there may be a case for arguing that in the development of cognitive historical and political skills lie the foundations for the acquisition of other skills. Further, that the use of role plays, simulations, fieldwork and other techniques used in history classrooms suggests that much can be done to develop relevant skills. For example, an ability to present a reasoned case, to undertake efforts at support mobilisation, and to evaluate the success of campaigns could become an accepted part of the aims of history lessons. The ability to think about topical issues, to justify, in writing and in speech, personal opinions about problems or events, and to contribute to a group discussion and debate are now statutory requirements. History teachers are well placed to meet them.

Developing skills of participation and responsible action

Comments made above about the perceived threats of bias and indoctrination imply that this area is likely to be the most problematic for history teachers. Careful professional action seems likely to be needed by teachers responding to the statutory requirement to 'negotiate, decide and take part responsibly in both school and community based activities' (DfEE/QCA 1999, p. 14). The difficulty becomes apparent when one reflects on the meaning of words such as 'responsibly'. Presumably it is not envisaged that school students will begin to form action groups that operate in sensitive and controversial contexts such as protesting publicly for or against fox hunting. The nature of values education suggests that some caution is needed before history teachers simply assume that appropriate work can be undertaken. There is a debate between those who perceive the need to supply 'right' answers (e.g. Bloom 1987) and others (e.g. Jonathan 1993) who place more emphasis on the exploration of different perspectives. It is vitally important that teachers feel confident in developing the skills of participation as a few ill-chosen activities that reach the front pages of certain newspapers could lead to a sharp decline in support for citizenship education.

The issue that provides a focus for debate and involvement needs to be carefully chosen. Stradling *et al.* (1984) discusses ways of recognising which issues are most controversial, based on the extent to which they divide the community, conflicting solutions being implied by different values held by different sections of the community or even the school itself. The nature of the rift exposed by an issue will be related to the perception of five factors. Firstly, its inherent importance will be considered. Nuclear energy, for example, will be regarded by some as more important than, perhaps, the nature of leisure interests. This inherent importance, of course, depends on a number of factors. The development of the leisure industry in particular ways is very much more controversial in some areas than nuclear energy. Secondly, the degree to which an argument is perceived as being extreme will affect the level of controversy. In this context, issues often become more controversial if they are presented as a proposal rather than just as an area for discussion. For example, discussion about the age of consent is probably not as controversial as it would be if someone made a specific proposal that it should be reduced or increased. Thirdly, how far an issue is perceived to relate to moral absolutes or culturally specific matters can raise the temperature of a debate. Some people think that an issue is less controversial if its discussion is limited in some way. Some, for example, may be content to concede that discussions about women's rights in a particular country should primarily or exclusively be the responsibility of people in that country. Debate will not then be conducted as fiercely as it would be if the matter was assumed to be relevant to all. Fourthly, how many people are likely to express agreement or disagreement on an issue is also relevant. This could mean that arguments about football could be more genuinely controversial in certain sections of the community than certain constitutional issues. Finally, the capacity of young people to be affected positively or negatively by an issue will be a crucial factor in determining the nature and level of controversy. It is vital for teachers to consider these issues, as it is perfectly possible for some topics to appear simply factual and yet lead in practice to fierce debate. For example, in certain parts of the country, only an unwise teacher would teach as an obvious and undisputed fact that London is the capital of the United Kingdom. Similarly, although a good educational debate can be held about certain topics in some areas, it may be necessary to avoid them in particular circumstances.

Nevertheless, the skills of participation can be developed by teaching about and working in local and other communities. At times the 'space' offered by distant historical events is useful. It is possible, for example, to raise good questions about contemporary welfare rights through local history that focuses on nineteenth-century poor relief. The scandal of the Andover workhouse is an example that can be used to good effect, particularly by teachers in Hampshire. The local history of villages involved in the Swing riots is a good way of illustrating themes to do with law and order. As long as the purpose of the activity is educational and teachers are not aiming at the achievement of a specific, perhaps party-political, goal, then involvement in a heritage campaign to abandon, preserve or restore a historical site could be very fruitful.

Conclusion

It is a cause of professional concern that the links between teaching and learning history and citizenship education have been neglected until recently by policy makers and teachers. An outpouring of rhetoric is a poor substitute for a few good lessons on a regular basis in all our schools. If evidence is sought for a democratic deficit, the absence of such work is all that is needed. A democracy that chooses to teach history to those who will not be historians, and science to those who will not be scientists, but refuses to teach citizenship explicitly and professionally to those who will be (or are already) citizens, is a democracy in name only. The simple proposition that political matters will always be in evidence in schools entails a pressing need for something to be done. The way forward is uncertain but attention to the following may be helpful:

- aiming to raise the status of work on citizenship education by supporting current official efforts which, while certainly not perfect, may lead to the establishment of some consensus within a broad framework about its importance and its nature
- looking for a meaningful structure in which citizenship can be taught and learned in schools which will give a heavy responsibility to the history teacher but also to others in what will hopefully lead to some sort of co-ordinated effort; this is preferable to unnecessary duplication or the development of unbalanced programmes that emphasise interpersonal understanding
- finding a way of making citizenship less of a goal and more of a process by establishing procedural concepts which will allow for classroom work to be explicitly focused on relevant ideas and issues

Key questions

1   What do you think about the arguments presented in this chapter concerning the ways in which history and citizenship interrelate? What are the key dividing lines between history and citizenship education? Where does one stop and the other begin?

2   Very generally, it could be said that there may be three levels of activity for citizenship education in history classrooms: the teacher is unaware or uninterested; the students are unaware of the teacher's intentions to promote citizenship education; students and teacher understand the common purpose of the work in the classroom. Do you think that school students have to be aware of what they are learning before they can make good progress? If so, what needs to be done to ensure as far as possible the development of a common focus?

Recommended reading

J. Appleby, L. Hunt and M. Jacob (1994) *Telling the Truth about History*. New York, W.W. Norton.

R. Phillips (1998) *History Teaching, Nationhood and the State: a study in educational politics*. London, Cassell.

Part II

Curriculum issues

Chapter 3

Securing a place for citizenship education in the history department

> We should like to see a fundamental review of the place of the humanities and social sciences within the curriculum. We believe it to be entirely unsatisfactory that significant elements of citizenship education should be relegated to second class status and left to the mercy of an individual school's curriculum policy.
>
> (Citizenship Foundation, quoted in National Commission on Education 1993)

The many calls for improved attention to be given to citizenship education have now been met, at least to some extent. It is a source of immense professional satisfaction that citizenship education is a National Curriculum subject in Key Stages 3 and 4 from the beginning of the academic year in 2002. The purpose of this chapter is to relate the detailed official guidance that has been provided for the history teacher. By promoting an awareness of the specifics of the guidance for teachers and by stressing some general ways in which departments can act, it is intended that a secure relationship will come to exist between history and citizenship. This chapter provides a brief sketch of policy-related details for the teacher that were not covered in Chapter 1 and suggests departmental strategies that are more focused than those given in Chapter 2. Once clarification has been achieved about locating citizenship within the history department, it will be possible, in the chapters that follow, to provide the guidance needed to tackle specific areas of citizenship.

Of course, this clarification for the purpose of anchoring citizenship is necessary. Some discussion has already been undertaken in this book about the contested nature of citizenship. Beyond these fundamental debates (that are both conceptual and practical) there are issues to do with the appropriate development of a strategy for educational change. The sensible and, some might argue, necessary approach that means that schools should 'choose how they organise their school curriculum to include the programmes of study for citizenship'(DfEE/QCA 1999b, p. 6) highlights the need for proactive, informed and skilful teachers who will develop appropriate frameworks and strategies. The challenges for history teachers are significant. History teachers will have particular responsibilities contained in the History Order for this area. History teachers may even lead the introduction of citizenship education in many schools: this means they will be required to provide a balanced view of citizenship education within their teaching. In order to adopt the principles of citizenship education found in the new Citizenship and History Orders, history teachers will also need to examine carefully the impact on their classroom practice and consider the ethos and organisation within their school which will influence the delivery of citizenship education. They will certainly need to consider confirming or adopting a participative and pupil-centred approach to learning as: 'It is difficult to conceive of pupils as active citizens if their experience of learning in citizenship education has been predominantly passive' (QCA 1998, p. 37, para 6.3.2).

It should be emphasised very strongly that history teachers are well placed to develop citizenship education. The attainment of intended learning outcomes in citizenship education is evident in and transferable to history. For example, at Key Stage 3 pupils are expected to:

- express and justify, orally and in writing, a personal opinion relevant to an issue
- contribute to small-group and class discussions on matters of personal and general significance and present the outcomes to a class
- work with others to meet a challenge of shared significance through negotiation, accommodation and agreed action, and be able to reflect on the process
- use imagination when considering the experience of others and be able to role play, express plausibly and reflect on viewpoints contrary to their own
- analyse, discuss and reflect on significant issues and events encountered within a community
- garner information about an issue from a range of sources including TV and radio news, documentary footage, newspapers and new communication technologies with some understanding of the different roles these sources play
- demonstrate an understanding of the use of statistics
- take part in informal debates and have opportunities to vote on issues

(QCA 1998, p. 49, para 6.13.1)

At Key Stage 4 pupils are expected to:

- express and justify, orally and in writing, a personal opinion relevant to an issue
- contribute to small-group and class discussions on matters of personal and general significance and present the outcomes to a wider audience
- work with others to meet a challenge of shared significance through negotiation, accommodation and agreed action, and be able to reflect on and critically evaluate the process
- use imagination when considering the experience of others and be able to role play, express plausibly viewpoints contrary to their own and reflect on and critically evaluate such viewpoints
- investigate, analyse, discuss and reflect on major challenges faced by communities
- research an issue from a range of sources including TV and radio news, documentary footage, newspapers and new communication technologies with particular reference to bias and the use of evidence
- demonstrate an understanding of the use and abuse of statistics

- take part in formal debates and have structured opportunities to vote on issues

(QCA 1998, pp. 50–1, para 6.14.1)

The content and intended learning outcomes of citizenship education overlap most significantly with history, especially in the following areas: teaching and learning about political, social and economic systems, development of the British democratic system, development of Britain as a pluralist society, consideration of international sustainable development, understanding of human rights, use of evidence, learning processes of enquiry and reaching informed judgements and conclusions. History subject leaders are both required, in the new History Order, and advised to identify aspects of their work which correspond with the programme of study for citizenship education. This will allow history teachers to identify activities and tasks that relate to the history programmes of study. In order to consider how history may contribute to citizenship education we need to look at earlier stages, especially Key Stage 2. The following is expected at the beginning of Year 7, but may not be realised:

- know how rules and laws are made, and understand right, wrong, fair, unfair, law, rule, forgiveness
- understand the need for laws, the role of the police, the consequences of anti-social behaviour; understand terms like punishment, cause, consequence, justice, fairness, evidence.
- know about the workings of local and national communities, sources of government and opportunities to participate; understand terms like mayor, council, councillor, parliament, MP, MEP, election, vote, political party
- recognise different types of government such as democracies and dictatorships, understanding terms like freedom of speech, opposition, vote, government, king, queen, prime minister, president
- know about voluntary organisations and understand the meaning of terms like voluntary service, volunteer, charity, protest, petition
- know that different economic systems exist, and understand terms like fairness, justice, choice, price, services, wealth, market, wage
- understand the concept of a global community, understanding terms like poverty, famine, disease, charity, aid, human rights

(adapted from QCA 1998, p. 47, para 6.12.1)

Consequently, a detailed audit of current provision in history is a good starting point for any history department. While the Orders for all subjects highlight potential linkages, some potential history linkages are illustrated in Table 3.1.

Table 3.1 provides a good baseline for secondary history teachers in conducting such an audit. This is not to argue, however, that the production of such a table is sufficient. Unfortunately, many tables like this have already been produced and have had no real impact. It would be possible, for example, to show in departmental schemes of work that Roman aqueducts can be used as an illustration of the power of the state and even of the

Table 3.1 Potential linkages between history and citizenship

Citizenship	History
Key Stage 3	
1a The legal and human rights and responsibilities underpinning society, basic aspects of the criminal justice system, and how both relate to young people	**10, 13** A study of how expansion of trade and colonisation, industrialisation and political changes affected the UK, including the local area A study of some of the significant individuals, events and developments from across the 20th century, including the two World Wars, the Holocaust, the Cold War and their impact on Britain, Europe and the wider world
1b The diversity of national, regional, religious and ethnic identities in the UK and the need for mutual respect and understanding	**2b** Pupils should be taught about the social, cultural, religious and ethnic diversity of the societies studied, both in Britain and the wider world
1c–e c Central and local government, the public services they offer and how they are financed, and the opportunities to contribute d The key characteristics of parliamentary and other forms of government e The electoral system and importance of voting	**9, 10** A study of crowns, parliaments and people: the major political, religious and social changes affecting people throughout the British Isles, including the local area if appropriate A study of how expansion of trade and colonisation, industrialisation and political changes affected the UK, including the local area
1i The world as a global community, and the political, economic, environmental and social implications of this, and the role of the European Union, the Commonwealth and the United Nations	**13** A study of some of the significant individuals, events and developments from across the 20th century, including the two World Wars, the Holocaust, the Cold War and their impact on Britain, Europe and the wider world
2a Think about topical political, spiritual, moral, social and cultural issues, problems and events by analysing information and its sources, including ICT-based resources	**4a** Identify, select and use a range of appropriate sources of information including oral accounts, documents, printed sources, the media, artefacts, pictures, photographs, music, museums, buildings and sites and ICT-based sources as a basis for independent historical enquiries

Table 3.1 continued

Citizenship	History
2b Justify orally and in writing a personal opinion about such issues, problems or events	**5b** Recall, prioritise and select historical information
2c Contribute to group and exploratory class discussions, and take part in debates	**5c** Communicate their knowledge and understanding of history, using a range of techniques, including spoken language, structured narratives, substantiated explanations and the use of ICT

Key Stage 4

Citizenship	History
II The UK's relations in Europe, including the EU, and relations with the Commonwealth and the United Nations	GCSE syllabuses, particularly those dealing with the 20th century world, include much relevant material
2a Research a topical political, spiritual, moral, social or cultural issue, problem or event by analysing information from different sources, including ICT-based resources, showing an awareness of the use and abuse of statistics	Social and economic history GCSE work commonly includes work on statistics that relate to contemporary issues (e.g. population increases in the 19th century that relate to issues of enduring concern such as standards of living)
2b Express, justify and defend orally and in writing a personal opinion about such issues, problems or events	An example can be given from Schools History Project work in which the past is understood in the context of the present (e.g. in modern China)
2c Contribute to group and exploratory class discussions, and take part in formal debates	Debates and discussions are one of the principal ways in which history students see the complexities of sources, evidence and interpretations.

Source: QCA (1998).

early development of some sort of social rights. But this does not ensure that teachers are explicitly promoting this sort of understanding in the classroom or that, even if they are, students recognise what is being taught. A number of different factors need to come together in an explicit treatment of citizenship.

One way to work towards this difficult goal of infusing citizenship through history is to look beyond the identification of aims and content and to focus on how pupils should learn. This can be tackled both structurally, in ensuring that there is an appropriate framework that recognises citizenship issues, and also in the classroom processes that are used to develop appropriate understanding and skills. It should be recognised that sequencing learning is a difficult procedure without level descriptions for citizenship education. At each key stage guidance is provided to help history teachers identify topics and activities within their own schemes of work which will reinforce work covered in citizenship lessons. There should be time for history teachers to evaluate current provision and to build plans to enable continual growth and development. It is important that each history department:

- audits current provision in terms of content and teaching methodology
- identifies areas of teachers' strengths and weaknesses in terms of developing independent and autonomous learning styles
- notes areas of common approach and content with other subjects
- develops a statement which justifies the contribution of a subject to citizenship education
- plans topics within schemes of work in collaboration with other subject areas which cover similar content
- arranges staff development to promote independent and autonomous learning styles
- researches opportunities for enhanced learning beyond the classroom and in the local community
- builds community activities into schemes of work

A team approach is essential and history departments must recognise the need for consistency and coherence. This requires careful attention to the teaching and learning of controversial issues. Teachers of history are already generally well equipped to avoid biased presention of controversial content, and so to make a balanced presentation possible. In citizenship studies the history teacher needs to continue such good practice, including allowing discussion and the presentation of conflicting viewpoints within a structured environment.

To avoid bias on controversial issues teachers will resist:

- highlighting a particular selection of facts or items of evidence, thereby giving them greater importance than other equally relevant information
- presenting information as if not open to alternative interpretation
- setting themselves up as the sole authority
- presenting opinions and value judgements on facts
- giving an account of others' views, instead of real sources
- revealing their own preferences
- implying preferences by not opening up discussion
- neglecting a challenging consensus of opinion

(QCA 1998, p. 58, para 10.9)

The team approach requires a sense of ownership and commitment on the part of teachers.

During Key Stage 4 pupils continue to study, think about and discuss work covered at Key Stage 3. The development of skills and understanding enables more learning to take place. Table 3.2 (QCA 1998, p. 47) provides a summary of what can be expected of pupils at the end of their period of compulsory education.

Of course, drawing attention to such outcomes is absolutely essential for demonstrating the vital importance of the work generally and showing that these are issues on which history teachers commonly focus. There is nothing in the above with which a good history teacher would disagree. However, such a list is also incredibly daunting. It is important to recognise what at times has been both a terrific advantage and a huge stumbling block for citizenship education: it is rich in goals and ambitions but under-provided with research knowledge and human resources. If we expect the history teacher to be the sole guarantor of such ambitions we will only raise hopes unrealistically and condemn teachers to take the blame for problems that are actually beyond their capabilities. The congruence (or at times confusion) between the nature of citizenship education and education itself is still an issue that needs resolution. However, while an entire school, or even the educational system as a whole, could not be expected to cover everything, the positive point should be made that the history teacher should not stand alone in these endeavours. The implications of citizenship education will permeate the whole school, with one – but only one – vital part including the teaching and learning of history. The formulation of a policy therefore requires a collaborative effort that addresses both the content of what is taught and learnt, and teaching and learning methodologies across the school. A clear history departmental policy needs to account for and allay any concerns. Due consideration should be given to auditing current provision, drawing on existing staff strengths, interests and expertise, and staff development. It is for individual history departments to consider working in collaboration with colleagues from other subject areas when there is obvious overlap. It is also important that the history departmental policy fits into an overarching whole-school approach to avoid inconsistencies. However, there are also many conceptual issues which history teachers need to consider and this book aims to outline them in the framework of possible practical ways forward.

Key questions

1   Does an audit of content and preferred teaching methodology in a history department of which you are aware suggest that the development of citizenship education will be straightforward? If change is necessary, what could you do to facilitate it?

2   What opportunities exist within a history department of which you are aware for collaborative work on citizenship education with colleagues from another subject area?

3   If you were able to spend a small amount of money on citizenship education that would assist the professional development of history staff, what would you purchase?

Table 3.2 QCA's summary of what can be expected of pupils at the end of their period of compulsory education

Key concepts	Values and dispositions	Skills and aptitudes	Knowledge and understanding
Democracy and autocracy	Concern for the common good	Ability to make a reasoned argument both verbally and in writing	Topical and contemporary issues and events at local, national, EU, Commonwealth and international levels
Co-operation and conflict	Belief in human dignity and equality	Ability to co-operate and work effectively with others	
Fairness, justice, the rule of law, rules, law and human rights	Concern to resolve conflicts	Ability to consider and appreciate the experience and perspective of others	The nature of democratic communities, including how they function and change
Freedom and order	A disposition to work with and for others with sympathetic understanding	Ability to tolerate other viewpoints	The interdependence of individuals and local and voluntary communities
Individual and the community		Ability to develop a problem-solving approach	The nature of diversity, dissent, and social conflict
Power and authority	Proclivity to act responsibly: that is to care for others and oneself; premeditation and calculation about the effect actions are likely to have on others; and acceptance of responsibility for unforeseen or unfortunate consequences	Ability to use modern media and technology critically to gather information	Legal and moral rights and responsibilities of individuals and communities
Rights and responsibilities		A critical approach to evidence put before one and ability to look for fresh evidence	The nature of social, moral and political challenges faced by individuals and communities
	Practice of tolerance	Ability to recognise forms of manipulation and persuasion	Britain's parliamentary political and legal systems at local, national, European, Commonwealth and international level, including how they function and change
	Judging and acting by a moral code	Ability to identify, respond to and influence social, moral and political challenges and situations	
	Courage to defend a point of view		The nature of political and voluntary action in communities
	Willingness to be open to changing one's opinions and attitudes in the light of discussion and evidence		The rights and responsibilities of citizens as consumers, employees, employers and family and community members
	Individual initiative and effort		
	Civility and respect for the rule of law		The economic system as it relates to individuals and communities
	Determination to act justly		
	Commitment to equal opportunities and gender equality		Human rights charters and issues
	Commitment to voluntary service		Sustainable development and environmental issues
	Concern for human rights		
	Concern for the environment		

Source: QCA (1998).

Recommended reading

D. Banham (2000) *King John*. London, John Murray.
An innovative, engaging textbook for use with school students, part of which explores citizenship.

M. Fullan (1982) *The Meaning of Educational Change*. Toronto, O.I.S.E.
A contemporary classic statement on educational change and how to achieve it.

Chapter 4

Communitarianism and the teaching of history
Community and identity

> The past is where our roots lie, and we have much to learn from it. What we urgently need today is a sense of our histories and cultures as a shared past, one that brings together our diverse experiences and informs our understanding of the present. Only then can we take a full and active part in realising our vision of a shared future.
>
> (Commission for Racial Equality 1996: p. 121)

Introduction

The relationship between communitarianism and the teaching of school history is not an obvious one that most teachers would notice. Communitarianism is, after all, a new philosophical stance originating from academia and there has been, in the context of British communitarianism, almost no literature on its implications for school history. There has also been practically no discussion in the educational literature of the potential worth of communitarian theory for the teaching of history or of how this new philosophical and political movement might assist our understanding of diverse communities in modern Britain or of the contribution it may make to an individual's personal identity (Goldby 1997; Arthur 1998, 2000). This chapter introduces and reviews the meaning of communitarianism and explains some of the possible implications for history teaching in British schools. It examines the potential relationship between communitarianism and the teaching of history, and discusses the teaching of 'British' history in the context of a communitarian understanding of community formation. The chapter will attempt to consider history teaching from a communitarian perspective and will present two examples of religious and racial controversy in the teaching of history in British schools to illustrate the 'contested' nature of school history. There are clear connections between communitarianism and the place of both history and citizenship education in the school curriculum. The Crick Report (QCA 1998) placed considerable emphasis on community involvement in schools, and communitarian theory has much to offer in this area. Communitarian theory also connects with history teaching in terms of how we think about national identity and the requirements for membership of a historical community.

Communitarianism

In the growing academic literature communitarianism is expressed in both radical and conservative forms which reflect the diverse understandings academics have of it. Nevertheless, the core understanding essentially holds that the community, rather than the individual or state, should be at the centre of our analysis and our value system. Communitarianism has been popularised in recent years and has had a considerable impact on both the Democrats in the USA and the New Labour Party in Britain where it is often referred to in political rhetoric as 'The Third Way'. The Prime Minister, Tony Blair, has adopted much of the communitarian message of social solidarity and community as the chief means by which individuals flourish and develop (Arthur 2000: p. 20). New Labour also uses the rhetoric of 'new Britain' and 'one nation' which has the advantage of being inclusive language, but it may be just language and not meant as a guide for action.

'Community' is certainly the key concept in any understanding of communitarianism. Communitarians generally make several claims about the nature of persons and human identity, not least that persons are embedded in communities. They claim that the self is constituted to some extent through a community which provides shared values, interests or practices. A person's individual values are formed in the social context of these communities and often pursued through communal attachments (Kymlicka 1993). Communitarians emphasise the embedded status of the person, and almost all communitarians are therefore united around a conception of human beings as 'integrally related to the communities of culture and language that they create, maintain and sustain' (Mulhall and Swift 1996: p. 162).

Bell (1993: pp. 93ff.) helps develop an understanding of the implications of the communitarian concept of community. He agrees that deeply felt attachments to a number of communities help constitute a person's identity. These *constitutive communities* define the sense of who we are and provide a largely background way of our being in the world of thinking, acting and deciding. Bell argues that we cannot easily shed what we are since we are principally connected with these constitutive features of our identity in a way which often resists articulation. To reject them can lead to a potential crisis of identity or a form of disorientation. Bell suggests that it is possible to answer the question of what these constitutive communities are by asking a very simple question: 'Who are you?' (Bell 1993: p. 97). The answer might involve such elements as family name, nationality, language, culture and religion – all of which relate to the community in which people grow. It is important to say that Bell does not have in mind a monolithic society where everyone has the same commitments and simply conforms, but he does claim that there is no such thing as the 'unencumbered self'. In other words, no individual can find an identity apart from others.

One of the basic premises of recent communitarian thinking is that modern society has lost a sense of social solidarity. It lacks the communal dimensions that might unite people around a conception of what is 'good' or 'worthwhile' to pursue in life. Therefore, communitarians argue that there should be an attempt to forge a new equilibrium between rights and responsibilities. The communitarian position is thus bound up with the concepts of fraternity, solidarity, civic pride, social obligation and tradition, and is seen as corrective to the recent 'cult of the individual'. While communitarians claim that we can critically examine our attachments to communities, they uphold the view that some attachments are so fundamental to our identity we cannot set them aside without harmful costs to ourselves and the community. Communitarians make it clear that our attachments to communities are not voluntary, that social attachments are not normally chosen ones (e.g. family, nationality, etc.), and that our upbringing and the values we adopt and live by are often acquired involuntarily rather than being a matter of rational choice by each individual.

Some communitarian theorists use historical theses of idyllic communities in past periods to support their moral and political theories. Popenoe (1994: p. 27) is most explicit in terms of policy implications. He calls for a return to 'natural communities' – small, village-like groups, protected, to some extent, from intrusion by outsiders. According to this overtly anachronistic vision, mobility of residents would be reduced, diversity would be resisted and strict moral standards would be enforced, all in the name of social stability and community. For MacIntyre (1981), you understand your life only by looking at your actions within a story, a 'narrative'. But this narrative converges with that of other people, who come to be part of one's own narrative. Thus an understanding of oneself can be attained only in the context of the community, that sets up the form and shape, as well as the circumstances and the background, of these narratives. Our identities are constructed by the stories we tell ourselves, and our virtues and values are prescribed by the very nature of the specific social practices in which they function. The elements that make up a community are shared history, shared practice, shared meanings, a common tradition and common ideas about life together.

Another contribution to the debate was the publication of *Habits of the Heart* (1985), in which Robert Bellah and his colleagues attempt to challenge conceptions of community. Drawing heavily upon the framework provided by MacIntyre's *After Virtue* (1981), these writers are convinced that individuals have become increasingly detached from their social and cultural contexts, and they seek to reverse this trend through the renewal of community. *Habits of the Heart* provides a definition of community which includes both a territorial and a relational dimension: territorial in the sense that a community is located within a specific geographical area, and relational in the sense that community exists when there is a quality to the relationships and associations among people. Bellah and his colleagues place great emphasis on the relational aspects of community and also emphasise the interdependence of these relationships. Such a community of memory tells its story or narrative of common values which are deeply rooted in its history. Members would involve themselves in shared practices and manifest loyalty and obligations that keep the community alive. There would be a sense of solidarity and a relationship of reciprocity with everyone else in the community. Phillips (1993: p. 14) draws his definition of community from this dimension of the communitarian position: 'A community is a group of people who live in a common territory, have a common history and shared values, participate together in various activities, and have a high degree of solidarity.'

There may well be an intuitive appeal to the idea of the serenity and order of a by-gone age, in which people grew, lived and died within a community characterised by reciprocity and stability. Perhaps it does not matter very much that such communities seem not to have existed, at least in the idyllic form portrayed by some communitarians. Much of the discussion of community in communitarian thought has a certain sense of nostalgia associated with it, but three broad strands can be identified. First, community can serve as a means of self-identification on the basis of shared circumstances – roots in community. Second, we can speak of 'the community of . . .' which represents a homogeneous community. Finally, community can be based on the principle of the 'common good': all have a say in what happens in society and all contribute to the general 'good'. It is to the third strand that many liberal communitarians subscribe, since for them it is only within a liberal democratic society that more effective participation by all for all is possible. More conservative communitarians subscribe to a process of strong formation in communal identity which results in a high degree of exclusivity of the community in order to provide members with a deep sense of belonging.

Communitarianism and the teaching of history

The history curriculum in English schools is expected to provide pupils with opportunities to develop a sense of identity, respect, tolerance and empathy through knowledge and appreciation of their own social and cultural heritage and traditions, and of the culture and traditions of people in other communities, countries, societies, ethnic groups, faiths and beliefs (QCA 1999c). History is explicitly intended to promote citizenship through 'providing opportunities for pupils to discuss the nature and diversity of societies in Britain' (DfEE/QCA 1999a: p. 8). Communitarianism is obviously concerned with what makes us into a community and also with what helps us form our community identity. It emphasises the need to belong, to be included within society. It is concerned with shared history and memory, what Nash (1998: p. 74) describes as 'collective history', knowledge of the community's traditions and memories. Continuity with a familiar past, a language, shared rituals and beliefs are core features of this view. Kincheloe and Steinberg (1997: p. 421) ask what part memory and historical knowledge play in our lives, and they focus on the word 'memory' which connects us to the present through the past–present relationship. The past lives in the present and consequently how we remember is important (1997: p. 242). The danger that they raise is that we may end up with a 'dominant memory' which is open to exploitation by national governments as a focus for encouraging a mechanistic loyalty and patriotism from the next generation.

Anthony Smith (1991) believes that many people in society seek to maintain their 'common myths and historical memories', but he warns that our identity can never be reduced to a single element as it is too multi-dimensional a concept. Anderson (1991) believes that Britain is whatever its citizens imagine it to be – 'an imagined community' – because its members will never know all fellow members. History is certainly still considered by many to be a socialising subject which transmits the culture and shared values of society to the next generation. Through this transmission identity is formed, and communitarianism appears to give support to the idea that history teaching in schools should be a reinforcer of community tradition and community identity. Liberal communitarians argue that there can be an inclusive ideal of a community of communities. It is why Tam (1998: p. 226) asserts that we belong to a multiplicity of communities, such as a Church, trade union, neighbourhood, town or region; all of these communities associate with each other in a vertical and horizontal way. The nation-state is only one of these communities. Etzioni (1997: pp. 187–205) describes these communities as 'layered loyalties' while Tam (1998: p. 227) concludes that: 'No communitarian theory can be sustained on the basis of a single overriding community which commands the exclusive allegiance of its members'. In order to establish some kind of identity everyone needs a past, but confining history to one's own story or community, and only seeing the *other* story or community in relation to the relevance it has for one's own, is limited and narrow. Nevertheless, it is often this type of history which is used to promote one particular community's identity and survival.

Consequently, if communitarians believe that communities must be preserved and that it is important to teach traditional values, would they also agree, for example, that the National Curriculum in history should continue to consist of mainly British history? What do they have to say to us about 'Britishness' as a value in education or as a part of our settled traditions and personal identity? It seems, very little. Communitarian theory uses a whole series of concepts which link easily with certain aims of history: identity and community are obvious, but shared rituals, memory, practices and values indicate that communitarianism has something to say about the teaching of history. However, such a link may be too simplistic since communitarianism is open to a range of interpretations and it is often difficult to provide exact definitions of what different communitarian writers believe or advocate as education policy.

In America some communitarians would object to a multicultural approach to history teaching which is particularistic, that is which encourages children to seek their identity in the cultures of their ancestors. Ravitch (1991) describes a California history syllabus with a section on 'National Identity' which advocates that history should be taught in such a way as to help American children realise that patriotism celebrates the moral force of the American idea of the nation that unites as one people the descendants of many cultures, races, religions and ethnic groups. She believes that a multicultural education in history is essential, but can be taken to extremes, leading to two different outcomes: first, pluralistic multiculturalism in which all citizens are members of one society and contribute their identity and religious beliefs to being responsible for all within society; second, particularistic multiculturalism which neglects the bonds of mutuality that exist among people of different races and religions and encourages children to seek their primary identity in the cultures and homelands of their ancestors. She argues for the first, as we should 'closely examine and try to understand that part of our national identity in which different groups competed, fought, suffered, but ultimately learned to live together in peace and even achieved a sense of common nationhood' (Ravitch 1991: p. 35). In other words, she believes that if there is no overall community then there can be no common good, for each community will fight for its own interests; and there will be no social good as each cultural group ends by teaching its own particular and distinctive history. Much of what Ravitch has to say appears to be about patriotism and very little else. She effectively holds up a model of patriotism which is both highly controversial and deeply contested. Not all communitarians would accept this model.

Ravitch (1991: p. 37) provides the example of a New York State report entitled 'A curriculum of inclusion', published in 1990, which claims that negative characterisations of, or the absence of positive references about, minority communities have a damaging effect on children. Ravitch observes that the report advocates that history teachers should portray non-European cultures positively. The report denounces bias without being able to identify a single instance of it in the curriculum and treats every disagreement with the curriculum as if it were proof of bias. European values are presented, she says, as being in themselves 'racist' and 'oppressive'. Much of the report, according to Ravitch, is clearly 'Europhobic' and what is highlighted is our differences. The report proposes that the purpose of history should be to promote 'self-esteem' among minority children so that they can think of their ancestors as also great and glorious. Ravitch believes that this teaches children that the culture they live in is not their native culture and that they must look elsewhere for their heritage. She says: 'Particularism is premised on the spurious notion that cultural traits may be inherited. It implies a dubious, perhaps dangerous, form of cultural predestination' (Ravitch 1991: p. 43). Ravitch's views are clearly controversial, but she does represent a significant number of those who claim the title, communitarian. The teaching of history in British schools has also faced the positive challenge of intercultural perspectives.

The contested nature of English school history

The English school curriculum is not neutral, and controversies will inevitably arise that reflect the differences in values among people in a diverse society. The curriculum is also often seen by interest groups as a means to shape the minds and values of the next generation. Haydn (1992) has illustrated how those from different political positions have attempted to use school history to develop in pupils values and attitudes linked to their own particular philosophies. Two concrete examples follow of contested history teaching from the perspective of two different communities. The first relates to how Catholics fought to remove the Protestant influence on textbooks and the school curriculum in the 1920s and 1930s while the second relates to how different ethnic communities sought to eliminate racial bias from schools in the 1980s and 1990s. Fowler (1995: p. 88) would call these two communities 'communities of memory' since they both are based on religious and/or traditional ideas of community. Both communities have a commitment to a shared history and identity – in effect, a particular world-view and culture. Demands to eradicate bias, ignorance and prejudice and to teach children to appreciate others whose religious and ethnic backgrounds are different from their own have a long history in Britain. Bias is understood here to mean an interpretation of evidence that lacks balance and expresses a partial view. Prejudice is a more difficult concept, more emotional, and usually implies a set of opinions independent of evidence. Both can be unconscious or deliberate. The Catholic campaigns in 1927 have much in common with the pressures that ethnic minorities in Britain brought to bear on the school curriculum in the 1990s – but also many important differences. Both movements sought to change the aims, content and methods of history teaching in schools in order to integrate their communities into British life in such a way that their own traditions, practices, values and beliefs were not simply tolerated, but accepted as part of British life.

Being British in 1927 meant accepting a significantly different set of values and beliefs from those of the early twenty-first century, and this is well illustrated in the school history curriculum. The Catholic community of Britain, still predominantly of Irish immigrant descent in the 1920s, was openly discriminated against even after the Catholic Emancipation Act of 1829. This Act only tolerated Catholics, while the general population treated Catholics as un-British and continued anti-Catholic discrimination at almost every level in society. Catholic children attending state schools studied a history syllabus which largely denied their faith, sometimes ignored it and even attempted to suppress it. The Westminster Catholic Federation (WCF), formed in 1927, established a Vigilance Committee to examine history textbooks and readers, and subsequently protested to publishers, authors and local councils about the 'manifest unfairness' with which the Catholic faith was treated in schools. There were 153 authorised history textbooks made available to schools by the London County Council. The WVF aim was to protest vigorously against three things:

- historical incorrectness
- misinterpretations of Catholic teaching
- offensive anti-Catholic bias

The list of publishers included Macmillan, Nelson, Cassell, Edward Arnold, Oxford Press, Chambers, and Longman. The WCF's activities may be illustrated by a letter it wrote to Thomas Nelson and Sons which stated that:

> History cannot, whatever our own view or prejudices would like to make it, be either Catholic or Protestant. History should relate facts as they occurred; the historian exceeds his function when of his own volition he imposes motives or gives a colouring which the facts themselves or the circumstances do not warrant. When divergent opinions are held the student should have both sides of every question submitted to his or her judgement.
>
> (WCF, 1927: pp. 22–3)

John Buchan replied on behalf of Nelson with the following statement:

> I am a Protestant, my firm is Protestant, the country is predominantly Protestant, and we publish educational books which are meant to be mainly for circulation among Protestants. That is to say, we believe that the Reformation was on the whole a very good thing, and that we have no desire to see its work undone.
>
> (WCF 1927: p. 69)

This open and honest attitude was typical of the period since Protestantism gave the British their identity. As Colley (1994: p. 53) says: 'Protestantism was the foundation that made the invention of Great Britain possible.' However, John Buchan was open enough to enter into discussion with another religious community, and he agreed with all the numerous corrections and suggestions made by the WCF. Edward Arnold, another publisher, was less sympathetic and responded to the same kind of letter with the statement that true and unbiased history cannot be written – end of matter (WCF 1927: p. 153).

The WCF found evidence in almost all of the 153 history textbooks used in schools of major Catholic figures being systematically discredited, their motives questioned, their actions disparaged, their names compromised. Mary Queen of Scots, monks, Catholic Europe, were all targets for this partial historical writing, and the poor people of Saragossa are described as 'slow, lazy, and careless' (WCF 1927: p. 154). In Edward Arnold's *Gateways to History* series the Pope and Spain, in particular, are attacked, and the offensive word 'Papist' is used to describe Catholics in many of the textbooks. The last Catholic Archbishop of Canterbury is compared with Mary Tudor in the following biased manner in one text: 'Pole, a narrow-minded bigot like herself' (WCF 1927: p. 557). In the Macmillan *Then and Now* series it is stated that '[St. Patrick] laid the foundation of a Cathedral and a bishopric; and to-day the Archbishop of Armagh is the head of the Irish Protestant Church'; this prompted the WCF to ask 'Was St. Patrick a Protestant?' (1927: p. 763). There are some odd and unexplained comments in the textbooks, like the statement in the *Pupil's Class Book of English History* that Elizabeth's refusal to marry Philip II of Spain 'was one of the causes that led him to send the Great Armada to attempt the conquest of England in 1588'. The history taught in these texts was largely English history and the presentation was often false, with particular views given in order to justify the status quo. Opinion was often presented as fact in many children's history textbooks. The Catholic campaign was largely successful and many of the texts were amended as a result of these campaigns in subsequent editions. However, there has been a widening of the field of school history since 1927 and while some would say that anti-Catholic bias and prejudice have not been removed entirely from texts it is certainly no longer obvious.

The main narrative of British history as taught in schools has largely ignored minority and immigrant communities in the attempt to minimise inter-community problems. The idea of Britishness assumed a common identity which became problematic for many immigrants to Britain, and various models were used in education to address the problem. First, attempts were made at assimilation, ignoring differences. Second, integration was tried, taking account of some differences. Third, cultural pluralism was adopted as the liberal answer to the problem, focussing on a concern for human rights and cultural diversity. However, even in the last model themes such as women's history or black history were often only add-ons to the main history curriculum. It is difficult to defend the grand historical narrative these days; at best it is provisional, at worst, it is biased and distorted. Yet it is our story telling which makes sense of our reality.

Britain today is an ethnically diverse country, but we must underscore the empirical fact that ethnic communities in Britain, including the white communities, belong to a variety of linguistic, regional and sectarian groups. There is no obvious unity between them. The hyphenated nationality used in the USA, e.g. African-American, Italian-American, is sometimes adopted in Britain, but there are difficulties with this. For example, to refer to people as Asian-British would imply that they were born in Asia or descended from parents or grandparents born in Asia, but how can Turks, Chinese, Japanese and Indians be placed in the same category when they do not have a great deal in common? In modern Britain (see Appiah 1999) people increasingly have multiple identities and we can no longer speak of the black/white dichotomy since this has broken down to be replaced with ethno-cultural dichotomies. However, by emphasising ethno-cultural identities, Appiah (1999: p. 5) goes further and claims that '40% of families are mixed origin families – their children are the embodiment of multiple identities'. Her definition of identity includes race, class, gender and sexuality and therefore the question arises: with these criteria why not 100 per cent 'mixed origin'?

A debate about school history, its aims, nature and justification, together with what it might be to be British, is well covered in the literature. R. Phillips (1998a, 1998b, 1999) summarises the debate between those who believe school history to be concerned with cultural transmission and those who see it as developing essential skills needed to deal with a diverse Britain. The fear in the 1980s was that the New Right wished to control the history school curriculum. A number of democratic groups have attempted to use history in schools to promote the cultural diversity of society and eradicate racist attitudes through the promotion of equal opportunity policies. There has also been a debate about the content of the history curriculum in English schools, in particular whether or not it should have a pluralist content base.

A number of positions are advocated. Josna Pankania, for example, is an Indian who attended an English grammar school after she immigrated to Britain as a child. She informs us that: 'My school was neither a place where my Indian identity was nurtured nor a source of knowledge about the history of my people', and that schools do not 'nurture the identity of black students' (1994: pp. 2–3). She advocates a kind of multiple citizenship and she also argues that perspectives on race, class and gender oppression should be interwoven into the National Curriculum. She dismisses the narrow pluralist model advocated by communitarians such as Ravitch. Multiculturalism, she says, masks the problem of racism and offers only a 'superficial debate on culture' (Pankania 1994: p. 52). She recommends parents to be vigilant and challenge history teaching and to be critical of the perceived intentions of teachers. She claims that the hidden values in a school could be racist. Britain, she asserts, is responsible for a catalogue of abuses and she concludes her argument: 'the National History Curriculum attempts to teach students a limited history, a history that does not threaten the British social order with its unequal race, gender, and class relations' (1994: pp. 148–9). However, if the aim of history is to make sense of the past, she is denying that history teachers teach their students a critical history of Britain. On this point she is supported by many others who argue that there has been a lack of critical perspective in teaching the history of Britain. Her book provides some very good examples of how to integrate various intercultural perspectives into the study units of the history National Curriculum.

In regard to the teaching of some kind of British national identity through history, Keith Robbins, a former President of the Historical Association, believes that the danger arises only if 'signposts' are transformed into exclusive 'badges', and pupils are taught that 'Britishness' is embodied most purely in a particular tradition. Rootedness, Robbins suggests, must be matched by an awareness of external diversity. John Slater (1995: p. 48) believes that:

> History does not explicitly seek to create a multicultural society or to argue an informed acceptance of it. But, without an informed understanding of the historical context of the experiences, attitudes and beliefs of other cultures, some necessary, if not sufficient, conditions for the existence of multicultural societies will not exist.

Insufficient serious attention may be being given to multicultural issues in our history classrooms. History will remain a contested subject, with debates about its nature and purpose. For example, Paul Goalen (1988) bemoans the fact that even the history teachers' professional journal *Teaching History* does not cover multicultural issues in sufficient detail. However, teachers today are much more sensitive about the need to avoid anything which erodes the human rights of young people. One of the underlying weaknesses of much multicultural writing on history, unlike the Catholic campaign of the 1920s, is the inability to identify many examples of factual error in the curriculum content of history. However, the leaders of both the Catholic community in the 1920s and the multicultural campaigns of the 1980s illustrated how suffering had been caused by ignorance, bias and prejudice in British school history teaching, often as a result of discrimination by omission. In a study of textbooks, Sherwood (1988) showed that such discrimination resulted in a failture to recognise the contribution of black people to the history of Britain.

Ernest Renan once said that: 'Forgetting, even getting history wrong, is an essential factor in the formation of a nation, which is why the progress of historical studies is often a danger to nationality' (quoted in Hobsbawm 1997: p. 270). History is inextricably bound to contemporary politics. Whilst Hobsbawm (1997: p. 275) notes that the most important channel for imparting historical information is the school, he says little about school history. Nevertheless, he says that bad history is dangerous and that teachers of history, especially national history, have a responsibility to be 'myth-slayers': 'The deconstruction of political or social myths dressed up as history has long been part of the historian's professional duties, independent of his or her sympathies' (1997: p. 273). Colley's (1994) impressive analysis of how Britain was forged as a nation indicates that British history can give the impression that Britain has existed for a long time, but really it is a fairly recent construction, an invented tradition. It could be argued that it is precisely because Britain is an invention that it allows for so much diversity. The impact of the new Scottish Parliament and Welsh Assembly will no doubt continue this process of reconstructing British national identity.

Communitarian perspectives

Some communitarians seek to use school-based history as a tool for teaching 'modern virtues' which, they believe, will help children reject their racist and sexist pasts in favour of some sort of cultural egalitarianism. Johnson (1995) offers a rationale for this, advocating a form of communitarian education which seeks to promote a love of learning and a tradition of excellence. He believes that:

> this love of learning and one's culture's traditions of excellence must finally be based in a love of the local place, the local community, the local people, no matter how small the place or humble the community and its people. Otherwise, our young will continue to learn their modern lessons of disdain for their folkways, their homeplaces, and the common people in our nation's schools. And we will 'educate' still another generation of 'rootless, emancipated, migrating individuals', who are 'cultural renegades believing in nothing but their own right to a good time'.
>
> (Johnson 1995: p. 103; quotes within from Lasch 1991)

He seems to imply that it is undesirable to be emancipated or to migrate. The virtues which communitarians have in mind include democratic habits, service to neighbours, collaboration and altruism, and they believe that all reasonable people with a democratic spirit will agree with them. It could be argued that these are not abstract concepts, but are rooted in history, indeed within a particular British tradition that needs therefore to be critically taught.

The communitarian perspective emphasises the local community, in particular its human rights and responsibilities. Nevertheless, the communitarian approach to history teaching in schools would undoubtedly emphasise the importance of understanding the history of a number of communities which constitute the individual in a modern, diverse Britain. It would recognise the existence of different tradition-based communities with their own memories and particular history and beliefs. It would also recognise that members of the Catholic or Asian communities would share a great deal with other communities in society, and that certain common bonds and common values would also be shared. In other words, there would exist a common core of values across various communities which would include ideas about the common good, human rights, solidarity in society, and democratic principles. Consequently, history teaching would need to reflect these concepts by ensuring that all children in every community have an understanding of the historical background to these concepts. This will inevitably mean the teaching of British history, but interwoven with a number of different perspectives including 'race', gender and class.

There are few communities in Britain which are so fundamentalist that they hold entirely closed belief systems: such communities would be totally authoritarian, conformist and oppressive if they were cut off from interaction with other communities in society. Distinctive communities in Britain are not monolithic, for they are neither isolated from outside pressures nor free from internal tensions. Communitarians seek a balance, and individual membership of a number of communities is necessary, preventing a monolithic community from being formed. Consequently, many communitarians do not seek a return to traditional communities embodied in history. Instead, they seek open but culturally distinctive communities which are committed to a set of core democratic values and are able to build society through open participation. Liberal critics accuse communitarians of being conservative, and Amy Gutman (1985: p. 319) has gone so far as to suggest that communitarians really 'want us to live in Salem'. She provides no evidence for this claim and, in any case, many communitarians have no difficulty with diverse traditions being included within the history curriculum. Communitarian thinking appears to seek mutual recognition of cultural diversity and a shared way of thinking about common problems across communities. Consequently, a communitarian approach to teaching a multicultural history may emphasise similarities as much as differences.

The aim of a communitarian approach to school history would be to produce citizens who place great emphasis on putting aside personal interests for the sake of community. Communitarians seek to balance the social good of the community against the good of the individual and they can be either progressive or conservative in orientation. Communitarian history education would emphasise the role, depending on the ideological perspective employed, of 'mediating' social institutions in addition to schools, in the belief that society as a whole is educative. At best, this would not restrict itself to the transmission of a set of historical perspectives, but would aim to strengthen the democratic and participative spirit within each individual. At worst, it could become majoritarian in approach, insisting on the acceptance of the moral position of the majority in society. New Labour's agenda is to devise a national framework of achievable outcomes which will mould a majority of citizens who express communitarian sentiments – just as Thatcherism attempted to encourage citizens to feel comfortable with libertarian sentiments (Arthur and Davison 2000). The new curriculum for September 2000 offers flexibility for teachers to reflect the various cultural traditions found in the school community itself, but at the same time ensures that all members of that community are aware that they are included within the British national identity. The story of Britain is not fixed, it is also the story of errors and how we have managed and failed to overcome them, and for that reason it is a story without an end. The task of the history teacher is not only to help pupils learn about a critical British history, but to help them participate in its construction. Communitarians would be sceptical about Dreyden's (1989) contention that cultural diversity means different approaches to historical knowledge and perhaps even a different acquisition of knowledge. The more conservative communitarians would not accept the idea of constructing a new historical canon in order to infuse into the National Curriculum the histories of particular ethnic communities. While multicultural perspectives on history teaching are important within communitarian thinking, the movement does not generally recommend particular histories which encourage ethnic communities in Britain to find their identities outside the country.

Conclusion

There will always be objections to the criteria for the selection of the content of history syllabuses in schools. Content selection is always biased in some way, and there will always be concern about the selection and combination of historical facts. However, history, fully appreciated, means that nothing is fixed; its subject matter is always being reinterpreted, and through new scholarship and debate a critical awareness is always seen as important. The new National Curriculum is no longer taught in chronological order and much of the content specification has been removed. The history teacher now has greater professional autonomy. British history can be taught in relation to international developments; indeed it does not make much sense otherwise. The new National Curriculum provides opportunities to approach the teaching of history from a number of perspectives. Indeed, the experience and education of history teachers, together with the bulk of historical evidence and sources used in schools today, ensure an endless supply of perspectives. The history curriculum also gives emphasis to interpretation, evidence and skills, and if it is successful all pupils will realise that there is no evidence base to justify racism. In short, if school history is taught in a critical way then there should be less need to agonise over how many British 'heroes' are included in its content.

It is nevertheless defensible to devote time and to give particular significance to British history in order to help the cohesion of society. At the very least, cultural diversity in Britain is generally accepted as inevitable and at best is increasingly welcomed as a bonus, something which enriches. John White (1996) has argued for the cultivation of a British national sentiment within a liberal framework. He argues that so long as national sentiment and nationalism are not confused, then it is not incompatible with liberal positions on education to promote an attachment to the nation. He explains, in communitarian fashion, how one can love one's family and local place without feeling superior to other families or local places. He describes the nation as a group of people – 'a community of communities' – and therefore ethnic identity should not necessarily challenge the overarching bonds of nation and citizenship. The liberal communitarian answer appears to be national identity, yes, but as part of a series of complex and numerous community identities.

Key questions

1   What are the underlying values that assist in the definition of Britishness?

2   If Britain comprises a 'community of communities', how can the teaching and content of history in schools assist children to learn about both their own community and the community of the British nation?

3   According to the Runnymede Trust (2000), the very idea of 'Britishness' could be 'racially coded'. Does this mean that the teaching of British history in schools is 'racially coded', especially if one of the aims of history is to give children a sense of identity?

4   How can the history teacher ensure that children develop an understanding of the diversity of human experience while seeking to help give them an understanding of their cultural roots and shared inheritance?

Recommended reading

J. Arthur (2000) *Schools and Community: the communitarian agenda in education*. London, Falmer Press. An introduction to what communitarianism might mean in the British education context.

L. Colley (1994) *Britons: forging the nation 1707–1837*. London, Pimlico.
An influential account of how Britain emerged. The author is an adviser to New Labour and the Prime Minister.

A. Etzioni (1997) *The New Golden Rule: community and morality in a democratic society*. New York, Basic Books.
Written by the 'media prophet' of communitarianism, this book sets out the idea of the importance of community.

Runnymede Trust (2000) *Commission on the Future of Multi-Ethnic Britain*. London, Runnymede Trust.
A controversial report with implications for history teaching in Britain.

Chapter 5

Citizenship, political literacy and history

Pupils learning about and how to make themselves effective in *public life* through knowledge, skills and values – what can be called 'political literacy', seeking for a term that is wider than political knowledge alone.

(QCA 1998)

How does political literacy relate to citizenship education?

'Political literacy' was one of the three strands of citizenship explored in T.H. Marshall's (1963) work on this subject. The definition of political literacy given above from the Crick Report was developed from his ideas. It views the concept of political literacy as being bound up with 'public life', in other words where the life of the individual citizen interacts with the political system, whether on a macro or national level or on a local or micro level. The Crick Report assumes that this broad understanding is desirable and that therefore teaching pupils 'political knowledge' alone is insufficient. 'Political literacy' (in Crick's definition) implies that pupils need to learn *how* to engage and participate in 'public life' (i.e. politics at whatever level), not just learn *about* it. In turn, the National Curriculum Orders for Citizenship (DfEE/ QCA 1999b) are based on the conclusions of the Crick Report. While direct references to 'political literacy' have been removed from the final Orders, the Crick Report's definition of it clearly influenced the drawing up of the programmes of study. It therefore makes sense to analyse the Orders in the light of Crick's definition of 'political literacy'. Many teachers will equate 'political knowledge' in the Crick definition to factual information about politics rather than political literacy. Such information litters the Orders. They make reference to 'legal and human rights', 'basic aspects of the criminal justice system', 'central and local government', 'the key characteristics of parliamentary and other forms of government', the 'electoral system and the importance of voting'.

However, this factual information about politics is not to be seen as inert or neutral, even if teachers view it as 'content'. From Crick's definition of political literacy, the purpose of learning 'about' this factual information is to prepare students for an effective part in 'public life'. This was defined by Crick as 'encompassing realistic knowledge of, and preparation for conflict resolution and decision-making, related to the main economic and social problems of the day'. Once again, the Orders for Citizenship do not repeat this definition of 'public life', but the skills listed in them incorporate aspects of it.

The Orders require teaching to reach beyond 'political knowledge' (i.e. what many teachers will interpret as factual details about politics) to 'skills of enquiry and communication, participation and responsible action'. In relation to the Final Report's definition of 'political literacy' as a preparation for active participation in 'public life', these 'skills' are highly relevant. Among the skills are listed the following:

> Pupils should be taught to: (a) think about topical, political . . . problems and events by analysing information and its sources . . . (b) justify orally and in writing a personal opinion about such issues, problems or events . . . (c) negotiate, decide and take part responsibly in both school and community based activities . . . (d) reflect on the process of participating.

The implications of these definitions of political knowledge and political literacy within citizenship education are potentially far reaching. Political 'knowledge', as the Orders define it, is vast.

Kerr's term 'education *about* citizenship' (see Chapter 1 above) relates closely to the Crick's Report's definition of 'political knowledge'. Kerr's 'knowledge and understanding' of 'the structures and processes of government and political life' can be equated with Crick's references to 'political knowledge' and 'public life'. The emphasis within Kerr's summary of 'education *about* citizenship' is on inert factual political information. This is where 'education *about* citizenship' largely departs from the definition of political literacy in the Crick Report, which argues that political literacy 'is wider than political knowledge alone'.

The ways 'political literacy' might be taught and the relationship of this strand of citizenship education to history are complex issues. To explore these issues in this chapter, examples of thinking and practice will be taken, not from the full scope of 'political knowledge' to which the Orders allude, but in the context of the national politics of the United Kingdom. Some of the conclusions reached in this chapter in regard to the treatment of national politics will readily serve as a means of addressing other areas of 'political knowledge' set out in the Citizenship Orders.

The State Opening of Parliament is a ceremony in which the British constitutional monarchy displays an aspect of its political role in 'public life'. The following fictional contexts will be used to begin to investigate how a videoed recording of the ceremony might be used with students to develop their 'political literacy'. To begin with, we perhaps need to appreciate how odd this ceremony might seem to a student, a teacher and a person with no knowledge of its context at all. Suppose an alien spaceship intercepted standard BBC coverage of the State Opening of Parliament. Its transmission back to its home planet might be interspersed in the following way with the BBC commentary.

Transmission XI to Planet Vlarg from Earth Orbit   Stardate 21738.

Our ship picked up an informative transmission from one of the alien broadcasting systems, which will be invaluable in determining the power structures upon this planet. Our monitor detected it signalling from a minor island off one of the landmasses and from a location we decoded as variously 'The Houses of Parliament' or 'The Palace of Westminster'. Many aliens were gathered in the spaces of this building and we immediately noted how colourful the garments were, especially by comparison with the aliens waiting outside. In due course silence fell, a strange braying noise came from the orifices of a few aliens on a balcony through metallic objects they put to their faces.

BBC commentary

. . . and as Her Majesty leaves the robing room for the Royal Gallery of the House of Lords, the state trumpeters raise the silver instruments to their lips and sound the time-honoured fanfare. The procession then moves forward, flanked by guardsmen, headed by heralds with the Lord Great Chamberlain sustaining the medieval custom of walking backwards in the presence of the monarch. The Black Prince's ruby in the Imperial state crown glitters . . .

Alien transmission

Then, through the rooms, processed rows of silent aliens, two walking backwards. One of the group was surely of greater importance. This alien [*HM the Queen*] wore elaborate coverings of many textures, but mostly red, yellow and white. Upon its head it balanced a bizarre metallic object that seemed to be held in place rather precariously [*the crown*]. The object was covered in brightly coloured rocks. In one of the spaces of the building, the alien sat down on a raised platform and sent a messenger to one of the other spaces down a long corridor. This space was filled with aliens in dull colours [*MPs*]. The door was slammed in the face of the messenger who banged on it three times before being let in. The aliens in this room then processed to the room with the raised platform.

BBC commentary

. . . and now we see the gladiators of the House of Commons, summoned by Black Rod to stand at the bar of the House of Lords. Those usual combatants, the Prime Minister and the Leader of the Opposition, exchange civil conversation. Perhaps the Leader of the Opposition is taking the opportunity to congratulate the Prime Minister on . . .

Alien transmission

The alien on the platform spoke at some length on matters we are still decoding. It then left.

Our initial conclusion is that the alien on the platform must be the absolute ruler of this race. The silent deference and the unusual headgear point to this. It appeared to summon its subjects to listen to its commands and after a ceremonial resistance from its least important slaves in the dull garments, it made its will known. In considering making actual contact with this species it will probably be necessary to discover the intentions of this ruler. We have tracked its main abode to a building known in the alien language as 'Buckingham Palace'.

Suppose the same BBC broadcast was taped and shown without much teacher comment or questioning in a statutory citizenship lesson. Sarah Green, aged 14, comments in her diary on her day at school in September 2003.

Then we had the most boring lesson of the day – Citizenship! – yawn!! I always find it hard to concentrate on a Friday afternoon, but today it was worse because it was raining and the wind was rattling the windows. As soon as we sat down, we told old Tucker that we wanted to go home. He told us he wanted to go home as well and was only teaching Citizenship anyway because there weren't enough students doing technology in Year 10. He said Mrs Bryant had given him a video we had to watch about the State Opening of Parliament. It was really boring, even the Queen looked bored. Tucker pointed out the Prime Minister and the Leader of the Opposition. What gets me is if the Prime Minister is so powerful why does he have to go and hear her say what he's written for her anyway? Why doesn't he stick a crown on his head and read it himself? We asked Tucker this and what banging the door shut was about and why they wear silly clothes. He said he didn't know, that he wasn't interested in politics anyway as they were all the same and we should get on with the worksheet so he could mark some books. Tracey and I scribbled notes about which member of that boyband we fancied most and I tried to catch Ahmed's eye. He was done by Tucker for playing with his gameboy under the desk. Next week proportional representation – ugh!

The State Opening of Parliament is an impressive ceremony with its pomp and colour. An alien watching it and knowing nothing about British politics might easily assume that the Queen was an absolute ruler. Yet we know that this piece of political theatre is a complex mix of real and invented traditions that disguise the actual nature of constitutional politics. The sovereign has opened Parliament for centuries and outlined his or her wishes to peers and MPs. But the current version of this tradition is at best Victorian, with the speech written for the monarch by the democratically elected Prime Minister of the day. He *appears* to defer to her, she talks of *her* government, yet they are *his* words and, despite all the trappings, real power lies with the Prime Minister, not the Queen. Therefore to make sense of this ceremony, our alien would need to understand some basics of the British political system. Sarah Green and her classmates seem to grasp a little more than the alien. They know that the Prime Minister holds real power and that he has written the Queen's speech for her. This much either Mr Tucker told them or the commentary on the video mentioned. However, they don't understand why this happens or how the ceremony came to exist in its present form. As a technology teacher, reluctantly drafted in to teach citizenship about which he neither cares nor knows, Mr Tucker cannot help the students. They could only really understand the significance of this ceremony if they were given a wider perspective. The modern State Opening, however much it fakes or reinvents tradition, broadly reflects a medieval and early modern framework of government: the sovereign at the pinnacle of society, ruling with three other estates, the aristocracy, the Church (both represented in the House of Lords) and, lastly, the Commons – the Crown-in-Parliament. Yet the supremacy of the Commons can also be seen in the choreography of the ceremony. The Queen's messenger, Black Rod, has the doors of the Commons banged in his face. This reflects the determination of successive parliamentarians to emphasise that Charles I's attempt to arrest the five members in 1642 will not be repeated. Sarah needs to *know about* this to understand the ceremony. She also needs to *know about* the development of Britain into a constitutional monarchy, and the different roles of the head of state and head of government within the system. The political knowledge and political literacy of Mr Tucker's class have been set back by his ignorance and the lack of a historical context to his teaching of citizenship. The teaching lacked any rigour, and so resulted in little effective learning. Political knowledge needed to be introduced by the teacher and it was not. Mr Tucker didn't have it.

How does education about citizenship relate to history?

Kerr (1999) summarised three approaches to citizenship education in a survey of provision in sixteen states, world-wide. He summed up one approach as 'education *about* citizenship' which 'focuses on providing students with sufficient knowledge and understanding of national history and the structures and processes of government and political life'. There is a strong overlap between the Orders for Citizenship and for History in the revised National Curriculum for England (DfEE/QCA 1999b). Both support the emphasis on political knowledge stressed in Kerr's 'education *about* citizenship'. By implication, the development of political knowledge and understanding is an essential element of breadth of study in Key Stage 3 history. The National Curriculum Orders for History (1999) require: '7. In their study of local, British, European and World history, pupils should be taught . . . (a) history from a variety of perspectives including political [ones].'

Part of students' experience of Key Stage 3 history should include a political perspective. The non-statutory exemplification for 'areas of study' in National Curriculum Key Stage 3 history gives ample scope for history departments to convey an understanding of aspects of British and world political developments. 'Britain 1066–1500' cites 'the development of the monarchy' as worthy of study. Dale Banham, a history teacher in Suffolk, devotes several weeks to an enquiry with Year 7 classes about the historical reputation of King John. As part of this study, students consider Magna Carta and compare John with other medieval rulers of England. Through the detailed study of this one monarch, a chronological overview of the development of medieval monarchy itself through other reigns is also 'covered'. Both 'Britain 1500–1750 and 'Britain 1750–1900' can be taught with an emphasis on political change and reform. Examples include 'Charles I and the civil wars' and 'Chartism'. Sue Arnold, head of history at Ernulf School in Cambridgeshire, devised a Key Stage 3 scheme of work that included role plays of the Rump Parliament's closure by Cromwell and the campaign by the suffragettes for the franchise in Edwardian Britain. Through references to political change, backward and forward across the Key

Stage 3 history curriculum, it should be possible to construct a strand of teaching that revisits and builds up knowledge of concepts such as 'monarchy' and 'democracy', as well as some understanding of the general forces that influence processes of political change. Year 8 students should not be embarking on study of the civil wars of the seventeenth century without ever having come across the term Parliament before. It should already be familiar to them from 'Britain 1066–1500' or from the significance of the role of Parliament during the English Reformation under the Tudors. By a rigorous emphasis on and recall of political concepts through sequences of lessons across Key Stage 3, and suitable 'content' across Key Stage 3 history, the subject provides an element of 'education *about* citizenship'. School history can provide students with sufficient 'knowledge and understanding of national history "and up to a point" the structures and processes of government and political life', cited in Kerr's 'education *about* citizenship'.

Even if this teaching of politically related historical 'content' were highlighted as contributing to citizenship requirements, it would not really be enough to justify a claim that school history was already 'doing' citizenship as such. By definition, the study of history, and therefore school history, concerns the past, while citizenship education is more concerned with the present. In order for students to make sense of the political perspective taught rigorously in their history lessons, they would need to relate this learning to the present. The danger for history as a school discipline is that if teachers of history fail to make links and comparisons between past and present, students will not grasp the role the past plays in shaping their own existence and therefore their future as citizens. Links between past political development and current political literacy need to be made explicit. Closing this gap between history teaching and current events should be relatively straightforward.

For history teachers, closing the gap between history and citizenship education may be a matter of bringing the past 'up to date' by legitimate analogies with the present or a demonstration of the lineage of ideas, concepts and institutions into the present. The National Curriculum Orders hint at this, in the list of knowledge, skills and understanding given for the programme of study at Key Stage 3: '2 (d) to identify trends, both within and across different periods, and links between local, British, European and World history'. If other examples of history, why not the present as well? This suggestion has a strong precedent. Since its development in the 1970s, schools history project syllabuses at the 14–16 level have included a 'Modern World Study'. This allows secondary history departments to set up units of study for coursework that take a political problem of the present and examine it in the light of its historical roots. For example, Ben Walsh (2000) has published a GCSE textbook on Northern Ireland, tracing the conflict through the Troubles and into the Good Friday Agreement. History departments can easily follow this pattern at Key Stage 3. Role plays on past parliamentary themes (as at Ernulf School) can lead directly into consideration of modern political systems. When students are taught about such terms as 'monarch', 'Parliament' and 'democracy', appreciating how their meanings and significance changed over time through sequences of history lessons over Key Stage 3, they should be able to relate this learning to the present. Most will not be able to do this unless their history teachers emphasise and explicitly draw out links and connections between past and present.

Linking the politics of the past and present, either through combined history and citizenship provision or through mutually supportive links co-ordinated across the curriculum, should only enhance the development of political knowledge in students not only as Kerr defines it in 'education *about* citizenship' but also according to Crick's definition of political literacy ('learning about and how to make themselves effective in *public life* through knowledge, skills and values').

For citizenship education, the support of a lively and interested secondary history department might bring the colourful stories and excitement of the past to bear on understanding 'education *about* citizenship' (i.e. 'factual political knowledge') which otherwise could appear a rather dry list of 'content'. However, there is more to it than making appropriate selections from the breadth of study in history and linking these to some means of meeting the statutory requirement for citizenship. The scenario set out at the beginning of this chapter, where Mr Tucker's class is bored and disaffected with a discrete citizenship lesson, might still not be improved significantly. Suppose Mr Tucker had been more motivated and knowledgeable. Suppose he had explained the role of the Queen and the Prime Minister in the constitution. Suppose he had conveyed the significance of the Commons barring their doors to Black Rod. Suppose the history department had 'covered' the development of Parliament in a one-off Year 8 'overview' lesson. Sarah and her low-attaining friends might still understand little and care even less.

Fortunately Kerr identified at least two further approaches to citizenship education from his international research.

Education *through* citizenship involves students learning by doing through active participative experiences in the school or local community and beyond. This learning reinforces the knowledge component.

Education *for* citizenship . . . involves equipping students with a set of tools (knowledge and understanding, skills and aptitudes, values and dispositions) which enable them to participate actively and sensibly in the roles and responsibilities they encounter in their adult lives. This approach links citizenship education with the whole education experience of students.

In other words, it is perfectly feasible for citizenship education to move beyond a narrow diet of 'given' fact and detail (political knowledge). McLaughlin (1992) claimed that definitions of citizenship and, as a consequence, citizenship education range from minimal to maximal interpretations.

Minimal	*Maximal*
thin	thick
exclusive	inclusive
elitist	activist
civics education	citizenship education
formal	participative
content led	process led
knowledge based	values based
didactic transmission	interactive interpretation
easier to achieve and measure in practice	more difficult to achieve and measure in practice

Despite the use of a video tape, Mr Tucker's citizenship lesson was fairly minimal in approach. It was in the formal setting of a discrete lesson. It was led by content and was in theory based on the didactic 'transmission' of knowledge about the State Opening of Parliament and its significance by the teacher. The students were like empty bottles, to be filled with 'political knowledge' by the teacher, but even this process failed because of his ignorance. Doubtless the lesson would have been made more effective if Mr Tucker had been able to explain more and 'come across' to the students with greater enthusiasm. This minimal approach, however, would still be wanting. 'Education about citizenship' is not enough in itself to motivate students. If developing political literacy as a strand of citizenship education is to include a *growing* knowledge of political processes and vocabulary in students, it is better for them to be *motivated* by what they are studying.

What is the relationship between 'education *through* citizenship' and 'education *for* citizenship' and history?

Kerr's definitions of 'education *through* citizenship' and 'education *for* citizenship' are fortunately reflected in the new National Curriculum Orders for Citizenship. It is stated in the National Curriculum Orders for citizenship that 'knowledge and understanding' are to be geared to the purpose of making the students 'informed citizens'. The implication of the wording is that students are being prepared *for* adult citizenship. It is assumed that they will need a certain degree of 'knowledge and understanding' in order to develop this adult identity. The 'knowledge and understanding' referred to in the National Curriculum Orders for Citizenship can be equated with Kerr's 'education *about* citizenship', the implied preparation for adult citizenship with Kerr's 'education *for* citizenship'. Moreover, the term 'informed' seems to imply that they will need to exercise judgement as adult citizens. 'Knowledge and understanding' must not only be 'acquired', but also 'applied'.

This application, according to the National Curriculum Orders for Citizenship, will be achieved through 'developing skills of enquiry and communication, and participation and responsible action'. The programmes of study at Key Stages 3 and 4 carefully list these 'skills' which can be equated to Kerr's 'education *through* citizenship'.

Pupils should be taught to:

(a) think about topical political, spiritual, moral, social and cultural issues, problems and events by analysing information and its sources, including ICT-based sources.

(b) justify orally and in writing a personal opinion about such issues, problems or events.

(c) contribute to group and exploratory class discussions, and take part in debates.

Pupils should be taught to:

(a) use their imagination to consider other people's experiences and be able to think about, express and explain views that are not their own.

(b) negotiate, decide and take part responsibly in both school and community-based activities.

(c) reflect on the process of participating.

The hybrid of citizenship education set out in the new Orders therefore contains an element of McLaughlin's minimal approach but arguably veers more towards the maximal. Adapting Kerr's definitions of citizenship education, the National Curriculum Orders for Citizenship might be represented as in Figure 5.1.

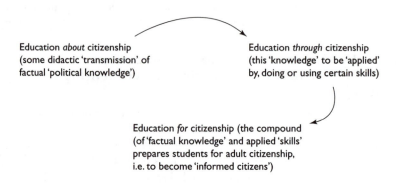

Education *about* citizenship (some didactic 'transmission' of factual 'political knowledge')

Education *through* citizenship (this 'knowledge' to be 'applied' by, doing or using certain skills)

Education *for* citizenship (the compound (of 'factual knowledge' and applied 'skills' prepares students for adult citizenship, i.e. to become 'informed citizens')

Figure 5.1 Education about, for and through citizenship

Thus all Mr Tucker has to do to motivate his class of reluctant learners, including the low attainers, to take their part in 'public life' is to make his lesson more active. This will allow them to practise the *skills* of citizenship. Mr Tucker might stop the video to prompt some interactive questioning of the ceremony. He might stage a role play of the State Opening. He could set up some groupwork leading to a whole-class discussion or debate on the role of the monarchy. In such activities Mr Tucker is arguably transmitting some factual knowledge *about* the State Opening of Parliament. *Through* the activities the students are thinking about topical political . . . issues, analysing information and its sources. They may be justifying orally a personal opinion about such issues, problems and events, and contributing to group and exploratory class discussions and debates. Thus he is preparing his students *for* adult citizenship. But why do these issues need to concern history teachers? The answer is because the structure of school history can support a more effective delivery of citizenship education. It is also in the enlightened self-interest of secondary history departments to offer this support. The introduction of citizenship in statutory form from 2002 may tempt some senior management teams in secondary schools to adopt a minimal approach. It would be easy enough to find time, certainly at Key Stage 3, to set up a discrete lesson of citizenship each week, probably staffed by a mixture of teachers from various subject areas. However this might lead to cuts in timetabled lessons elsewhere, perhaps in history. School history has always had to fight hard to defend its place in the curriculum. How much better to find a more creative, maximal approach to citizenship education that best practice in school history can support.

Davies *et al.* (1998: 17) reported a one-day off-timetable 'Democracy Day' held in a northern comprehensive (see Figure 5.2). Aimed at Years 7 to 9 with the involvement of some Year 10s, the day sought to develop political literacy in students. The authors quote from the stated aims of the staged House of Commons debate.

> Prepare for a debate on the issue of corporal punishment in schools. They will view relevant video extracts of Question Time in the Commons. They will be allocated roles to play and parties to represent. After preparation of their arguments and questions in the first half of the session, they will debate and vote in the second half with a debriefing at the end.

The Democracy Day took a maximal approach towards citizenship education and met many of the criteria for the knowledge, skills and understanding of citizenship set out in the National Curriculum Orders for Citizenship for the Key Stage 3 programme of study. It can also be matched to Kerr's three definitions of citizenship education.

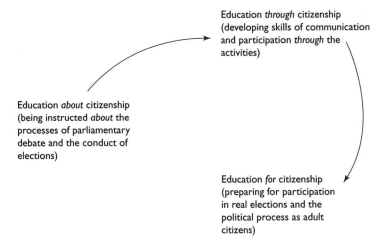

Education *through* citizenship
(developing skills of communication
and participation *through* the
activities)

Education *about* citizenship
(being instructed *about* the
processes of parliamentary
debate and the conduct of
elections)

Education *for* citizenship
(preparing for participation
in real elections and the
political process as adult
citizens)

Figure 5.2 Citizenship education in the form of a Democracy Day

This predominantly maximal approach would probably succeed in motivating students to a greater degree than any lesson by Mr Tucker. However, it may still not go far enough. The Democracy Day was one of several organised off timetable on various cross-curricular themes. Such events, however worthy and exciting in themselves, may not be incorporated into the subject-based curriculum. They risk being seen by students as bearing no relationship to the taught curriculum. Without integrated planning, the lasting impact of the Democracy Day may be as ineffective to students' learning as a didactic civics lesson on a wet and windy Friday afternoon. A model for more integrated curricular planning can be borrowed from the Passport Project, a research initiative on PSHE teaching supported by the Gulbenkian Foundation. This project proposed that personal, social and health education should be delivered at secondary level through three curriculum vehicles: (1) a core of designated, discrete teaching time; (2) linked to related content and 'skills' in other 'lead' subjects; (3) extending out into enrichment activities. The model could be adapted for use by citizenship education. Where certain citizenship 'content' (e.g. political knowledge) dovetails with discrete PSHE provision, citizenship might be taught alongside it in a designated core. This would be supported through lead subjects and branch out further into enrichment (see Figure 5.3).

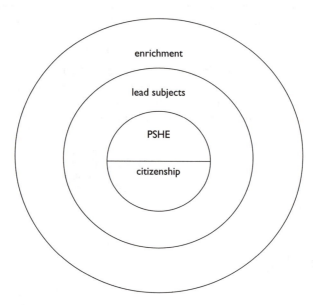

Figure 5.3 Citizenship: lead subjects and enrichment

Source: Wrenn (1999).

History was named as a 'lead' subject for the delivery of citizenship education by the Final Report of the Advisory Group on Citizenship (QCA 1998). History's support of citizenship education could be fitted into the adapted Passport model. Lang (1999) makes the following suggestions for making history teaching about democracy interesting for students.

> Why not run a mock old-style election, with a restricted franchise? Perhaps only girls have the vote (as a fitting counter-balance to what actually happened for so long!), or only those with certain postcodes. But really to get the idea of the issues the successful candidates must have some real power over those – franchised and unfranchised – they represent. Why not give the elected representatives the power

to dispose, for real, of a fund into which everyone has paid a modest sum – say 50p: not enough to hurt but enough not to want to waste. One can predict an instant resurgence of interest in the process of parliamentary reform.

If the Reform Act of 1832 was the object of study for all Year 9 classes at the same time in their history lessons, Lang's suggestions could be adapted as shown in Figure 5.4.

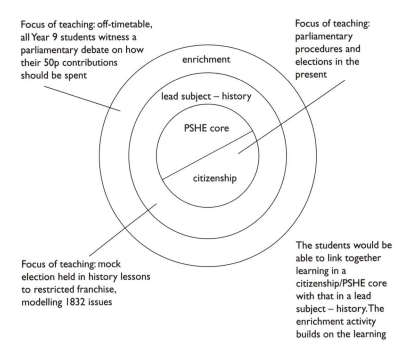

Figure 5.4 Citizenship education through work on the 1832 Reform Act

The sequence of activities veers towards a lively, maximalist approach to citizenship education. Yet it deepens students' knowledge and understanding of the development of democratic processes into the present in a way that citizenship taught in isolation would not. The role of history as the lead subject is crucial in making this happen. At Eurnulf School in Cambridgeshire the role plays enacted as part of Key Stage 3 history based on Cromwell's expulsion of the Rump Parliament and the suffragettes' campaign in Edwardian Britain fed into elections for the school council. Students' understanding of the democratic process of this election was deepened and enriched by the inclusion of a lively, historical context.

The skills of 'communication and enquiry' as set out in the Orders for Citizenship can also be strongly supported by school history. Again the 1970s 'skills-based' methods of the Schools Council History Project, and its widespread influence in the secondary history curriculum, provide a distinguished tradition of source analysis. It is unnecessary for citizenship education in English schools to reinvent this wheel. However, the legitimate ideological concerns of history teachers might come into play here. The analysis and evaluation of sources in history teaching have been seen by many teachers as a part of the armoury used by the historian to uncover the truth about the past. Citizenship education may seek to deploy the same methods but for a different purpose from that of the history teacher. In citizenship the analysis and evaluation of sources serve the purpose of students 'becoming informed citizens'.

But surely this depends on what an 'informed citizen' is. The Labour Party or the Tories might like 'informed citizens' to support their party. A central government-sponsored Citizenship Order leaves schools and their students open to political manipulation and indoctrination. History teachers might feel that they did not enter teaching to propagandise on behalf of the state. Peter Kellner said of citizenship in the *Independent* in 1988: 'It is a precious, exhilarating, anti-establishment word which politicians the world over have tried to steal. Only in dictatorships and enfeebled democracies do they ever succeed.' A careful scan of the membership of the working party on whose report the Citizenship Orders were based should bring some reassurance. It is true that it was chaired by Professor Bernard Crick, a former university tutor of David Blunkett, the then Education Secretary. However, members included Lord Baker, architect of the 1988 Education Act that set in motion the National Curriculum, and Sir Stephen Tumim, another Conservative. The proposals were approved by an all-party committee and had cross-party support in Parliament. The bias towards a maximal approach in the orders and cross-party agreement on their content, provide a secure defence against the exploitation of citizenship education for party-political purposes. The strand of citizenship education that requires a developing political literacy does not translate into an equivalent fluency in the language of any one party.

Similar tensions between the interests of the state and the professional independence of teachers were played out in the development of the National Curriculum for history. At first glance, the National Curriculum Orders for History (DfEE/QCA 1999a) retain the broad outline of historical content set for study at Key Stage 3 in their first statutory form (DES, 1991). In particular, the three British 'areas of study' from 1066 to 1900 apparently perpetuate an Anglo-centric history curriculum based on a hopelessly outdated, whig version of 'our island story'. The National Curriculum Orders for History still have about them the stamp of the boyhood history of a Conservative cabinet minister. It might seem tempting to dismiss such a history curriculum on ideological grounds. Yet this would ignore the insurance carefully built into all three versions of the National Curriculum Orders for History (DES, 1991, DfEE 1995; DfEE/QCA 1999a). The first National Curriculum Orders for History set out a new curriculum construct, 'Interpretations of history'. School history was already characterised by the rigour of the analysis and evaluation of sources, popularised by the Schools Council History Project. The History Working Group appointed to draw up the first National Curriculum for history reinforced this earlier tradition by planning a fresh emphasis upon the study of secondary sources. The Group justified this in their report (DES, 1990) by reference to the need to protect students against indoctrination and political bias. The History Working Group argued that students needed to study the context in which an 'interpretation' was constructed. They should be required to understand the cultural settings and audiences which shape a *subsequent* interpretation. Later developmental projects, most notably that commissioned by the National Curriculum Council and led by Tony McAleavy, devised new theoretical models and practical approaches for teaching students how to evaluate existing 'interpretations'. Evaluations had to examine factors such as the political, cultural or social context in which the interpretation was written (NCC 1993; McAleavy 1993).

The scrutiny of secondary sources was not new. Teachers were accustomed to analyse secondary sources and notions of bias and reliability. McAleavy emphasised that the distinctive purpose of the new curriculum construct was to alert students to the way in which subsequent 'interpretations' had been constructed. This attempted to shift the evaluation of secondary sources away from their relationship to primary sources and closer to evaluation of the factors that shaped these sources at the *time they were produced*. He later defined an 'interpretation' as 'any conscious reflection on the past'.

NCC (1993) guidance defined an interpretation of history as a mix of 'fact and fiction, imagination and point of view . . . dependent for its historical worth . . . among other things' on the purpose for which it was written and the audience intended to read it. McAleavy (1993) carefully defined five types of 'interpretation' (Table 5.1). Perhaps the most obvious category was the academic. Yet beyond the academic lay many other kinds of 'interpretation' which could all be rigorously tested against the same criteria. In addition, the category of personal reflection must also logically include the views of students themselves, consciously reflecting on the past. The writing of an academic historian and an 11-year-old student therefore fall within the same definition. They are both 'interpretations' and the validity of either can be tested by the same criteria.

Table 5.1 McAleavy's five types of interpretation

Types of interpretation	Examples
Academic	Books and journals by professional historians; excavation reports; lectures
Educational	Textbooks; museums; TV documentaries; artists' interpretations
Fictional	Novels; feature films; TV dramas; plays
Popular	Folk wisdom about the past; theme parks; nostalgic depictions in advertising
Personal	Personal reflection

Source: McAleavy (1993).

As an example of the application of this idea of interpretations in history teaching, let us take a complex historical interpretation quite separate from British national politics. The following source of information has commonly been used to illustrate the environmental attitudes of Native Americans in teaching on the American West in Year 8 or at GCSE.

The earth is our mother. I have seen a thousand rotting buffaloes on the prairies left by the white man who shot them from a passing train. What will happen when the buffaloes are all slaughtered? The wild horses tamed? . . . when the secret corners of the forest are heavy with the scent of many men and view of the ripe hills is blotted by talking wires?

(Letter from Chief Seattle to US President Franklin Pierce 1854)

Yet, as Bage (1999) states, 'Unfortunately Seattle's "speech" as quoted was apparently bogus, the result of a fictionalised retelling by a screen writer in 1972 who admitted "I did not check the historical accuracy of anything I wrote".' Moreover, Seattle's tribe lived 600 miles away from the Great Plains and he died before the slaughter of the buffalo began. So is this source to be dismissed as an anachronistic fake? There are grounds for doing so, yet some of the details incorporated into the text are based on fact. The value of this piece of historical evidence depends on what you want to find out and therefore the criteria by which you judge it. If, as teachers, we want to help our students to discover more about the attitudes of nineteenth-century Native Americans, then Seattle's letter is not much use; it is a bogus forgery. However, if we need evidence of how a white environmentalist in the 1970s viewed nineteenth-century Native Americans, this text is extremely useful. It is an interpretation of history and 'a conscious reflection on the past', not by a nineteenth-century Native American but by a white twentieth-century American environmentalist putting words in Chief Seattle's mouth. In an 'Interpretations' context (using 'Interpretations' in its technical post-1991 curriculum sense), the focus of historical learning here would be upon what this text tells us about late twentieth-century American attitudes. One learning activity that might realign this objective is shown in Figure 5.5. Students might be asked to place a cross representing this interpretation in the triangle which reflects McAleavy's definition of an interpretation as a combination of 'fact and fiction, imagination and point of view'. Much debate will be provoked. Is the interpretation mostly imagination? To what extent is it factual? What does it tell us about the writer's attitude? This 'Interpretation' tells us little about nineteenth-century Native Americans. It tells us a lot more about what a subsequent white, twentieth-century American writer thought about Native Americans.

'Interpretations of history' is a curriculum lock preventing any one view of the past from being allowed to dominate school history. Interpretations can be linked with National Curriculum Skills, knowledge and understanding 2a, which requires that pupils be taught 'to describe and analyse the relationships between the characteristic features of the periods and societies studied, including the experiences and range of ideas, beliefs and attitudes of men, women, and children in the past', and 2b, 'about the social, cultural, religious and ethnic diversity of the societies studied, both in Britain and the wider world' (DfEE/QCA 1999a). The 'breadth of study' at Key Stage 3 may remain whiggish in outline, yet history should not be taught as 'our island story'. There is an obligation to 'cover' more than traditional English and later British political history. Not only that, the requirement to study 'Interpretations' should equip students with analytical tools for sophisticated historical questioning. Nothing, including the views of the teacher, should escape critical scrutiny.

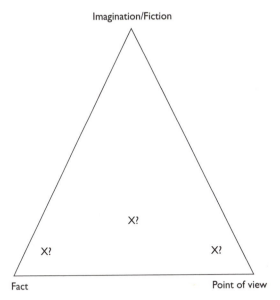

Figure 5.5 Imagination/fact/point of view

Source: Wrenn (1999).

The maximal bias and all-party support of the Citizenship Orders should prevent party-political manipulation. This dovetails well with the role of 'Interpretations' in ensuring that a range of views of the same events are examined in history teaching. Both the traditions of source evaluation and 'Interpretations' in school history provide the rigour necessary for the development of systematic approaches to citizenship education.

On the eve of St George's Day, 1993, the then Prime Minister, John Major, made this speech to a Conservative Party split over Britain's role in the European Union:

> Fifty years from now Britain will still be the country of long shadows on county grounds, warm beer, invincible green suburbs, dog lovers and pools fillers and – as George Orwell said – 'Old maids cycling to Communion through the morning mist'.

Here is another 'conscious reflection on the past'. A Conservative politician, evoking nostalgic images of an idyllic Britain (or, perhaps more accurately, the England of the 1950s Ealing comedies), ironically quoting the socialist, George Orwell, sends important messages of reassurance to his party and the country. Does this interpretation tell us about Britain in 1993 or what John Major wanted us to believe about Britain in 1993 for reasons of his own? If included as part of a 'World study since 1900' in Year 9 History, this interpretation might place developments in modern British political history in a recent context. The study of this interpretation would enhance students' political literacy, deepening awareness of how politicians can mine the past for political purposes in the present.

A teacher wishing to use this 'Interpretation' might ask students to place this extract in the 'Interpretations' frame (Figure 5.5). Students will be able to debate and analyse this modern politician's 'Interpretation' of British history, provided that the activity is positioned within a sequence of lessons carefully constructed to build relevant historical knowledge. How much of what he said was fact, how much fiction, imagination or point of view? Arguably, Britain still possesses county grounds, warm beer, dog lovers and pools fillers, perhaps even a few old maids cycling to Communion. But what has been left out and why?

Conclusion

1   While the National Curriculum Orders for Citizenship do not explicitly refer to 'political literacy', there is a clear expectation that it should be taught.
2   Even a maximal approach to citizenship as a discrete subject may not be enough to motivate students.
3   The development of 'political literacy' as a strand of citizenship education requires systematic rigour. Two features of such rigour are the clear building of concepts and reinforcement of knowledge and skills over time. History education can already provide models of such rigorous practice. The collective professional knowledge of history teachers as enshrined by curriculum research and development should be taken into account.
4   The overlap between school history and citizenship education falls into two broad areas.

   • The Orders for Citizenship make frequent reference to factual 'political knowledge'. Much of this equates to Kerr's 'education *about* citizenship'. There are similar requirements within the 'breadth of study' for Key Stage 3 required by the National Curriculum Orders for History.
   • The Orders for Citizenship require teaching to reach beyond 'political knowledge' with 'skills of enquiry and communication'. Much of this equates to Kerr's 'education *through* citizenship'. National Curriculum Orders for History strongly emphasise critical and reflective processes, particularly through source evaluation and the more recent development, 'Interpretations'.

5   'Interpretations' builds insurance against manipulation for party political purposes into the Orders for History. This safeguard strongly overlaps with the maximal approach of the Orders for Citizenship and their all-party support.

Key questions

1   Do you agree that Kerr's proposed 'education *about* citizenship', 'education *through* citizenship' and 'education *for* citizenship' help to provide a coherent interpretation of the Crick Report and National Curriculum Orders for Citizenship?

2   How does the subject of history combined with citizenship give more systematic rigour to teaching and learning than stand-alone citizenship lessons or enrichment activities?

Recommended reading

I. Davies, G. Gray and P. Stephens (1998) 'Education for citizenship; a case study of "Democracy Day" at a comprehensive school', *Educational Review*, 50(1) pp. 15–27.

D. Kerr (1999) *Citizenship Education; an international comparison.* London, QCA.

A. Wrenn (1999) 'Build it in, don't bolt it on; history's opportunity to support critical Citizenship', *Teaching History*, 96.

Chapter 6

The moral dimensions of promoting citizenship through the teaching of history

> What matters at this stage is the construction of local forms of community within which civility and the intellectual and moral life can be sustained through the new dark ages which are already upon us. And if the tradition of the virtues was able to survive the horrors of the last dark ages, we are not entirely without grounds for hope.
>
> MacIntyre 1981: p. 244)

Introduction

At the turn of the last century the teaching of history was generally conceived by teachers in terms of a contribution to the formation of moral citizens. One of the chief arguments advanced for school history teaching was that it served as a vehicle for the moral instruction of British citizens. Not only is this widely contested today, but some teachers may even doubt whether there are any links between morality and the teaching of school history. MacIntyre (1981) interprets this association of history with morality as part of a general liberalism which has no coherent conception of the moral life and consequently ends up in moral subjectivism. It is not surprising that MacIntyre strikes an apocalyptic note in contemplating the last days of the Roman Empire; he pessimistically concludes that our civility and moral life are now in severe danger. It seems therefore timely to reconsider the moral nature and purposes of the study of history in classrooms. This chapter traces the development of moral and citizenship goals for history teaching and links this to the various purposes of and justifications for the place of history in the contemporary school curriculum. Government involvement in the political debate, principally through the construction of a National Curriculum, is also reviewed and analysed, together with the various views among the teaching profession about the use of history in schools. The chapter seeks to outline what the connections are and could be between citizenship, moral education and the teaching of history. Throughout this chapter it is recognised that, although some doubt it, there is indeed a close relationship between history teaching, moral education and citizenship.

School history has a moral dimension in the broad sense that any study of a people or a culture will normally engage the pupil in an examination of behaviour and institutions. Each culture will have its own norms which guide action and help its adherents preserve their identity. In teaching about different historical cultures, school history will offer pupils an increased awareness of alternative value systems, since history takes as its content human activity over time and explores what it means to be human. Pupils will understand that change is generally brought about by human actions, and that it can have advantages and disadvantages for individuals and society. However, it also offers a frame of reference in which the pupils' present place in time is perceived and ultimately understood. This moral dimension in history is therefore about the pupils' immersion in a moral discourse, and it comprises at least three important elements. First, through an understanding of the moral vocabulary of any historical period pupils are able to contextualise and understand, for example, that nineteenth-century England was, in many ways, an age of high moral rhetoric, independent of whether people held religious beliefs and whether they lived up to the public moral standards they set themselves and others. This ability to recognise and use moral language appropriately in history needs to be learnt. Second, through an ability to form moral judgements based on historical evidence pupils not only learn about other ways of living, but reflect critically on their own and society's values. The study of school history is often highly charged with moral content and can provide pupils with exercises in moral thinking, for example by explaining the horrors of intolerance ranging from witch-hunts and religious persecution to sectarian or racial violence. Third, through history teaching which is directed at moral education teachers can move their pupils to use a moral vocabulary in a way which views some things as good and others as wrong, wicked or vicious. For example, teachers may emphasise a method which encourages their pupils to view the racist policies and practices of Nazi Germany as morally unacceptable. Many teachers already understand and successfully employ these three elements in teaching school history, but others do not fully explore the moral dimension in their history teaching, largely because they may perceive it to be too sensitive, controversial or difficult to analyse.

Nevertheless, it is recognised here that any considerations of the role that history teaching can and should play in the moral development of pupils as citizens are themselves subject to controversy. Both Piaget and Kohlberg have been influential figures in moral education, but their observations concerning the development of moral ideas are also derived from philosophical assumptions and are thus questionable and highly debatable. Piaget (1932: p. 134) recognised the complexities of moral reasoning in children and advocated nearly seventy years ago that children should not be subject to ritualistic and external obedience, but develop obligations to each other out of mutual respect. Kohlberg (Power et al., 1989) has proposed that children form ways of thinking through their experiences which include understandings of moral concepts central to history teaching, such as justice, rights, equality and human welfare. While he believes that children must operate as moral agents within communities, Kohlberg claims that in much classroom practice teachers arbitrarily impose values based upon their societal, cultural or personal beliefs. He rejects the idea that there is a single or correct answer to moral questions, and also rejects traditional methods of teaching morality on the grounds that they assume a community consensus. However, the moral dimensions of the aims for the new National Curriculum, it could be said, are based on the premise of community consensus. The history curriculum (DfEE/QCA 1999a: p. 8) is designed to promote moral development 'through helping pupils to recognise that actions have consequences by considering the results of events and decisions, and to explore how different interpretations of the past reflect different viewpoints and values'. It needs to be remembered that the Kohlberg approach does not underpin the aims and rationale of the new National Curriculum.

Purposes of school history

Two reasons have generally been given to justify history's place in the school curriculum. First, history had a major role in the transmission of identity; second, as a subject it formed part of a pupil's moral education (Burston and Green 1972). History was often used by teachers to judge or allocate praise or blame, and in their teaching it was unusual to disjoin political principle from moral character; this was especially so in the nineteenth century (see Carr 1961: p. 76). History has often been concerned not simply with recognising facts, but also with promoting virtue and an awareness of what is right and wrong. Morality and citizenship were therefore integral to the teaching of history and teachers incorporated explicit moral aims when teaching the subject. It was believed that history could successfully be mined for moral values and exemplars for application in the contemporary world. Henry Bourne (1905: pp. 93–4), writing on the teaching of history at the beginning of the twentieth century, believed that:

> pupils may be instructed in the duties of citizenship in two ways: first, by studying the structure of government and the duties of the individual in relation to it; and, second, by discipline in the performance of such social duties as fall to them during school life, with the expectation that thereby sound habits may be created and good citizenship may be only a continuation of the earlier training in conduct.

This moral education through history has a long tradition in England and has its origins in the emphasis placed upon the acquisition of virtue in the thought of Aristotle, Plato and Aquinas. By the time of the Renaissance the study of history was thought necessary for statecraft, but Machiavelli reminds us that the acquisition of virtue was not perhaps the main purpose of the subject: 'the things done by our princes, abroad and at home, cannot, like those of the ancients, be read of with wonder because of their virtues and greatness'.

History teaching continued to be explicitly linked to moral, rather than intellectual, values through a range of publications by professional history teachers which were more concerned with training better citizens than with educating competent historians (Madeley 1920; Showman 1923; Firth 1929; Gooch 1936; Happold 1935; Wort 1935). Each of these texts gave precedence to ethical over intellectual values, and Sylvester (1994: p. 10) quotes from the Board of Education's 1905 publication, *Suggestions for the Consideration of Teachers and Others Concerned in the Work of Public Elementary Schools*:

> All boys and girls in Great Britain have rights and duties which they will someday exercise. The province of history is to trace how these rights and duties arise . . . examples put before them, whether for imitation or the reverse, of the great men and women that have lived in the past.

The moral aim of history is clearly stated. In a Memorandum on the Study of History in Schools issued by the Scottish Education Department (1907) the moral position is even more carefully summarised, as the document states that compared with the laws of evidence and a 'clarified moral sense', the mere accumulation of knowledge of historical facts is of secondary importance.

During the inter-war years there was renewed concern in Britain for teaching citizenship. Helen Madeley (1920: p. 9) accurately reflected the mood of history teachers of the time when she wrote that if history was to survive it must serve the ends of citizenship and that 'the curriculum of the school shall be definitely and recognisably related to life as we mean it to be lived'. Her book is full of sensible suggestions about teaching with sources, the use of evidence and the importance of a variety of teaching methods in history which most teachers today would endorse. Her book, however, essentially conceived the purpose of history in terms of nurturing moral growth and developing in children abilities to make responsible moral decisions. History was part of a school curriculum which was designed to teach children to become certain kinds of adults, based upon the virtues and moral tradition within the Western heritage. History had a clear instrumental use and promoted particular moral values through historical narratives in the teaching of which children learned how to recognise 'heroes and villains'; an attempt was made to uphold virtue and avoid vice. History played a significant part in maintaining the identity, myths and values of society, and was also directly used to encourage patriotism until the late 1950s (Marsden 1989). It was thought that by introducing children to 'exceptional' and 'great' national figures, patriotism could be established. Children were largely trained to conform to an ethical code by simply learning and repeating the one interpretation found in their history textbook.

Choice of interpretations in history textbooks was certainly lacking and these were almost entirely conventional in their outline of British history. In Chapter 5 it was shown that the history curriculum is not neutral, and has a long tradition of use based upon the promotion of certain values and attitudes. Systematic state propaganda reinforced the idea that anything prior to the Protestant Reformation was to be treated with suspicion and deemed bad, while anything since was naturally good. One of the most widely known problems or questions Kohlberg posed to children was whether in the American Civil War it was right for people to help runaway slaves, who were regarded as the legal property of their masters. Kohlberg described levels of response which ranged from those motivated by the child's need for praise through to recognising that the answer may not fit in with existing moral rules – a stage in which the child adopts an independent and reflective position. To describe or interpret what you believe is the case in history may reveal what is sociologically normative in a particular society, for it tells you what *is*, not what *ought to be*, and children may be left with the impression in history that *what is* equals *what ought to be*. Something is not morally acceptable or legitimate simply because it is widely accepted, voted for or practised in society. Slavish adherence to a set of laws and norms, leaving little room for personal responsibility, is effectively a training in conformity and one is not historically educated if one simply repeats one view to the exclusion of all others. Interpretation in history requires knowledge and understanding, not just facts. Denis Shemilt (1980: pp. 7–8, 19) found that pupils on traditional history courses tended to see history as a corpus of 'pre-existent, pre-digested and inalienable facts. These facts were construed as absolutely true and absolutely unchanging.' Shemilt would not go as far as Butterfield (1951), who was one of the first to suggest that we should generally avoid moral judgements in teaching history. It seems likely that Shemilt is suggesting that history offered pupils the opportunity to clarify their own values by thinking through the various moral issues in the subject.

Is it the role of history to help develop virtue in pupils? This, of course, will depend on what we mean by virtue. Patrick Walsh (1992: p. 180) warns about the danger of a moralistic approach in history teaching and suggests it may lead 'to premature and artificial synopses of broad historical development, based on a simplistic division of historical agents and ideas into "good" and "bad", "progressive" and "reactionary", or – in other words – "loyal" and "subversive"'. However, Walsh questions whether there is such a thing as the impartiality of the historian and concludes that: 'the refusal of an ethical encounter with the past is a denial of spontaneous expectations, a methodological exclusion of a range of responses that naturally seem appropriate'. Do these responses impede objectivity? Pluralist and multiculturalist approaches often require a methodological exclusion of certain value judgements, but value-free history is not possible since there is an endless set of perspectives and moral beliefs which 'participate inevitably in shaping historical enquiry' and, therefore, our historical moral outlook.

Arthur Marwick (1981: p. 102) agrees that 'history is implicated in the making of moral judgements' and he accepts that in the selection of facts morality cannot be avoided. He points us to the moral overtones of the phrases used in history writing, such as 'atrocities' and 'massacres', to demonstrate that we cannot avoid making moral judgements about events. There is recognition, though, that there are problems of objectivity and he suggests that the best evidence is the truth (1981: p. 189). Nevertheless, Marwick (1981: p. 190) is absolutely clear that history has a moral element, and he concludes that: 'The "moral" quality to be found in historical writing actually arises from two circumstances; first, that historians deal with human and social issues . . . second . . . they also have to work with highly imperfect evidence.' Marwick (1981: p. 207) is also conscious of the dangers that can arise from this moral element in history writing and warns us that it can turn to hatred of others:

> Very often the desire for human justice is in essence a sombre and heavily moralised desire for revenge. The demand for justice at the bar of history is no exception to this. The motive behind it is very often the fact that those who feel it to be their duty to recount and stigmatise what they consider to have been the misdeeds of the past do so because in some way they identify themselves with the victims of those misdeeds and some other still existing groups or historic personality with those who perpetrated them. Thereby hatred is sustained and increased.

As Hill (1953) reminds us: 'History properly taught can help men to become critical and humane, just as wrongly taught, it can turn them into bigots and fanatics.'

During the last two to three decades the role of history in the school curriculum has been justified in many different ways. Many of the aims and benefits in terms of the various kinds of skills advocated for the subject are the same type of skills claimed for other subjects. History is essentially, and perhaps even uniquely, about the study of change over time. History is also a source of skills, but not uniquely so. There has been a reaction against the past teaching of history by teachers and some, like Smith (1986), have argued that we must not teach substantive values. He adopts a relativism in which one thing is no better than anything else, and everything is open for discussion leading to informed personal judgement. This has often led to an attempt to confine the presentation of the past to a study of evidence and to a neutral technical language. Some others have advocated a procedural method or 'neutral' position to be adopted on the part of teacher. Yet others, such as Denis Shemilt (see Lee *et al.* 1992), believe that 'the aims of history should relate to the potentialities of the individual as well as to the needs of society, and must be broadly civilising rather than narrowly instrumental'. History's aim, in this view, is to promote the liberal democracy that we live in. There is also debate about whether history is part of the aims of education or has its own intrinsic aims separate from those of the school curriculum (Lee *et al.* 1992). In addition, there is a lack of clarity about the nature and purpose of moral education, and disagreement about what citizenship education means. We need to return to these themes and tensions, but first we need to survey the government position in the form of the National Curriculum.

Government and political intervention, 1979–99

Moral education was very much at the foundation of the 1988 Education Reform Act (section 1, part 1), for the curriculum was seen as basically intellectual and moral in character. A culturally conservative curriculum was formulated which included most of the traditional subjects as a hierarchy of disciplines together with moral values. In the list of subjects history was viewed by many as vitally important, and even before the Act was proposed Conservative politicians repeated the more traditional aims and justifications for history in the school curriculum. Sir Keith Joseph, in an address to the Historical Association in 1984, claimed that: 'History, properly taught, justifies its place in the school curriculum by what it does to prepare all pupils for the requirements of citizenship.' For Joseph, promoting citizenship through history was a means to understanding the contemporary world and obviously had a moral dimension. Beck (1998) is very critical of such views which he, together with many other critics, collectively label 'New Right', an ideology which, he says, combines nation, culture, identity, social cohesion and the educational curriculum and treats them as interdependent in an attempt to promote particular values in society. However, this ignores the traditional aims of history teaching which were still held by many teachers and parents in the 1980s. HMIs continued to reflect this traditional view, however diluted, by retaining the idea that history was connected to moral values. In an HMI discussion document it was stated that by the age of 16, a pupil 'can identify the values and attitudes on which human actions have been based in the past' (DES 1985: p. 19).

The debate over National Curriculum history which took place after the passing of the Education Reform Act in 1988 was largely and primarily concerned with national identity, not factual coverage of a particular period in British history. This debate has a long tradition. It was not initiated by the New Right, which did, however, together with the press, exploit it and used it to promote a particular line. There was and still is a widespread belief that civility, patriotism, discipline, and respect for law and property have disappeared. This belief motivated some people's decision to promote certain virtues in education which included: responsibility, prudence, honesty, self-respect and reverence. This line of argument had a responsive chord with the public and the Interim Report on History agreed that history must contribute to the education of informed citizens, but it did not explicitly address the question of whether history included moral goals. Clearly, the teaching of history was to have an educational role in the question of what it is to be human and what form of human behaviour best promotes responsibility.

The National Curriculum Council issued a paper (April 1993) which explicitly addressed the question of moral education in the curriculum and linked it to the development of pupils educated to be able to choose for themselves a set of social values (see White 1994). The paper was clear that 'all subjects in the curriculum' had to contribute to this moral education. It provided a framework for the role of history in moral education, but was rather vague on specific links with the subject of history. This was also the case with OfSTED's (February 1994) discussion paper OfSTED (May 1994) nonetheless incorporated the requirement that each subject must address the moral dimension in its teaching. This provision was also incorporated into the TTA's *Teaching Standards* (1999) which state that history teachers must 'plan opportunities to contribute to pupils' personal, spiritual, moral, social and cultural development'. Samuel (1996) endorsed this view of history's contribution to moral education in an address to the QCA conference 'Curriculum, Culture and Society', claiming that:

> History is an argument about the past as well as a record of it, and its terms are forever changing. It is, or ought to be, contentious. It has always provided, though many historians have preferred not to acknowledge this, an arena for moral debate, distinguishing 'fact' and 'values' at one moment, but at the next treating the two as one.

In a submission to the White Paper *Excellence in Schools* (House of Commons, 1997) the Citizenship Foundation stated that 'We believe that citizenship has a clear conceptual core which relates to the induction of young people into the legal, moral and political arena of public life' (quoted in QCA 1998: p. 11). In defining citizenship education, the Crick Report (QCA 1998: pp. 11, 52–3) first mentioned that 'morally responsible behaviour' was part of citizenship, for which 'guidance on moral matters' was a precondition. History was recognised as contributing to this aim, and it was stated that the subject's use of evidence and the processes of enquiry employed would help pupils to discuss and reach informed judgements about contemporary issues.

In government, New Labour reviewed the National Curriculum in order to make it less prescriptive and increase the professional autonomy of teachers. In the stated rationale for the curriculum entitled *Rationale for the School Curriculum and Functions of the National Curriculum* (QCA 1999b) comprising two short pages, the word 'moral' appears no less than six times and 'virtues' are also mentioned in connection with the aims of the school curriculum. If this rationale for the curriculum had been proposed under a Conservative government, critics would certainly have interpreted it as influenced by the New Right. Under New Labour, criticism has been muted, if voiced at all. In stating the rationale for teaching history under the section 'The Distinctive Contribution of History to the School Curriculum', the new curriculum outlines the moral purpose of school history: 'They are able to clarify their own life choices, attitudes and values in context . . .'. The links between the programmes of study for history and citizenship at Key Stage 3 are to be made clear through non-statutory information to accompany the revised curriculum. The role of history is 'officially' seen as contributing to both citizenship and moral education, and there also appears to be a political consensus about this.

History teaching: moral rhetoric and reality

This 'official' view of history, incorporating civil and moral aims, sits easily with White's (see Lee *et al.* 1992) understanding of history, which begins with the aims of education and then sees how school history fits in. Lee argues that history has its own aims and should not be used to transmit values or moral education. He argues that to incorporate essentially broad educational aims in history teaching will offend against the values of detachment and objectivity that are found in historical research. Aims, according to Lee, are intrinsic to the study of history and must not be subordinated to moral education. Therefore, there is a need to distinguish the aims of history from the aims of education, otherwise history becomes distorted as a subject. White rejects this view and argues that history serves the aims of education by throwing light on particular choices made by pupils. This debate captures the essential problem that many history teachers have about the purpose of school history.

There appears to be a deep-seated ambivalence among history teachers about the role and nature of moral values in history teaching. Many history teachers believe that moral education and citizenship education must not be allowed to shape the primary analytical goals of history itself. The concepts and methodology of history are not those of moral education. History teachers are right to avoid moralising in history, but they also know that the National Curriculum requires some discussion of the moral dimension in history. While history teachers should be aware of the moral dimension of their work, at the same time they need to preserve the discipline of history itself. Yet there are many teachers who see their subject as intellectual, not moral, and argue that substantive moral values should be avoided in the teaching of the subject. It is often argued that all moral ideas are subjective and relative, and therefore are mere customs and conventions which have a purely instrumental purpose; thus values are peculiar to specific individuals and societies. Values can be beliefs, feelings, opinions, preferences, prejudices; they become 'value-free' as a result of our non-judgemental approach to history. Nothing is fixed or certain. Can this relativist argument be sustained?

The revised National Curriculum details the values and purposes underpinning the whole school curriculum and states: 'Education should . . . reaffirm our commitment to the virtues of truth, justice, honesty, trust and a sense of duty.' These are all substantive or procedural values. It adds: 'The school curriculum should contribute to the development of pupils' sense of identity.' Values here refer in their most general sense to that which is good, desirable and worthwhile. There is a recognition in the National Curriculum that history expands our picture of the world and human beings and, therefore what is possible for us. The curriculum attempts to integrate ethical and intellectual values. In the very study of the subject pupils explore moral dilemmas, reflect on moral situations, rethink and evaluate these historical situations and ultimately learn to argue and support a point of view. History teaching needs therefore to embrace moral reasoning, for no one can effectively study history without some form of moral deliberation or judgement. As we reflect on the many morally perplexing situations in history we seek some response of feeling, whether of attraction or repulsion. How do we decide on a moral stance in history? History is about judgement and therefore it is about moral reasoning. Pupils learn to examine people as responsible agents, the consequences of their actions, their general policies, their traits of character, their motives in a given historical situation; all of this is the stuff of history. History offers opportunities to examine what it is to be human. This is a complex area for history teachers and one in which their own understanding of morality influences their approach to the subject. The aims normally outlined in school history departments often refer to a skills-based subject while there is hardly ever any explicit mention of morality or moral reasoning.

Peter Knight (1987) argues that it is the values dimension of history that makes the subject distinctive. He suggests that skills can be developed more successfully by other subject areas. Values, he says, are not value free. Critical historians claim to eschew ethical judgement, but while the intrusion of moral judgement in historical enquiry can lead to a loss of objectivity and even to the falsification of history, without it pupils would fail to identify the morally relevant properties in any historical situation and also fail to distinguish the context in which moral activity takes place. History would not be able to enlarge on human experience by teaching about human behaviour in the past. Questions such as: What governs our behaviour? What is it that people should aspire to? What ideals do we put before them? might disappear from history teaching. This is perhaps why the American National Center for History in the Schools (1994) argued that:

> without history, a society shares no common memory of where it has been, what its core values are, or what decisions of the past account for present circumstances. Without history, we cannot undertake any sensible inquiry into the political, social, or moral issues in society. And without historical knowledge and inquiry, we cannot achieve the informed discriminating citizenship essential to effective participation in the democratic processes or governance and the fulfilment for all our citizens of the nation's democratic ideals.

R.J. Unstead, a writer whose works, mainly school history textbooks, were widely available and used in the 1960s through to the early 1980s, gave great emphasis to the coverage of British history, or English history, which he presented largely as facts in a story form, not as evidence to be debated. Sallie Purkis (1980) is very critical of Unstead. She notes that we now have comprehensive schools and multi-racial classrooms, and consequently she dismisses Unstead's efforts as past their sell-by date. Unstead, she concludes, is prejudiced and: 'His belief that one of the main reasons for teaching history, what might be called moral values, is unacceptable'. She fears indoctrination and claims his work is insulting in an age 'where children see and sympathise with the Vietnamese boat people and become involved in schemes to buy medi-bikes for Tanzania'. While Unstead's selection of historical materials appears dated now, what should replace it? Unstead certainly attempted to build identity through history and anything which built on a pupil's ability to identify with the British state was celebrated, commemorated and deemed to be good while other historical figures and events were condemned or ignored. Purkis has her own moral agenda and whatever she would replace it with would be no less moral in character. What is interesting, and ironic, about her argument that school history is unacceptable if it carries ideological messages is that the only objections she raises are an appeal to the emotive and to the type of 'history' pupils receive from the television age.

There is confusion in this important area and some teachers still see morality as too controversial and may even talk of the futility of teaching values. It reminds me of Richard McCloud, a history teacher who wrote: in the *Washington Post* in 1989: 'When I read and study the Declaration of Independence with my junior students . . . I am not teaching historical facts as an end in themselves. Instead, I am implicitly teaching Thomas Jefferson's commitment to freedom and high moral standards.' However, this teacher began the letter by writing that moral values and history teaching did not mix. But history teachers are often involved with moral questions, whether they are conscious of them or not (see Holden 1996). Martin Boult (1980) provides some limited evidence that 'history can modify favourably and positively . . . attitudes towards racial groups'. In other words, he claims it can make school students less racist and more inclusive, which is of itself a moral response to the selection of historical materials for teaching. This selection of historical content is intended to change, develop or modify a pupil's moral outlook and is equivalent to what P.W. Musgrave (1983) said was the intention of much history teaching:

> The stories of national heroes, Nelson and Florence Nightingale, have been taught in the hope that they would be seen as moral exemplars. Great victories, for example that of Drake over the Spanish Armada, have been emphasised in the hope of building patriotism. Material has been chosen with such lessons in mind.

Selection of content is not morally neutral.

In the 1970s there was a reaction against syllabuses which were simply chronological outline surveys of British history in favour of history defined as a mode of enquiry. Ben Jones (1973) divided teachers into 'traditionalists', who favoured content, and 'progressives', who favoured methods. Lawrence Stenhouse (1970), in his work with the Humanities Curriculum Project, advocated the role of the 'impartial chairperson' by which a teacher could avoid stating his or her own position and keep to procedural rules – in effect the teacher renounces authority as 'expert'. Evidence is respected and the pupils' statements and viewpoints, however inaccurate, are deemed important. The idea behind this teaching method was the development of the autonomy of the child; this meant the avoidance of any potential beliefs or morals in teaching. This view also tended to fit well with the 'progressive' mode of enquiry in history and saw the development of individual capacities as not tied to any particular view of culture or transmission. Basil Singh (1988) criticised this concept of neutrality on the basis that, whether evidence or argument, history teaching is someone's interpretation. Is it not also the case, he argued, that some kinds of evidence are more relevant or more compelling than others and that teachers should be in a better position than their pupils to assess the various views and claims grounded upon evidence in relation to certain historical topics? Stenhouse (Stenhouse and Verma 1981: pp. 103–5) researched his own 'impartial chair' teaching method, and found that attitudes and values were formed nevertheless. Pupils were just as likely to be influenced at home as at school, and he reminded us that pupils are not *tabulae rasae*. Nevertheless, this 'progressive' lobby in both teaching methods and skills found qualified support among postmodernists who argued that history is too diffuse, complex and multilayered to be reduced to narrowly defined tradition. They called for transnational perspectives on history. Henry Giroux (Giroux *et al.* 1996: p. 51) commented:

> Historical learning . . . is not about constructing a linear narrative but about blasting history open, rupturing its silences, highlighting its detours, and organising its limits within an open and honest concern for human suffering, values and the legacy of the often unrepresentable or misrepresented.

However, this postmodernist approach opens up a whole range of values and moral questions.

Controversy and conflict are the essence of history and controversial moral issues are an integral and inescapable part of this. Since it is not directly possible to verify the truth of historical events, how to interpret events and understand different perspectives requires procedures agreed by historians for validating historical statements in the light of relevant evidence. Nevertheless, there is widespread disagreement about historical events, and alternative interpretations based on the same evidence and on the same use of skills are common place. A narrow conception of moral education through history is simply not good enough. History can promote basic morality, but not as conformity. Moral situations in history have their own particular characteristics, and this implies that we cannot simply copy them. Reflection and judgement are required and moral judgements need as much scrutiny as historical evidence, for human life is rule-governed by general principles, laws, codes of conduct, advisory codes to which school history makes a contribution. We need to ask again to what extent we are highlighting history's moral relevance in the classroom, and to what extent moral relevance should influence the selection of content and the emphasis of teaching.

Conclusion

When history was established as a school subject at the beginning of the twentieth century patriotic and moral objectives predominated. Today, at the start of the twenty-first century there is once again a growing political demand for the educational system to instil notions of citizenship and ethical codes. Should history teachers attempt to convey a sense of sympathy with the kind of society in which their pupils live? The moral positions adopted by the pupils are not a matter of indifference for the teacher. Pupils can and do acquire moral values and moral reasoning skills in history. There are of course limitations to what history can contribute in this field, but the relationship between moral reasoning and moral action, between moral cognition and moral character, and whether the subject should be taught as a way of thinking or as a way of acting – or both – are important questions for history teachers. Through the knowledge of laws, constitution and political institutions, which are all necessary to democracy, citizens are helped to become self-governing. Pupils are taught through history's contribution to the aims of education that they have obligations, need to practise tolerance, fairness and self-discipline, and should develop and practise certain virtues and seek to avoid particular vices. A sense of balance in the selection and presentation of moral concepts is crucial here, especially as the National Curriculum does not define the word moral in its documents. There is no official guidance on the moral dimension of history or any specified content of what this moral dimension is.

History teaching has a moral dimension and moral concepts are taught through the teaching of history. Those who teach about protests, wars, uprisings, genocide, religious conflict and ethnic cleansing do not confine themselves to factual information, but include moral reasoning and judgement in their interpretation of these events. The words which describe these events are deliberately selected by historians to evoke an affective response from their readers and may even function to redirect the readers' attitudes to accord more fully with the historians'. Moral words are emotive and they are widely used in history. In the same way that 'great' or 'exceptional' figures in the past are examined, the moral climate of the age is considered: we reflect on moral attitudes, feelings and conduct, and we consider the moral implications of a political event or military response. The scope for raising moral questions in history is practically endless. There is no promise that history will improve people, or make them better human beings, but to sympathise with the predicament of others is to make a significant moral response. This requires emotional and psychological maturity on the part of the pupil. Teachers often feel uneasy about the moral dimension of history, partly in reaction against what is generally understood to have been too restrictive a moral outlook in the past. School history, like education itself, is not morally neutral about what being a human person means, and it has moral outcomes. An understanding of the moral dimension in teaching or studying history will place considerable demands on the personal resources of the teacher. In the end, if history is to prove of some value to pupils it must be a basis upon which to make moral judgements.

Key questions

1   How do the moral values of teachers influence the teaching of history in schools? Are teachers aware of their own viewpoints and moral values when teaching history?

2   Heater (1990) considers that schools convey moral values in three ways: selection of material, deliberate identification of certain objectives to provide a certain moral outcome, and the hidden curriculum. Is this a useful framework for history teachers to consider when planning their teaching?

3   Should the moral dimension in history be a focus for assessment?

Recommended reading

J. Beck (1998) *Morality and Citizenship in Education*. London, Cassell.
    An academic account of the moral dimension of citizenship.

P. Coman (1999) 'Mentioning the War: does studying World War II make any difference to pupils' sense of British achievement and identity', *Teaching History*, 96 October.

T. Haydn (2000) 'Teaching the Holocaust through History', in I. Davies (ed.) *Teaching the Holocaust: educational dimensions, principles and practice*. London, Continuum.
    A good introduction to the teaching of a moral theme in history.

R. Nash (1998) *Answering the 'Virtuecrats': a moral conversation on character education*. New York, Columbia University, Teachers College Press.
    An excellent introduction to the place of moral education in the school curriculum.

D. Rowe (1998) 'Moral and Civic Education: the search for a robust entitlement model', *Curriculum*, 19(2) pp. 74–83.
    A brief description of the link between morality and citizenship written by one of the key figures in the Citizenship Foundation.

Chapter 7

History, citizenship and diversity

Some principles, problems and past mistakes

There is nothing artificial about the link between history and citizenship. Whereas teachers in some school subjects may be scratching their heads and thinking that they have not really done much of this sort of thing before, it would be a fairly odd history curriculum which did not at some points raise questions about what it means to be a citizen, about different ideas of 'the good citizen' over time, and about the changing relationships between rulers and the ruled. Similarly, given that history involves the study of human behaviour over time, one obvious area of interest would be how different groups have related to each other and treated each other in the past, and what light this might throw on present and future relations between different groups in society. This is not a 'bolt-on' extra. Just as disciplines such as science and philosophy have their 'big questions', citizenship and diversity are at the heart of good, relevant history teaching: some of our 'big questions' are in this area.

History, well taught, can help to develop young people's intellectual autonomy, and 'informed and responsible scepticism' (Slater, 1989: 16). In helping pupils to understand the factors influencing relations between different groups in society, history can help to develop 'a passionate drive for clarity, fair mindedness, a fervour for getting to the bottom of things, for listening sympathetically to opposing points of view, a compelling drive to seek out evidence, a devotion to truth as against self-interest' (Paul, 1998); or, put less elegantly by Postman and Weingartner (1998), history is a 'crap-detecting' subject.

One important proposition which will be advanced in this chapter, as a suggested principle of good history teaching, is that if school history is to be worthwhile, connections must be made between the past and the present. Aldrich (1997: 3) makes the point that history is about human activity with particular reference to the whole dimension of time – past, present and future. Without the ability to make connections and comparisons with the present, what is the point of learning about the past? It becomes a harmless diversion, a quaint hobby like collecting matchboxes or trainspotting, and this is one of the reasons why some pupils think that history is 'boring and useless' (Adey, 2000; Price, 1968).

Is there any present-day problem or question into which it might not be possible to glean some further degree of insight by considering what has gone before? As Husbands (1996: 34) notes:

Learning about the concept of kingship (*or whatever*) frequently involves two sets of simultaneous learning: learning about power and its distribution in past societies, and learning about power and its distribution in modern society. The former cannot be given real meaning until pupils have some more contemporary knowledge against which to calibrate their historical understandings.

If we fail to make connections between the past and the present, there is the danger that pupils will be left asking 'So what?' and wondering what history has to do with their lives. If we want politically literate citizens, they will need to relate their political understandings of the past to present-day political issues and problems. Although religious strife in Britain in the sixteenth and seventeenth centuries is part of the National Curriculum, how many school leavers would be able to explain why there are problems between Catholics and Protestants in Scotland and Ireland, but not in England and Wales? How many would be able to explain the slogan, 'A bayonet is a weapon with a worker at both ends'? If one of the aims of school history is 'to help understand the present in the context of the past' (DES, 1990: 1) there is no point in 'pulling up the drawbridge' before the present day. In 1952, the Ministry of Education (1952: 32) made an important point relating to history and political literacy which went unheeded by some of the architects of the National Curriculum for history:

> The divorce between current affairs and history, so that they are regarded as two different subjects, gravely weakens both. It accentuates the natural tendency of children to regard history as something remote and irrelevant instead of something which has formed the world around them and which is continuously being formed by that world. And, it accentuates equally the tendency to look at contemporary questions as though they had no context in time, no parallels or precedents.

One further point might be made here about how we approach these issues. We need to teach citizenship and diversity in a way which is consistent with the integrity of the discipline of history. School history is not about 'preaching' to pupils, or conflating moral fables with the attempt to get at the truth of what happened in the past. John Arnold (2000: 13) makes the point that history is above all else 'an argument':

> If the evidence always spoke plainly, truthfully and clearly to us, not only would historians have no work to do, we would have no opportunity to argue with each other. History . . . is an argument between different historians, and perhaps, an argument between the past and the present, an argument between what actually happened and what is going to happen next. Arguments are important; they create the possibility of changing things.

One of the uses of school history is to help young people to handle information intelligently; to learn to subject sources to critical scrutiny in order to get at the truth in a society which has become increasingly adroit at manipulating and distorting information. One of the corollaries of this is that we cannot always derive comforting or positive messages from how societies in the past (whether in Britain or elsewhere) handled issues of cultural, ethnic or religious diversity. It would be wrong to think that a well-intentioned desire to promote 'fairness, social justice, respect for democracy and diversity', and the need for 'mutual respect and understanding' between diverse national, regional, religious and ethnic identities in the UK (DfEE/QCA, 1999b: 15), can be unproblematically delivered by exposing young people to the study of the past. Although Edgington (1982) talks of the 'healing role' of history teaching, it could be argued that the abuse of school history, worldwide, has done more harm than good in this area (see, for instance, Ferro, 1981). The answer is not to get rid of school history, or traduce the discipline of history by turning it into moral fairy tales or an advert for cultural pluralism. Slater (1989: 16) makes the point that history 'cannot guarantee tolerance, though it can give it some intellectual weapons'. As soon as we start trying to use history to engineer a change in pupils' values and attitudes, and get them to arrive at a predetermined conclusion, it stops being history and becomes something else. The idea with history is that you study the evidence first and *then* come to some conclusions. Moreover, often the evidence does not produce tidy and unproblematic outcomes. History is not like the Michael Jackson/Paul McCartney record, which presents 'ebony and ivory living together in harmony', as on the piano keyboard. School history gives pupils a methodology or framework for looking at issues of diversity and citizenship, together with contexts derived from past examples. If religious toleration or democracy or cultural pluralism or whatever is 'a good thing', it ought to be able to stand up to critical scrutiny. In Lee's words,

> The reason for teaching history is not that it changes society, but that it changes *pupils*; it changes what they see in the world, and how they see it. . . . To say someone has learnt history is to say something very wide ranging about the way in which he or she is likely to make sense of the world. History offers a way of seeing almost any substantive issue in human affairs, subject to certain procedures and standards, whatever feelings one may have.
>
> (Lee, 1992: 23–4)

What questions do we ask?

If we want to equip young people with the intellectual equipment to resist the blandishments of *Bulldog* and other National Front publications, we need to do more than simply tell pupils that racism is wrong; we need to provide the tools to help pupils detect ulterior motives, factual elisions and dubious claims. This is not cultural relativism. If we simply tell pupils about the wickedness of Hitler, slave traders, Pol Pot, etc., are we equipping them with the intellectual foundations which will enable them to subject contemporary values and policies to intelligent scrutiny? As Lord Lane remarked, 'Oppression does not stand on the doorstep with a toothbrush moustache and a swastika armband. It creeps up insidiously, step by step' (quoted in Supple, 1994). So when teaching important topics in history involving discrimination by groups of people in the past in their treatment of other groups, whether the Nazis' treatment of the Jews, or European traders' treatment of African slaves, we need to get beyond 'This is what happened, wasn't it awful', and ask some of the more difficult questions. These might include:

- How did people who burned Catholics/traded in slaves/killed Jews justify their actions?
- Why did some people commit atrocities and others stand aside or protect persecuted groups?
- Who gained what from the instigation of discrimination and persecution?
- Why did persecution and violence occur at some times and places but not others?
- On what grounds is it morally or ethically justifiable to treat particular groups or individuals differently from others?
- Is it possible to value people and groups differently, but treat them with equal respect and consideration?
- Is it possible to identify preconditions for the harmonious coexistence of differing ethnic and religious groupings?
- What factors influence the outbreak of persecution and discrimination of minorities?
- Why did supposedly civilised people commit barbaric acts?
- Why did so many 'ordinary' people fail to do anything to prevent such acts?
- Why do explanations and accounts of these events differ, and how can we find out which accounts and explanations are most valid? (Which can we trust?)
- Why is it worth studying? Why does it matter?
- What light does it shed on current problems and issues?

Although some pupils may well have racist or sexist attitudes, many young people do not regard themselves as prejudiced, and see equal opportunities as a fairly unproblematic issue. The study of past societies can help to make young people more aware of some of the complexities of equal opportunities issues, not least in looking at the different philosophies of resource allocation and political rights which have been prevalent at different times in different places. The Levellers, the Jacobins, nineteenth-century venture capitalists, the Bolsheviks and New Labour had very different views about meritocracy and the franchise. Although the Crick Report, *Education for Citizenship* (QCA, 1998), talks of the 'skills' of citizenship, it may well be that enhanced *understanding* of the complexities of citizenship and equal opportunities issues may be more important than an accretion of knowledge and skills pertaining to these areas. Through the study of the past, young people can examine propositions such as:

- Equal treatment of people sometimes has a lower priority as an operating principle than other factors.
- There is often a tension between equal treatment of people and other concerns, e.g. profit.
- Different societies have had differing views on the extent to which 'efficiency' rather than 'equity' should determine resource allocation in areas such as personal income and primary social goods such as health care and education.
- 'Equal treatment' becomes a more powerful operating principle if it concerns the people whose treatment is involved, rather than consideration of other groups.

- The relation between equality of opportunity and equality of outcome is a complex one; increasing one may not increase the other.

A similar list could be drawn up with the object of developing young people's understanding of democracy. The study of topics such as the French Revolution, the Russian Revolution, the Puritan communities in New England in the seventeenth century, the Salem Witch Trials, the history of Northern Ireland since 1922, Weimar Germany and de Tocqueville's (1835) observations on democracy can give an understanding of the flaws and limitations of democratic systems. Better that young people have a developed understanding of the ways in which democratic systems can be flawed, or subverted and undermined, than that they are taught to believe that democracy is a good thing without having an intelligent understanding of the ways in which democracies work.

Mistakes from the past

The recent history of multicultural and anti-racist initiatives in humanities education points to mistakes which might be avoided, as well as possible ways forward. It is not the case that 'the more attention we give to multicultural and diversity issues, the more tolerant and humane school leavers will be'. Like anything else, diversity issues can be handled well or badly in the history classroom. The Macdonald Report (1989) graphically illustrates that multicultural and anti-racist initiatives, in the humanities and elsewhere, can be handled in a way which causes more harm than good.

Diversity issues in history can be approached in ways that are posturing, intellectually shallow, misguided and tokenistic. The BBC Radio 3 series looking at inventions by men and women from around the world was doubtless well intended, but was the invention of the ironing board (by Sarah Moore) the best example of an initiative by a woman that they could come up with? When I taught in Manchester, the school had an anti-apartheid week. When I asked my Year 10 pupils whether they thought apartheid was a bad thing, they all put their hands up, but when I asked them if they knew what apartheid *was*, no one knew the answer. If apartheid is *per se* a bad thing, are single-sex schools also necessarily a bad thing? Anti-racist zeal can sometimes lead to a 'four legs good, two legs bad' approach to history – history with the thinking taken out, which leaves pupils without a proper understanding of some of the concepts we are trying to teach. Often, playing devil's advocate, problematising the past, and requiring pupils to think through the intellectual rationale for taking positions can be more helpful than asking them to accept judgements about history at face value, or to believe things 'just because the teacher says so'. While I was working in the same local authority, the Section 11 library would only loan out pictures and resources about Third World countries if they portrayed 'positive images' of undeveloped countries. Are children to grow up thinking that India is mainly skyscrapers and motorways? Similarly, at an exam board meeting for the modern world syllabus, it was suggested that 50 per cent of the questions should be about women. As DES (1985: 29) pointed out, 'It would be naive to expect evidence and its interpretation to suggest that women dominated political and military history.' Pupils need to be given a picture of the past which is consistent with reality. If there are inequities, the point is to try and explain them, not to pretend that they do not exist. Another example of the 'wishful thinking' school of history is Kenneth Baker's assertion (1988) that history 'promotes tolerance . . . shows virtue continuously triumphing over wickedness, courage over cowardice, and that a good little 'un can beat the big bad 'un' (try telling that to the people of Poland). Nor should it be assumed that pupils from ethnic minority backgrounds necessarily prefer to do 'black' history, or that white pupils in some way share a heritage of guilt for the colonial misdemeanours of their predecessors. Content which has the potential to provide insights into contemporary problems in the area of social, cultural and religious diversity can be helpful, but it must be handled in a way which is consistent with the procedures and conventions of the discipline.

> Whatever decisions are taken about content, they will go for naught unless they are founded firmly on the skills of historical thinking with their insistence on the absolute necessity of having to support statements made about those individuals or groups. Thus historical thinking is the implacable enemy of unexamined and stridently asserted stereotypes. . . . History teaching will be a powerful weapon *against* indoctrination provided that it constantly insists on the necessary relationship between statements about people and available evidence.
>
> (DES, 1985: 32)

Principles of procedure

Given that there are different ideas about the aims of political and social education (see, for example, Porter, 1983), and that there is no universally accepted consensus as to which values should be promoted through the study of school history, how should history teachers approach issues of citizenship and diversity so as to avoid allegations of political bias or inappropriate indoctrination of pupils? As Nick Tate (1996c) remarked,

> If we find that there are certain values which are shared by society, it would be appropriate for any moral education in schools to have these as their object. Where there are disputes in society between values, schools have to be neutral.

One way forward is to adhere to the guidance provided by the National Curriculum documentation for history (DfEE/QCA, 1999a: 8) and for citizenship (DfEE/QCA, 1999b: 14–15). These documents include specific reference to studying the 'social, cultural, religious and ethnic diversity of the societies studied, both in Britain and the wider world', and learning about 'fairness, social justice, respect for democracy and diversity at school, local, national and global level'. Furthermore if we take the utterances of the Secretary of State for Education at face value, young people need to be taught to 'discern between information and propaganda' (Blunkett, 1999), to develop 'a full understanding of their roles and responsibilities as citizens in a modern democracy', and be better equipped to deal with 'the difficult moral and social questions that arise in their lives and in society' (Blunkett, 2000). This means that young people must be taught to think for themselves rather than being told what to think. Slater's (1989) conception of the discipline of history as providing objectivity of *procedures* for discussion and debate of controversial issues offers history teachers a *modus operandi* for dealing with issues of diversity and citizenship. School history provides a framework for pupils to discuss contentious issues within academic canons of reliability, explanation and justification (Husbands, 1996). Although teachers may experiment with different roles in conducting discussions, from neutral chair to devil's advocate, stated commitment or 'balanced approach' (Stradling *et al.*, 1984), the overarching question is 'How would someone adhering to the rules and procedures of the discipline of history conduct the enquiry into this matter?' This is the position which helps to guide history teachers through some of the sensitive areas which diversity issues sometimes generate.

Teaching approaches

(a) How should we present the national past to pupils?

One British historian has argued that pupils should learn that 'to be born British is to win first prize in the lottery of life' (Johnson, 1994) and at least one politician has expressed regret at the passing of what Sylvester (1994) terms 'The Great Tradition' in British history teaching, celebrating our glorious heritage of empire, independence and parliamentary democracy: 'Why cannot we go back to the good old days when we learnt by heart the names of the kings and queens of England, the feats of our warriors and our battles, and the glorious deeds of our past?' (Stokes, 1990).

In the same way that most people would accept the truism that 'nobody's perfect', most historians would acknowledge that all nations have their 'skeletons' – lost battles, periods of decline, moments of shame, insalubrious and discreditable episodes, and leaders and governments who have behaved dishonourably. How are history teachers in the United Kingdom to handle these elements of 'bad heritage'? Should we, as one leading statesman suggested, 'Reshape our system of national education so that attention can be concentrated on great heroes and go beyond "objective presentation" towards the more urgent goal of inspiring national pride' (Hitler, quoted in Ferro, 1981: 98–9)? What about Drogheda and Wexford, Yorktown, Amritsar, the Fall of Singapore, the introduction of the concentration camp? If we expunge less glorious elements of the national past, are we not grossly misrepresenting ('doing an Irving') with the historical record? Shouldn't pupils examine both the successes and failures of Britain's past? And if part of the purpose of school history is to understand the present in the light of the past, don't pupils need to learn about how we lost an empire as well as how we built one? If they are to understand Britain's changing role in the world, shouldn't they learn about Suez and 'the wind of change', as well as Waterloo and the Great Exhibition? In a country which has had its moments of greatness and triumph, and its share of great men and women, shouldn't it be acceptable to be open about less glorious moments and personnel? Perhaps a democracy that is confident and at ease enough to examine its weaknesses and mistakes is more healthy and robust than one that censors or distorts the national past. It is also possible to problematise the criteria for national success. Is it about size, power, military success and size of empire, or prosperity, tolerance and social cohesion? Are twentieth-century Sweden, Switzerland and Luxembourg the really successful nations? Much of the recent debate about school history has focused on national identity and the question, 'What does it mean to be British at the start of the twenty first century?' (See, for instance, Phillips, 1996, 1998a; Tate, 1995a, 1995b.) School history does not, however, have to be framed exclusively or predominantly in national terms. Acton makes the point that the importance of national identity has perhaps been overstated, compared to other important elements of history, for instance the extent to which power in different societies is used for the general good (Acton, 2000). This is particularly important in considering issues of diversity, and the rights of minority and marginalised groups. One of the tests of a civilised society is the way that it treats those without power and status.

(b) The discourse of citizenship and diversity

It has been increasingly common practice in history classrooms to display history-specific vocabulary on classroom walls: a glossary of the words, terms and phrases that are part of the discourse of history. One object of this exercise should be the gradual development of pupils' grasp of vocabulary and concepts related to citizenship and diversity. As pupils progress through the school, they should become familiar with terms and phrases such as 'sovereignty', 'social mobility', 'Little Englander', 'hegemony', 'assimilation', 'xenophobia', 'interdependence', 'playing the race card', 'political correctness', 'authoritarian', 'liberal', 'whistle-blower', 'cultural pluralism', 'coexistence', 'separate development', 'meritocracy', 'moral panic', 'beyond the pale' and 'crusade'; they should be able to understand the difference between 'bias', 'prejudice' and 'indoctrination', and have a grasp of concepts such as 'outsider groups', 'the tyranny of the majority', 'the military-industrial complex' and 'economic imperialism'. If young people are, as the Crick Report suggests (QCA, 1998), to be participative contributors to a democratic society, they will need to possess the language of political discourse.

(c) Learning to handle information intelligently

Perhaps the biggest single contribution which school history can make in the area of citizenship and diversity (and political literacy in general) is to teach pupils not to accept information at face value, and to develop the skills to 'decode', analyse and assess the validity of the information they are presented with. The idea of the (politically) educated citizen as the best defence of civil and political liberties has a stronger tradition in the United States than in Great Britain (see, for example, Haydn, 1999). The idea that school history might serve as a protection against one's own government rather than as a support for it is comparatively new, and has elicited a hostile counter-reaction from some right-wing commentators (see, for instance, Naismith, 1988; Major, 1993). However, given the ability of modern technocratic governments (and multinational corporations) to control and 'spin' information, it is not unreasonable to suggest that citizens should be able to subject the statements of their rulers to the same 'tests' and critical scrutiny as any other sources. Can we always rely on governments to tell the truth, the whole truth and nothing but the truth about, for example, radioactive leakage from nuclear plants, or whether it is safe to eat beef? This suggests not that our governments are particularly or unusually wicked, but that one part of political literacy is the awareness that, given the nature of politics, full disclosure and transparency are sometimes difficult, even in liberal democratic societies. The recent debate over asylum seekers is a good example of how important it is for citizens to be aware of the complexities and motives of policies in this area. Teaching pupils to develop an understanding of how contextual factors can influence the ways in which information is presented is an important part of producing politically literate citizens.

(d) The importance of overviews and the making of connections

Gold (2000) makes the perhaps obvious point that 'If you teach citizenship, then you must teach children what it means to be a citizen.' The study of history is invaluable in this respect, because it makes pupils aware that what is entailed in being a citizen varies in both time and place. One of the criticisms which has been made about the National Curriculum for history is its tendency to atomise topics within a study unit, rather than consider themes of development across whole key stages. Being a citizen in medieval times was a very different matter from being a citizen in early modern Britain or in the Victorian era. There are various similarities and differences in being a citizen of Sparta, Athens, Rome, France at the time of the Revolution, nineteenth-century Prussia, Soviet Russia or Nazi Germany, not least in terms of the boundaries between the rights of individuals and duties to the state, and the 'order of loyalties' between family, religion, state, employer, co-workers, etc. Addressing these changes and differences explicitly, and making comparisons with the present-day tensions and dilemmas of citizenship, can help to broaden pupils' global conception of citizenship issues by developing their knowledge of the wide range and variety of views on what it can mean to be a citizen. Wrenn's suggestion (1999) of pursuing a 'big theme' over time, such as 'dissent and the formation of the concept of "rights"' is a good example of this approach. In Year 7, the enquiry question is 'Why did Muslims only tolerate Jews and Christians but not other faiths?' In Year 8, the enquiry questions on the same overarching theme are 'Why did European Christians *stop* burning each other?' and 'Why did the French revolutionaries *fail* to stick to the Rights of Man?' In Year 9, the theme is continued with the questions 'Why did the Americans who signed the US constitution *not* free black slaves?' and 'Has the UN Charter made any difference to human rights in the last fifty years?' Following through ideas such as what constitutes a 'deserving' or 'undeserving' citizen, or what constitutes 'the virtuous citizen' in different times and places, suggests other possible themes. Such approaches not only help to build in progression to pupils' learning, they can help to give coherence and understanding to pupils' views of the past, so that history does not appear as a bewildering series of dismembered and unconnected gobbets of information. It also helps us to put across the complexity of many of the issues surrounding citizenship and diversity.

(e) Linking the past with the present

Sometimes, a helpful starting point can be the present rather than the past. This can be particularly useful in persuading pupils of the relevance and importance of history. Almost every week it is possible to access some controversy, story or debate relevant to citizenship and diversity. Recent examples include the right of Muslim pupils to wear headscarves in school, the report that 'Racial mix leads to greater tolerance' in German schools (*Times Educational Supplement*, 20 October 2000), two schools' fight to prevent the deportation of pupils (*Guardian Education*, 21 November 2000), debate on the Act of Settlement (*Guardian*, 8 December 2000) and a plethora of articles with very differing views on the impact of asylum seekers, and suggestions for social policy in this area.

This is not to suggest that such articles should be presented as neat and unproblematic moral exemplars to pupils; rather, that they serve as a starting point for discussing the historical context of such issues, and examining the ways in which such study might provide insight into present-day concerns. Various politicians have recently claimed that Britain is a tolerant and outward-looking nation. Examination of the historical record shows that at various points in the past, Britain exhibited differing degrees of tolerance and 'outward-lookingness' to religious minorities and immigrants. Part of pupils' political education is that one example does not prove a case, and that issues and positions are not always as simple and unproblematic as they are presented to be. Exposure to articles or programmes about religious or ethnic conflict in other societies, in the Balkans or the Middle East for example, can also help to develop pupils' grasp of diversity issues. It can also be interesting to draw on what pupils already know about women in history or non-European figures from the past (how many could they list?).

Rather than searching for examples of 'significant' or important women in history, we can ask the question: how did the First World War (or the factory system, or whatever) affect the lives of women? Some sources help to make the point that developing an understanding of the effects of war entails more than just looking at the actions of generals, politicians and soldiers.

Conclusion

There is a danger that if approaches to citizenship and diversity are not considered thoughtfully, materials may be simplistic, 'politically correct' and stultifying. One publisher recently described its materials as 'a one-stop shop' for citizenship (*Times Educational Supplement*, 2000). What next? 'The little book of citizenship' as a quick, cheap fix which will provide the required 'social glue'? The attempt to reduce citizenship to a simple and easy-to-digest form, however well intentioned, will not equip young people to understand the difficult issues involved in citizenship and diversity. The role of school history should be to develop in young people an understanding that these issues are interesting, complex, multi-faceted and very relevant to the sort of lives that they will lead, and the sort of society they will live in.

Key questions

1   What counts as a good history question? Teachers wish to ensure that their questions and those used by the school students can be understood and are appropriately targeted on important educational goals. What do you think about the examples of questions that are given in this chapter? Could you develop a list of questions that would lead to good work in classrooms?

2   How should history teachers approach issues of citizenship and diversity so as to avoid allegations of political bias? Unless a teacher manages to get this issue right serious problems may emerge.

3   What can a teacher do to help students understand the present in the context of the past? How could a teacher avoid the accusation that using the lens of the present to study the past may lead to a distortion of 'real' history?

Recommended resources

Books

H. Bourdillon (ed.) (1994) *Teaching History*, London, Routledge.
Succinct and well-written chapters on 'Black perspectives', 'Gender' and 'Four nations or one?'

A. Cardinal, D. Goldman and J. Hattaway (2000) *Women's Writing on the First World War*, Oxford, Oxford University Press.

H. Clare (1996) *Reclaiming our Pasts: equality and diversity in the primary history curriculum*, London, Trentham.
Practical suggestions for primary teachers.

Council of Europe (1999) *Towards a Pluralist and Tolerant Approach to Teaching History: a range of sources and new didactics*, Strasbourg, Council of Europe.
With an introductory keynote address by Marc Ferro, this book provides interesting insights into how different societies are approaching this challenge.

R. Darnton (1984) *The Great Cat Massacre and Other Episodes in French Cultural History*, New York, Norton.
Provides interesting insights into why human beings sometimes do nasty things.

J. Glover (2001) *Humanity: a moral history of the twentieth century*, London, Pimlico.
Some chapters provide very powerful and interesting introductions to moral and ethical issues. The chapter on My Lai in particular is revealing in terms of the argument that people were simply 'obeying orders' or conforming to social norms.

R. Hoss, P. Broad and J. Kremer (1995) *KL Auschwitz seen by the SS*, Oswiecim, Auschwitz-Birkenau State Museum.
Recommended by the guides at Auschwitz State Museum, and based on the idea that if we want to understand the Holocaust, we need to gain insight into the minds of the perpetrators as well as the victims.

A. Porter (1983) *Teaching Political Literacy*, London, Bedford Way.
The appendix to this book gives a very helpful analysis of five different models of citizenship education. Helpful to see whether your conceptions of what citizenship education might be are unthinkingly narrow.

D. Smart (2001) *Citizenship in History: a guide for teachers*, Cheltenham, Nelsonthornes.
One of the earliest of what will presumably be a deluge of school texts in this field, which gives an indication of likely approaches. It includes sections on 'Who are the British?', 'The empire and beyond', 'Civil rights', 'Towards democracy', 'How does the economy shape our lives?', 'How do living conditions shape our lives?' and 'Conflict, war and aggression'.

O. Thomson (1999) *Easily Led: a history of propaganda*, Stroud, Sutton.
The first section powerfully makes a point about the breadth of ways in which information can be used and distorted.

Newspaper articles

Internet archiving of newspapers has made them a valuable resource for history teachers, although some newspapers keep more accessible and comprehensive recent archives than others. A meta-site for searching for newspaper articles is http://www.thepaperboy.com

M. Bright (2000) 'Revealed: why evil lurks in us all', *Observer*, 17 December.
A review of the BBC documentary, 'Five steps to tyranny' (BBC2, 19 December 2000), which profiled research evidence from a range of psychological experiments documenting the compliance of ordinary citizens in aggression against others. The documentary itself provides very powerful footage of the experiments.

L. Colley (1999) 'Blueprint for Britain', *Observer*, 12 December.
Puts forward the distinction between identity and citizenship as a first step in 'convincing all of the inhabitants of these islands that they are equal and valued citizens, irrespective of whatever identity they may select to prioritise'.

A. Grayling (2000) 'The last word on nationalism', *Guardian*, 26 February, and 'The last word on racism', *Guardian*, 4 March.
Short polemics, including interesting quotes from Hitler. (See Quotations section below.)

W. Hutton (2001) 'We have blood on our hands too', *Observer*, 21 January.
One of several articles commenting on the introduction of a Holocaust Memorial Day in Great Britain, it argues that British schoolchildren should be told that 'the English once mass-murdered Jews and made them wear the Star of David', and that the Holocaust should be put in the context of other genocides.

D. Margolick (2001) 'Civil rights, civil wrongs', *Guardian*, 16 February.
Gives the interesting history of the civil rights protest song, 'Strange fruit'.

Journal articles

A. Dixon (2000) 'Fire blankets or depth charges: choices in education for citizenship', *Forum*, Vol. 42, No. 3, 94–9.
Examines different approaches to citizenship education, drawing on research findings from initiatives in Europe and the United States.

N. Evans (2001) 'Red summers', *History Today*, Vol. 51, No. 2, 28–33.
Examines the outbreak of racial tension in Britain, France and the United States after the end of the First World War.

P. Gray and K. Oliver (2001) 'The memory of catastrophe', *History Today*, Vol. 51, No. 2, 9–15.
Reviews debates surrounding the commemoration of historical disasters.

Teaching History (1999) 'Citizenship', No. 96.
Issue devoted exclusively to citizenship education in history, ranging from teaching approaches to pupil preconceptions.

Film

As well as films such as *Schindler's List* and *Amistad*, there are potentially useful extracts about democracy and citizenship in *Danton* (especially the opening and closing scenes), *The Remains of the Day* and *The Crucible*.

The Internet

Typing in Citizenship and History will bring up a wide (and possibly unmanageable) range of possible resources; these three addresses are an idiosyncratic selection:

http://www.remember.org
Cybrary of the Holocaust; a massive and eclectic resource on Holocaust materials.

http://www.self-gov.org/quiz.html
'The world's smallest political quiz', a very quick but interesting exercise to find out 'your true political identity'; it can help pupils to develop an understanding of terms such as 'libertarian', 'liberal' and 'authoritarian'.

http://www.facinghistory.org
Site whose aim is to promote civic education, and provide resources to help young people to investigate moral and ethical issues in history and education.

Quotations

Several quotations I have come across which address various aspects of history, citizenship education and diversity can be accessed at http://www.uea.ac.uk/~m242/historypgce/cit

Chapter 8

Teaching and learning European citizenship in history lessons

Introduction

European citizenship is now a reality in that there are political institutions such as the European Parliament, Commission and Court of Justice, and in that individual citizens have legal rights and duties associated with those institutions. There is also the strong possibility that European citizenship exists in other less tangible (and, possibly, wider) forms relating to a sense of what it means to be European. There are opportunities for history teaching to contribute to a number of different aspects of European citizenship. This would not, of course, necessarily mean an uncritical promotion of the supposed virtues of the European Union but perhaps allow for a critical and constructive exploration of the means by which European citizenship came into being and what it might mean in the future.

The general purposes of the teaching and learning of history as outlined in Chapter 2 show that various targets are used. Normally, those targets include three areas: the acquisition of knowledge and understanding of the past by the pupils as they become educated people; the development of a historical perspective and understanding; and the acquisition of historical knowledge and skills as a means to other ends which could include socialisation, preparation for citizenship and international understanding. In the light of these targets, it seems obvious that teaching and learning history are directly relevant to European citizenship, and also that the connections that are and could be made between history and European citizenship should be examined. In other words, as well as showing in this chapter that there are potential links between history education and European citizenship, it will be necessary to discuss the particular form and purposes of each area and to show the different possible interactions between them. Both history and citizenship education have many dimensions, and without an explicit justification for how and why they could relate, teachers and others would be left clutching only a sense of undifferentiated altruism.

This chapter begins with some brief comments on the nature of three important contexts: Europe; European citizenship; and citizenship education within Europe. The next main section of the chapter deals with the nature of history education in Europe. There is a detailed exploration of the possible overarching approaches to history education that may allow for a fruitful interaction with the nature and purposes of citizenship education. It is argued that there are a number of possible approaches but only if the nature of history, history education, citizenship and citizenship education are perceived positively and democratically is there likely to be an opportunity of doing more than providing an academic introduction to conceptual matters. The final section searches for issues associated with the way in which a valuable form of history education could be introduced. This is followed by an outline of what sort of European history is taught in schools and what could be taught. Finally, a brief account is given of one project that took place recently in England.

Europe

What sort of Europe exists for history teachers? Europe may, for some, extend from the Atlantic to the Urals. It may include those who associate themselves with the Judaeo-Christian tradition, or, to phrase that slightly differently, refer to an individual who in James Baldwin's words is 'able to enter Chartres Cathedral and feel it has something to do with him' (quoted in Slater 1995, p. 5). A history of Europe may include issues arising from, for example, the Reformation and the Renaissance. A history of Europe may also involve seeing trends and events from a particular perspective: the First World War as a European war, and the so-called 'voyages of discovery' as being the responsibility of European explorers. An economic Europe may be associated with the development of a Common Market and in a wider sense the trade links between regions and nations within and beyond Europe. A political Europe is commonly associated with the development of the institutions of the European Union but could also be seen in a way that would allow themes of power and authority to be explored in 'low' rather than 'high' political contexts. Ultimately, however, there seems no reason to regard the above characterisations as being exhaustive, or for perceiving them as separate entities. There will be many who do not fit easily into any of the categories mentioned above. Any individual from any of the countries normally regarded as being within Europe could take exception to some of the points mentioned above. To give concrete examples of these difficulties would be straightforward. Someone from Turkey, Switzerland or Northern Ireland (or, indeed, anywhere else) might well reject some aspects of the above but embrace others.

Together with debates on the nature and significance of these characterisations, there are significant differences within each area. To take the European Union as an example, two quotations can be used to illustrate something of the range of opinions. Firstly, McCormick (1996, p. 300) believes that the European 'train' cannot now be stopped. Others dispute such certainty. Thatcher's (1993, p. 728) ringing words on the nature of the European Union come through clearly in her autobiography: 'If there was ever an idea whose time had come and gone it was that of the artificial mega-state.'

It is likely that these opposing perspectives are not wholly reliable. Just as the separate characterisations above are probably inadequate for a portrayal of any individual European, a little more subtlety is needed when judging the intended nature and purpose of one aspect of Europe. In the case of the European Union, for example, it is unlikely that there are stark choices between 'widening' and 'deepening'. It is perfectly possible for both to happen at the same time. Similarly, the debate over flexibility may well be an unhelpful way to understand the issues at stake, as a stark choice is usually presented between, on the one hand, a multi-speed Europe with all countries having the same destination but arriving at it at different times, and, on the other, a variable Europe in which different countries may choose different destinations (Brittan 1996).

European citizenship

There is, of course, some degree of overlap between notions of Europe, as described above, and European citizenship. However, there are also differences both between citizens and non-citizens and also within each of those groups (Bryant 1997). Within different European countries there is a wide variation between the 'constitution of citizenries' (Bryant 1997, p. 157). The Council of Europe recently placed on the Internet a questionnaire about citizenship presenting fourteen options (for each of which respondents could express their level of agreement on a five-point scale). The picture is further complicated if we consider a citizen's capacity to act (Turner 1993). Legal status is not enough.

To some extent the difficulties of characterising citizenship referred to above arise from a failure to distinguish between the different possible forms of citizenship. A brief account will be given of the three main ways of portraying citizenship: legal and political; civic virtue; and identity. It will be argued that these different characterisations and features of citizenship are useful in a number of ways. While it would be wrong to suggest that the following discussion will show simply what should be taught, it is nevertheless possible for history teachers to consider these areas as a sort of guide for their selection of content and methods.

The legal and political dimensions

I would not wish to suggest that history teachers should force students to memorise inert constitutional information. However, the issues that arise from the legal rights and duties of European citizens and how they came about can be developed into useful classroom material.

Article 17 (1) of the Maastricht Treaty establishes Union citizenship for nationals of member states. This form of citizenship complements but does not replace national citizenship. Articles 18 to 21 then give a list of the rights of a European citizen. A European citizen has the right to vote and stand as a candidate in municipal and parliamentary elections in his or her state of residence regardless of nationality. Member states are committed to the principles of democracy and subsidiarity, and the latter may mean that civic rights can be exercised at local, regional, state and Union levels. There is the right of free movement and there are social rights arising from the Social Chapter of the Maastricht Treaty as well as from earlier Community provisions. The rights of civil citizenship exist in the context of the operation of the European Court of Justice and the Court of Human Rights. These provisions are important but it should be noted that (as with all legal frameworks) there is room for interpretation of the meaning of the various clauses, and, more important, that legal force exists only in the context of rights for members of national states as opposed to the creation of a new nationality. The great strength of European citizenship may be that it exists in legal and political form. There is a tangibility about it which is reassuring and can be contrasted with the more elusive expressions of citizenship described in relation to civic virtue and identity. It also has the great advantage for teachers that something can be taught. However, some commentators (e.g. Evans 1999, p. 17) have drawn attention to the weaknesses of European citizenship, arguing that:

> In effect the Treaty apparently means no more than that a national of one Member State can enjoy limited citizenship rights in another Member State. Respect for the 'bond of nationality' apparently survives the establishment of Union Citizenship. As a result, the potential of Union Citizenship for tackling social problems is not being realised.

It would be rather straightforward for a history teacher to draw attention to cases that have come before the European courts. The historical background of a case could be examined. Considerations of how different judgements would have been reached at different times could be explored. The class could become fully involved in such matters. Some cases are potentially sensitive but, with careful treatment, very educational. For example, Britain's record in treating prisoners in Northern Ireland provides interesting data for any classes studying that topic.

Civic virtue

Another key aspect of citizenship is the extent to which a person or group can engage with issues relevant to that citizenship. In other words, it is important to analyse the extent to which people can become involved. It should be noted that, in terms of civic virtue, it is very difficult to be a 'good European'. There are few Europe-wide institutions in which people can participate or spend their time and money. Data from Eurobarometer 45 (autumn 1996) (http://europa.eu.int/comm/DGIO/EPO/) show that on average about 80 per cent of citizens across the Union have little confidence that they can influence the political process. There are many possible conflicts of interest across and within the various levels and forms of citizenship. Kymlicka (1995) and Torres (1998) raise difficult issues about the nature of citizenship in multicultural societies and some of those dilemmas are clearly in evidence within Europe of potential conflicts between patriotism and multiple citizenship. Again, classroom material readily flows from these matters. It would be interesting, for example, to explore the franchise in terms of excluded groups. Two contrasting case studies of the suffragettes in England and the very low voting figures for European elections could provide very useful material for those teachers who really want to help pupils develop new perspectives on contemporary society.

Identity

The identity of Europeans is the final area that should be mentioned within this discussion of the meaning of European citizenship. A number of recent surveys point to positive perspectives about European integration. Eurobarometer 50 (1999) (same website as above) shows that more than half of Europeans (55 per cent) feel that a great deal or a fair amount has been achieved during the past fifty years in terms of European integration; many Europeans (52 per cent) believe that the European Union will play a more important role in their daily lives at the beginning of the twenty-first century and 75 per cent believe that it should play a more important role or the same role in their daily lives. Support for the European Union as revealed in this 1999 survey shows a third consecutive increase. More than half of the EU population regard their country's membership as a good thing and around half of the population feel that their country has benefited from EU membership; 64 per cent of EU citizens were in favour of the Euro and only 25 per cent opposed it.

A European survey published by the *Guardian* newspaper in the United Kingdom on 1 June 1999 (Travis 1999, p. 1) showed that: 'European voters want to see a common European army, a directly elected European president and admission [to the EU] for eastern European countries.'

Eurobarometer also recently produced (Ahrendt 1998) a survey of young people's attitudes to the European Union and this too was very positive. This must be regarded as particularly important for the sort of work that can be done by teachers. Among young people (aged 15 to 30), 38 per cent are classified as Sympathisers – dedicated supporters who want a powerful Union. The next group are classified as the Positive Pragmatists (33 per cent), who have decided that the EU represents a positive development but they are less inclined to give it as much decision-making power as the Sympathisers. The Sceptics (28 per cent) hold largely negative feelings about the EU. But the authors of the report containing these data take an almost dismissive approach to this final group, members of which are classified as the most pessimistic as regards their own country and their own personal life. They are the least well-educated people in the survey, are the most likely to be in manual occupations and are the least likely to use the news media. They are to be found mainly in Sweden, Finland, Austria, the UK, Denmark and Germany.

It is important to view these findings carefully. The variations between as well as within the European states are significant. There is conflicting evidence about the nature and extent of convergence occurring in Europe (Sobisch and Immerfall 1997; Micklewright and Stewart 1999). Although there is some indication of the types of people who are likely to express certain views there is no real sense of what sort of Europe people are referring to when they respond to a questionnaire asking about Europe. While various outcomes are suggested in the questionnaire results, there is no clear, overarching sense of the Europe which is preferred. Further, there is no indication of the sorts of values that people are using when they express a desire for one option over another. There may or may not be a European heritage and it is very difficult to identify commonly held European values or beliefs. Indeed, it is important to remember that there are some very worrying data which show that 33 per cent of those interviewed openly described themselves as 'quite racist' or 'very racist' (European Commission 1997a). Voting intentions generally prove very different from actual voting figures. The surveys referred to above showed that more than seven in ten EU citizens intended to vote in the June 1999 European Parliament elections. The actual figures were rather different. It is true that Belgium registered a 90 per cent turnout but voting is compulsory in that country. In the UK the figure was only 25 per cent, with a rough average across Europe of 48 per cent. Therefore, although there are some grounds for seeing Europeans as having at least the intention to co-operate, there are many difficult issues. We need to be careful about the precise nature of the educational goals and processes that are stated and what is realised. Some of the statistics mentioned above show that there is perhaps a trend towards a greater commitment to being European.

This will have to be monitored closely, however, to ensure that the trend is not actually towards greater confidence or optimism among respondents about their own individual nation's ability to do well within Europe. The symbols of Europe are being used more obviously. In the words of an EU publication, the blue flag with gold stars is 'the emblem of European unification, a rallying point for all citizens of the European Community' and 'the Ode to Joy from Beethoven's Ninth Symphony is regarded as the anthem of European unification' (Fontaine 1991, pp. 7, 8). Arguments about replacing pictures of British scientists, novelists and railway pioneers as well as the Queen with a European symbol are regularly conducted in a rather deadening fashion in the British press. It is unsure what the relationship is between the development of these symbols and anything more substantial. Even some of the symbols themselves, especially those used within official EU documentation, are somewhat less than inspiring.

The material on European identity provides many opportunities for classroom work. The history of various European countries could be used to explore their contemporary perspectives. There are clear historical reasons why Germany, for example, is usually seen as being more European than Britain. A history of some of the attempts at European integration (Charlemagne, Napoleon and others were Europeans of sorts) could provide an interesting development study. A comparison of Britain's transition from losing an empire and, possibly, not finding Europe could be interesting. Alternatively, a study of regionalism could be of interest, with particular attention paid to places within Europe where complex allegiances exist. Is, for example, Scotland more European than British? Is the Basque country more Spanish than an independent state? This could develop into a study of conflicting loyalties, with examples drawn from the lives of individual conscientious objectors who had families on the 'wrong' side or of our reactions to refugees during the Second World War and beyond. The flags and anthems of the European Union (mentioned above) could be incorporated into other studies on the use of symbols and compared with acceptable and unacceptable uses of propaganda.

Citizenship education in Europe

International comparisons of citizenship education are becoming increasingly available although it is not easy to make simple generalisations (e.g. Torney-Purta et al. 1999; Ichilov 1998; Hahn 1998; Cogan and Derricott 1998).

In a comparison of the various initiatives across Europe, different types of indicator can be used: input indicators (the resources that go into education); process indicators (enrolment, drop-out and retention rates); and output indicators (what people actually learn). Micklewright and Stewart (1999, p. 45) argue that there is some evidence of convergence between the first two types of indicator but that information for the third, and most important, area is 'next to impossible to put together'. Citizenship education, however, has not lacked for another kind of indicator: the provision of ambitious aims. The rhetoric associated with education for European citizenship is extremely strong. An analysis of documentation produced by various EU agencies has led Dekker and Portengen (1996, pp. 178–9) to argue that knowledge of Europe, as well as a willingness to participate and to see oneself as a European, are seen as desirable.

The most obvious starting point for an examination of the extent to which the aims of European citizenship may be realised is a brief summary of the actions undertaken by the EU. Educational initiatives were not an early priority (the Treaty of Rome does not mention education as such) and the first truly significant act was a resolution of 1988 which encouraged member states to strengthen the European dimension in education. Article 126 of the Maastricht Treaty is more explicit about the need to act. More recently, although there is still a firm commitment not to establish a Europe-wide education policy and there has always been a specific commitment to linguistic diversity, the pace has quickened to some extent. The 1996 European Year of Lifelong Learning, a number of recent reports (European Commission 1997b, 1997c, 1998) and the 1997 Treaty of Amsterdam make it clear that a more active and participatory citizenship is to be encouraged; education is often seen as one of the key catalysts. There are a large number of initiatives and many people are part of networking, research and special interest projects involving co-operation within and beyond the EU and supported by the Commission. Four action programmes (of which Socrates is the most relevant to history teachers) are normally given particular prominence in EU documentation:

- Socrates, which seeks to promote the European dimension in higher education (Erasmus), school contexts (Comenius) or in a number of horizontal measures focusing for example on language learning; exchanges of staff and students around particular themes are often undertaken
- Youth for Europe III, which addresses young people in non-formal contexts
- the European Voluntary Service
- the Leonardo da Vinci programme, which focuses on vocational education

A recent study of the above four action programmes undertaken by DG XXII (European Commission 1998) has drawn attention to the following:

- the most significant contribution made by the programmes is their promotion of transnational and intercultural co-operation and exchange (p. 19)
- the action programmes may need to rebalance the profiles of projects they fund in the coming years (p. 20). This comment is made in the context of a finding that the groups best served by the action programmes are those young people and adults who

could be described as being in mainstream or high-status contexts. Further, there is an awareness that 'the action programmes' commitment to furthering equal opportunities between the sexes does not yet seem to be sufficiently reflected in the range of projects relevant to the theme of learning for active citizenship' (p. 23)

- perhaps most important, the study found that 'in practice, it could not be said that the majority of the projects they looked at had a primary, explicit and concrete orientation towards learning for active citizenship' (p. 24). In fact, 'all the researchers underlined that few of those with whom they spoke – including project promoters and co-ordinators – were able to articulate clearly just what active citizenship with a European dimension meant for them' (p. 24).

In the light of these findings, greater attention should be paid to ways in which citizenship education can be promoted. There may be very fundamental difficulties as support for the relatively small (in EU terms) budget for the ERASMUS programme is periodically in doubt (e.g. Rafferty 1999). There may be a need to respond in a number of ways: simplification of the administrative process necessary to secure funding; greater attention to the training of trainers; clearer identification of procedures for measuring the value added by a project to particular target groups; and, above all, a way of encouraging a more explicit focus on citizenship education. Students and trainers (or, in the jargon of the EU 'mediators and multipliers') taking advantage of the travel opportunities and qualifications offered in the emerging civil society of education appear to be the main beneficiaries of EU programmes while areas such as citizenship education for the majority or aid to the marginalised remain neglected.

Some evidence about education for European citizenship from member states

It is far less easy to establish an overarching account of the actions for European citizenship taken by individual member states. The official responses from government departments (following requests to all member states and members of the European Economic Area) do not always complement the accounts given by participants from those member states in Council of Europe reports (Di Gennaro 1998); nor do they show clearly what they mean by citizenship education even in terms of the phase in which relevant work may be taking place. There is some evidence to suggest little is taking place. The covering letters sent with the documentation from countries were interesting. Some countries (e.g. Finland) refer to the European dimension as being 'part and parcel of subjects like History, Social Studies, geography and languages' but an examination of the documents sent with the letter do not reveal any significant input on education for European citizenship. Some states almost seem to exclude education for European citizenship. The Portuguese comprehensive law on the education system passed in 1986 and the 1989 curricular organisation law make it clear that 'the education system is organised so as to contribute to preserving the national identity and strengthening loyalty to the historical background of Portugal', and that the emphasis placed on PSE where European citizenship might be taught is not great. For some states (e.g. Eire), there is obvious enthusiasm for civil, social and political education with the generation of many documents for teachers and pupils. But even Eire, where documentation for teachers and pupils that relates directly and explicitly to European citizenship is among the largest in Europe, has produced only four booklets on the subject, of which the longest is twelve pages. This coverage is obviously not great and, as some of the pages are devoted to basic geographical information, there are in reality few opportunities to probe issues deeply.

This avoidance of the European dimension in terms of the legal rights, identities and civic practices of European citizens may be positive. Of course, it avoids the development of a new form of exclusive nationalism (one that is simply geographically bigger than that of existing states) and this must be welcomed. In a global age the avoidance of the European dimension does not necessarily mean an exclusive focus on the nation-state. But it is somewhat disconcerting to see so little attention being paid to European citizenship by the EU or by individual member states whose peoples enjoy legal and political citizenship of the European Union.

European history and citizenship education; or, European citizenship education through history?

There are potential tensions between teaching European history and promoting European citizenship education through history. Do we want pupils to know more about the European past, or are we concerned to promote understanding and action as an expression of citizenship? The tensions within these different aims can be seen in the work of a number of authors. Convery *et al.* (1997) show five approaches to what they refer to as the European dimension in education. Teaching European history is seen as the lowest level. Merely teaching about the European past is not the same as promoting education for European citizenship.

Audigier (1998), in work for the Council of Europe, used the words *Education for Democratic Citizenship* in his title. This seems to foreground citizenship more strongly than would the word 'dimension', but Audigier's approach seems almost to ignore Europe. He suggests that there are competences which can be represented in three broad categories:

1   Cognitive competences would include four subgroups: competences of a legal and political nature (e.g. knowledge concerning the rules of collective life); knowledge of the present world; competences of a procedural nature (e.g. the ability to speak, argue and reflect); knowledge of the principles and values of human rights and democratic citizenship (e.g. a conception of the freedom and equal dignity of each individual).

2   Affective competences centre on freedom, equality and solidarity. The emphasis on this area recognises that 'Citizenship cannot be reduced to a catalogue of rights and duties, it is also belonging to a group or groups. It thus requires a personal and affective dimension' (Audigier 1998, p. 10).

3   Social competences (also referred to as capacities for action) include three subgroups: the capacity to live and co-operate with others, the capacity to resolve conflicts in accordance with the principles of democratic law; and the capacity to take part in public debate, to argue and choose in a real-life situation.

Osler and Starkey (1999) provide a useful way of asking questions about a project which aims to promote education for European citizenship. It is shown in Figure 8.1.

INFORMATION	**IDENTITIES**
• Is there a focus on specific information about democracy, human rights or European values?	• Does it explore/affirm various identities, including European identity? • Does it promote intercultural development?
INCLUSION	**SKILLS**
• Does it prepare participants for social/economic inclusion? • Does it have an equal opportunities focus, or one which addresses the specific needs of women/girls in addressing their citizenship rights? • Does the project have active methods/encourage participation?	• Does it develop skills for democratic participation, including skills of working through transnational links?

Figure 8.1 Questions about European citizenship education

Source: Osler and Starkey (1999).

This model seems to combine the European perspective used by Convery with the stronger focus on citizenship used by Audigier. But although Convery *et al.* see history education as the lowest level of awareness, Audigier, like Osler and Starkey, using a more tightly focused and more explicit attachment to citizenship, make no real mention of history at all.

Generally, then, there is a need to make clear just what sort of contribution, or what sort of justifications are given for including history in a programme which may be designed to promote some sense of 'European-ness'. Stradling (1995, p. 8) suggests the following:

- a greater sense of European identity and understanding of a common cultural heritage
- more tolerance for diversity between peoples of different cultural and ethnic backgrounds
- an appreciation of the growing political and economic interdependence among European nations
- an understanding of the historical origins of current developments towards greater political and economic co-operation and understanding

Various examples of practical projects can be found in a number of publications (e.g. Davies and Sobisch 1997). Osler and Starkey (1999) provide examples (which can be seen in more detail in European Commission (1998) and at http://europa.eu.int/en/comm/dg22/citizen) of some recent projects. Council of Europe documentation (e.g. Ahrendt 1998) shows the types of history projects discussed when teachers come together in teacher training conferences of that organsiation. Four different approaches are given:

- projects concerned with individuals or families whose lives or life's work is of significance to several of the participating countries (e.g. the tracing of a common past)
- projects concerned with minorities (e.g. an investigation into the minorities within the Gyor-Moson-Sopron region or in Neusiediam See)
- projects which explore everyday living conditions in the individual countries in a particular historical period (e.g. everyday life from 1945 to 1950)
- projects concerned with national symbols, that is the various social factors which shape national identities (e.g. comparisons of history textbooks)

When reviewing these various initiatives it is usually possible to discern two distinct approaches to Europe. Stradling (1995, pp. 17–20) clearly outlines these approaches. He argues that the first approach characterises Europe in terms of its common heritage. Teaching associated with this approach gives pupils an overview of European history (including a sense of its chronology) as well as a means of relating what was happening in their own country to broader European issues. There are a number of disadvantages to this framework which need to be considered carefully by those who wish to promote or explore a sense of European citizenship. Pupils may come to think that there is a linear development of European history which seems to unfold continuously. This method risks distracting attention from external forces and overemphasising cultural and political history and the history of ideas. Some have preferred a different overarching framework that stresses the diversity of Europe. This style tends to rely on the 'compare and contrast' model that might have the benefit of drawing pupils' attention to the power of dynamism and difference within a whole. However, this approach makes the selection of content very difficult. It would be possible to develop inappropriately complex lessons that lead to a fragmentary approach in which content has been selected not necessarily for its own significance but rather for its power to illustrate a contrast with another event. Those who seek to develop a history education aligned to European citizenship would have to take care to ensure that the whole was not destroyed by the comparative parts of such an approach.

The European history and citizenship project

A brief description of this project is given as an example of the attempts teachers are making to develop citizenship education through history teaching. It has been reported on in more detail elsewhere (Davies 1994b, 1995a, 1995b). The project was successful and a credit to the hard work and professionalism of the teachers who were principally involved, but it is not suggested that all difficult issues were entirely resolved. The description is given here not as an illustration of perfect work, but rather as an example of one approach that may be of interest to others.

The aim of the project was to develop a short scheme of work in history that would develop pupils' understandings of European citizenship and also allow for some academic and professional reflection upon the nature of this area. An initial characterisation of education for European citizenship was given in terms of the importance of the practices of civil, social and political rights and responsibilities of individuals, groups and nations within the EU, and within other conceptions of Europe. The project would attempt to promote this form of education by raising controversial questions in a variety of contexts and by illuminating relevant concepts as well as established and alternative societal frameworks. The project members sought to operate within a context in which pupils were seen to hold multiple citizenships and in which people could develop critical understanding and potential for action for Europe. The project team hoped that pupils would:

- develop enquiring, analytical minds and so become more capable of making reasoned judgements
- go beyond thinking about Europe, and begin to explore the potential for action
- develop a futures perspective which builds on a practical and theoretical study of recent and contemporary Europe
- explore the nature of tolerance, prejudice and discrimination in Europe in order to strengthen constructive toleration

The project team wanted to know more about the essential elements of education for European citizenship that might be taught in secondary schools and the extent to which the project materials supported education for European citizenship. The project had three distinct phases. Firstly, a series of interviews with experts and with history teachers involved in the project were undertaken to gain a clearer understanding of the nature of the key concepts and to gather suggestions about the best way to shape the curriculum materials and to develop teaching styles for the project. Secondly, the results of the initial data collection were presented to the project team for use as guidance in the writing of the teaching materials. Finally, the materials were tested in schools, and the project team held meetings to develop results. The materials provided a broad overview of the main social and political developments in European history during the last fifty years. They aimed to allow pupils to develop a deeper understanding of the economic, social and cultural forces which shaped the lives of people on both sides of the Iron Curtain during that period. The learning activities were structured around four key questions:

- How has Europe changed since 1945?
- Why has Europe changed?
- What was life like on different sides of the Iron Curtain?
- Should the European Union be enlarged to include the countries of eastern Europe?

The emphasis was on small-group discussion and problem solving though there were also opportunities for individual written work. In the activity related to the first of the four questions given above, pupils were asked to sequence a series of pictures and texts in the form of a timeline presenting some important events in European history since 1945 (e.g. the building and collapse of the Berlin Wall; the Prague Spring of 1968; the signing of the Maastricht Treaty). The purpose of the activities relating to the second of the four questions was to develop an understanding of some of the underlying causes of the events shown on the timeline. A video was used to allow pupils to see something of the events that they had sequenced. Three questions were used in connection with the video: Why was Europe divided after the Second World War? Why have some of the western European countries moved closer together since the war? How have some of the countries of eastern Europe reacted against communism? In the third activity pupils were asked to consider the advantages and disadvantages of life on either side of the Iron Curtain. Classes were split into small groups with half working on the west, and half working on the east. Pupils were provided with source sheets which covered four aspects of life: industry and work; standard of living; welfare; and freedom and protest. A range of material was included covering different countries during the period from the early 1950s to the early 1980s. In the freedom and protest sources, however, a more specific emphasis was placed on Britain and Czechoslovakia in the 1960s. In the final activity pupils were asked to use their historical knowledge to develop a point of view on a contemporary European issue. In preparing their reports pupils were encouraged to go beyond the information provided and use their wider historical knowledge of political, social, economic and cultural change in Europe since 1945. They also had to consider whether integration would be easier for some European countries than others.

The project was successfully developed by teachers and many pupils revealed complex understandings of some of the issues associated with European citizenship. The EU was the principal but not exclusive focus for the work, and the fourth activity explicitly allowed for a futures perspective. The pupils also said that they had found the activities enjoyable and there was a surprisingly positive approach towards being European. There may also have been benefits in terms of professional development for members of the project team as constructive discussions took place and tangible results were achieved with the development of teaching materials and the writing of reports and articles. The basic framework of this project could be used for further projects on European history or other types of work. We found that if teachers have an opportunity to engage in this simple three-stage structure (discussion, resource production, evaluation) the benefits are very significant for both students and staff. It is a format by which all partners gain and can see the immediate benefits of their efforts. The opportunity to discuss with colleagues from different institutions (schools and a university department of education or local education authority) is welcomed; the production of classroom resources means that the project is focused on 'real' work; and the testing process means that the whole exercise is taken seriously and professionally. In addition to the classroom materials and an enhanced sense of professional collaboration, this sort of work usually carries another advantage. With careful planning from the outset there is a wealth of data that can be analysed for the purposes of identifying the nature of the next project.

Some of the more critical issues about this project have been explored in a general way in Chapter 2. It remained an open question at the end of the project whether citizenship education had been sufficiently explored or whether European history and perhaps

European awareness had been the principal objects of the work. Members of the project team were at times positive about the overlap between the project materials and those materials normally available in schools. This seemed to suggest that history education and citizenship education are fundamentally very closely related. An exacting debate was held on the extent to which history and citizenship education differ and how these can be explicitly stated in a way that pupils can understand and rigorously explore. At the end of the project it was felt that there could be satisfaction with the very many good results achieved by teachers and, generally, that there were grounds for optimism in that teaching resources have become rather less xenophobic. Further, there is some evidence that a more investigative and critical approach to history education is being developed in at least some parts of Europe. However, all these positive points should not disguise the lack of knowledge that we still have about the power of history to contribute to the development of European citizens. This lack of knowledge and the limited positive work that has been done (conceptually and pedagogically) provides, at the very least, a strong case for continuing to investigate what history teachers can do to develop European citizenship education.

Conclusion

European citizenship has a number of potential disadvantages. It can be a 'rich man's club'. It can speak less about citizenship and more about economic exclusivity and education that 'merely' focuses on exchanges. But it is a reality. To emphasise the commonsense need to understand this, one only has to consider just how unacceptable and dangerous any proposal would be for European citizens not to know something about their own democracy. We need to understand more about Europe because so many people are part of it. Further, we need to understand of what European citizenship means in narrower (local, regional and national) and wider (international) contexts.

The meaning of citizenship in transnational settings can quickly become lost in vague hopes for some sort of better world through co-operative endeavour. But we should never underestimate the value of understanding, and contributing to, international co-operation. When dialogue can take place within a legal and political framework particular opportunities arise for the teacher of history. History lessons can do much to help students understand the development of Europe. The knowledge, skills and dispositions teachers and students acquire and develop can be most useful in the exploration and possible further elaboration of what it means to be a European citizen in a democratically organised international society.

Key questions

1   What comes to mind when you hear the word 'Europe'? Do you immediately think about the European Union or a wider Europe? Do you emphasise the political, economic, social, cultural or something else? What do these initial

reactions imply for the way European history and citizenship should be taught in schools?

2 What opportunities are offered for history teachers and students in the various European Union programmes? Are colleagues in your local area taking advantage of the programmes described in this chapter? If so, what are their experiences? Alternatively, review some of the projects that are described at the websites given in this chapter.

3 What are the differences between teaching European history and promoting education for European citizenship through history? Which would you prefer and why?

Recommended reading

N. Davies (1996) *Europe: a history*. Oxford, Oxford University Press.
A comprehensive and interesting account of European history that puts more emphasis on the east than that provided by other historians. The author is known for his argument that national history is best understood in a European context. A fascinating book to dip into for both anecdotes and statistical information.

A. Osler, H.-F. Rathenow and H. Starkey (eds) (1996) *Teaching for Citizenship in the New Europe*. Stoke on Trent, Trentham.
Most of the chapters in this edited book describe classroom based projects.

R. Watts (2000) 'History in Europe: the benefits and challenges of co-operation', in J. Arthur and R. Phillips (eds) *Issues in History Teaching*. London, Routledge.
A good account of the state of the art of history teaching in Europe with some very useful practical ideas and references that can be followed up.

Chapter 9

The history teacher and global citizenship

Introduction

The concept of global citizenship is attracting increasing attention. Many argue that our perspectives on globalisation determine the way we already respond to key issues. This chapter will explore whether globalisation is actually significant (as opposed merely to attracting increased attention from academics); it will attempt a characterisation of the nature of globalisation, global citizenship and global education. The key debates within global education will be described and some of the potential links with teaching and learning history will be outlined. A number of examples of classroom work will be given prior to a conclusion.

Are ideas about globalisation important?

It is undeniable that since 1990 there have been an increasing number of publications focusing on global trends (e.g. Kennedy 1993; Hertz 2001). Academic centres such as the Centre for the Study of Global Governance at the London School of Economics have been established to increase understanding and knowledge of global problems and to encourage interaction between both international organisations and national governments. Key texts from political science are focused on the global order (e.g. Held 1995) and there is an increasing number of publications relating directly to education within a global framework. A proliferation of international research projects explore teachers' perceptions of citizenship (e.g. Albala-Bertrand 1995; Cogan and Derricott 1998; Angell and Hahn 1996; Hahn 1998; Torney-Purta *et al.* 1999; Fouts in press). The number of fundamental discussions within an educational context about the nature of citizenship has expanded massively (e.g. Lynch 1992; Torres 1998). Many texts provide support for those involved in teacher education (e.g. Steiner 1996) and for work in classrooms with school students (e.g. Pike and Selby 1988, 1995; Claire 1996; Hill *et al.* 1998). This is, of course, in addition to – and partly as a result of – the huge interest shown in citizenship in individual states across the globe. High-status action including academic, media and governmental initiatives is taking place in the USA, Australia, the United Kingdom and many other countries. There is little doubt that an international dimension to citizenship education can easily be demonstrated. It seems obvious to suggest that this must be one of the main avenues for teachers and others to explore in the development of clearer thinking and better practice in citizenship education.

What is globalisation?

Although it is relatively straightforward to demonstrate the amount of attention being given to globalisation, it is less easy to suggest its meaning. Cogan (1998) has outlined several themes which emerge from the literature of globalisation. These themes, he asserts, are interwoven rather than mutually exclusive. They are:

- *the global economy*, in which nothing counts as external and a mesh of interlocking transnational ties focusing more on services and less on goods supplants more traditional activity
- *technology and communication*, more people having access principally to computers but also to other systems
- *population and environment*, where pollution, genetic engineering and disparities between the 'haves' and 'have-nots' are the focal points of discussions about sustainability

There are a number of debates around these issues. Cogan (1998) makes it clear that not all these developments may be positive. Although some argue that, generally, 'globalisation is not the prime source of new inequalities' and offers more benefit than harm (Giddens 1999), not all agree. There are also disagreements about the nature of globalisation in terms of, for example, the speed at which it is occurring. But there are also more fundamental disagreements. Green (1997) questions the whole basis of the globalisation debate. He refers to the large number of new national states. He also argues that 'economic globalization is a highly contested phenomenon' (1997, p. 161) by showing that internationalisation of trade and investment has a long history and that population movements are possibly slowing down. According to some theorists, the degree of uniqueness and innovation suggested by the term 'globalisation' is merely the most recent version of internationalisation which may depend heavily upon the actions of governments and individuals operating from the perspective of nation-states. As a further illustration of how wary we should be of the claims of the globalisation lobby, it can be useful to examine the efforts made to represent the past. It will be of interest to history teachers that those in the vanguard of the promotion of global education are at times guilty of remarkably ahistorical accounts. It is not helpful, for example, to argue that: 'The children of the 1880s belonged, perhaps, to the last generation to which teachers with any assuredness could teach from the premise that their charges would live in a world similar to their own' (Pike and Selby 1995, p. 4).

The word 'perhaps' in the above quotation does give some room for doubt about the wisdom of the statement and it may be that the speed of change is being discussed as opposed to globalisation. However, it is extremely unlikely that many people actually alive in the 1880s would have recognised this mythical golden age, supported by Pike and Selby only by reference to Flora Thompson's *Lark Rise to Candleford*. There are great tensions within debates about the degree to which globalisation is actually occurring and there are great differences between the proponents of particular perspectives. This uncertainty, however, provides part of the justification for work by history teachers and the contrasting statements will provide useful lesson material. A development study on globalisation would be a fascinating and very popular topic with history students.

What is global citizenship?

A number of models exist to clarify the nature of global citizenship. As shown in Figure 9.1 (from Heater 1997) illustrates how citizenship can be discussed alongside that which is sanctioned within a state.

Legally defined	Dual – citizenship of two states held simultaneously
	Layered – in federal constitutions; and in a few multinational communities
Mainly attitude: limited legal definition	Below state level – municipal, local allegiance/sense of identity
	Above state level – world citizenship

Figure 9.1 Forms of citizenship held in conjunction with state citizenship

Source: Heater (1997).

Heater goes on to explain (1997, pp. 36–8) that a range of meanings can be applied to global citizenship. He places four main meanings on a spectrum of which the opposite ends are 'vague' and 'precise' (see Figure 9.2).

VAGUE .... PRECISE

| Member of the human race | Responsible for the condition of the planet | Individual subject to moral law | Promotion of world government |

Figure 9.2 The meanings of world citizenship

Source: Heater (1997)

Heater explains that the first category would include those people who feel themselves to be linked to others and who often take it upon themselves to act in the interests of the world community. The second category is slightly less vague than the first, as the range and nature of the resulting thinking and actions are more closely defined (in, for example, working for conservation in an organisation such as Greenpeace). Wringe (1999, p. 6), for example, puts himself towards this 'vague' end of Heater's spectrum by being keen to dispel 'a prime misconception' that a global polity is necessary before global citizenship can exist. He dismisses the notion that global citizenship is simply 'international do-goodery', emphasising the importance of affective considerations and arguing for citizenship as 'the establishment of acceptable collective arrangements, which if not properly attended to may ultimately result in a worse life for everyone' (1999, p. 6). In the third category, a number of different forms of law are relevant: natural law; international law (e.g. the European Convention on Human Rights); and international criminal law (e.g. the trials at Nuremberg). This formulation is used by staff at the Centre for the Study of Global Governance at the London School of Economics who claim at their web site (http://www.lse.ac.uk/Depts/global/About-CsGG.htm) that: 'Global governance was understood not as government but as a minimum framework of rules necessary to tackle global problems guaranteed by a diverse set of institutions including both international organisations and national governments.'

Finally, in Heater's spectrum it is important to note that some aspire to a world government. David Held is probably the best-known current advocate of this position. Held (1995) argues for cosmopolitan democracy which would involve complementary regional, national and international assemblies, all with opportunities for popular participation.

Just as there are debates about the nature and degree of globalisation, difficult issues arise concerning global citizenship. These debates have been explored by various authors including Lynch (1992), Heater (1990), Oliver and Heater (1994) and Kymlicka (1995). Almost inevitably, some of these authors regard others as writing on very different topics. Heater, for example, sees some of Lynch's work as useful but essentially related to multiculturalism and not citizenship. Other strands of the debates are revealed by those who occupy different positions within the universalist or relativist spectrum. The former would (in simple terms) claim that some form of global approach can be embraced through something like the Universal Declaration of Human Rights. The universalists would argue that such a declaration does not offer a complete moral theory or provide a guide for action in specific circumstances but, rather, offers a guideline which may help decision making and improve the possibility of justice. The relativists (in simple terms) would be suspicious of solutions arrived at by reference to statements which are largely 'western' inspired and which may fail to recognise the 'local' needs inspired by cultural values which are expressed differently from those of debates in the United Nations buildings in New York and Geneva. Related to the universalist–relativist debate are the intellectual challenges associated with postmodern perspectives. Although postmodernism is a highly diverse field, it is reasonable to refer to its supporters' willingness to rely less heavily than others on claims deriving from objectivity and to depend instead on the construction of 'texts' that explore subjectivities in a world characterised by diversity.

This chapter is written, generally, from the universalist perspective of historians such as Appleby *et al.* (1994) who discuss at length how best to avoiding elitist approaches to writing about the past. This perspective is more likely to rescue the experiences of those who have been neglected (such as women, black people and the working class), as well as giving a perhaps more accurate representation of what happened than the stimulating but ultimately self-defeating work of the postmodernists (e.g. Jenkins 1991, 1995; and see also comments by Evans 1997). Finally, explicit mention should be made of questions of identity which normally arise when such issues are being discussed. The ability and willingness of individuals to characterise themselves as global actors form the subject of lengthy debate, being another of the key dividing lines in this field.

Thus, in this section of this chapter some of the different meanings of global citizenship have been described. These positions could lead to a reliance upon a global common feeling or to a desire for a legal framework or even a polity. I have also tried to show that the spectrum of opinion shown in Figure 9.2 contains a wide range of tremendously difficult issues. It is useful to be aware of at least some of these debates as teachers and others decide to develop particular initiatives.

Issues in global education

It is, of course, important to attempt to relate the debates about globalisation and citizenship to what educational action can be taken. Rauner (1997) has suggested the contrasts between national and post-national frameworks but has also added some comments about the implications of each approach for education (Table 9.1).

This table is useful as it attempts to draw together global (or post-national) citizenship and education. Normally the links are not made very clearly when suggestions are made for educational action. It is true that there have been some useful reviews of the impact of transnational organisations upon global civic education. Rauner (1999), for example, argues that there has been an increasing emphasis upon civics education as opposed to more generalised education about the dignity of humankind, and shows that wealthier countries (with the possible exception of those in western Europe) are more likely to emphasise civic content that is global in orientation. However, it is not possible to characterise global education in straightforward terms. At times global education is an umbrella term which is sometimes described as 'new'. The 'new' or adjectival (e.g. peace, gender, development) educations probably received most attention in the United Kingdom in the 1980s.

The 'new' educations are perhaps not a coherent school of thought or action other than in their commitment to social justice. Some, such as peace education and world studies, had existed from the period immediately following the First World War (Heater 1984); others, such as anti-sexist and anti-racist education, are more recent. Academics in 'new' areas such as women's studies as well as trade unionists, workers for aid organisations and teachers were regarded as those involved in the promotion of relevant projects. These various camps often competed between themselves for resources and curriculum space.

The initiatives of the 1980s, while for the most part having impeccably democratic credentials, were perceived to have a harder edge than earlier work and were not supported by key decision makers. Instead of having a broad framework of politics which

Table 9.1 National and post-national models of society

	National model of society	*Post-national model of society*
Nature	Internal focus on narrow national interests	External focus
	Concerned with strengthening or maintaining national identity	Global interdependence of countries or regions
Citizenship education	Emphasis on:	Emphasis on:
	Patriotism	Extra-national perspectives
	National history and societal structures	Inclusion of historically excluded groups
	National membership of the individual	Notion of citizenship tied to transnational personhood
		Regional and global level political structures
	Rights and responsibilities:	Rights and responsibilities:
	Rights and obligations that come with legal status in a country	Universal human rights (political, social economic)

Source: Rauner (1997).

was applied to issues affecting everyday lives, the 'new' educations seemed to give more attention to specific issues. Supporters argued both that those issues were vitally important in themselves and that also there could be some way in which the specifics could be made to generate a more decent society.

Four issues were always seen as the most important: the bomb; gender; development; and 'race' (the latter in inverted commas as the very existence of 'race' can be challenged). All four were concerned with social justice and had a number of strengths. The issues were undeniably important. A number of local education authorities (e.g. Newcastle) gave a lead at a time when many perceived there to be grave dangers for world safety. Those active in these movements were reflecting wider debates and actions, and were very much a part of the context of the early 1980s. Some of that context was characterised by: the 1978–9 winter of discontent; the 1981 riots in Liverpool, Bristol and London; reactions against the excesses of monetarist government policy and the controversies of Howe's 1981 budget; the teachers' strikes of the mid-1980s, together with actions by women who were developing far more developed versions of what was needed for a just society than had been allowed for by the 1975 Sex Discrimination Act.

The teachers who became involved with such work were not (or at least not as obviously as those associated with previous initiatives) academics moving from high-status disciplines, making comments about teachers and schools. The new groups included many intelligent and creative teachers who developed many curriculum packs, books, guides and schemes of work. Hicks's (1988) book on peace education has a subtitle which stresses action in the classroom; the work on world studies and later on global education by Pike and Selby (e.g. 1988), while always being academically respectable, is largely concerned with what teachers can do in their day-to-day work with children.

However, some of these strengths could also be seen as weaknesses and would mean that although much of this work continues in the form of, for example, education for the future (e.g. Hicks and Holden 1995; Hicks 1994) there were serious problems with the overarching coherence of the ideas and the likelihood of these movements being accepted. Intellectually, the 'new' educations were fragmented. This is not simply a matter of divisions between those favouring, for example, peace as opposed to another focal point. Rather, within each of the different camps there are very different conceptions. Conflict resolution, for example, can be seen as needing investigations into international crises and/or an exploration of the inner self (e.g. Kragh 1995). Feminism is a very broad church, with little possibility of a united front between the different elements (Bryson 1993). The shifts in other areas are readily apparent, with the multiculturalism of the 1970s being replaced by the anti-racist education of the 1980s which in turn now seems to be being replaced by intercultural education. Intellectual fragmentation and commitment to particular objectives which are perceived as being radical do not lead to widespread acceptance. Rather, certain local education authorities became associated with what seemed to be party political aims. Peace education guidelines produced separately by Avon and Manchester were in some ways open to easy attack (Lister 1984). As Scruton (1985) attacked Pike and Selby, sections 44 and 45 of the 1986 Education Act (number 2) were forbidding political activity in schools and requiring teachers in secondary schools to ensure that there was always a balanced presentation of opposing views. The 'new' educations, however unfairly, were now perceived as edging young people towards the margins of politics rather than saving them from that fate. Consequently, despite all their strengths (particularly their acceptance in the form of continued use by teachers of some of the teaching materials), the radical agenda is not seen either as a key determinant of policy or as a feature of widespread action. It is true that some attention has been given to global education by influential government advisers such as Michael Barber (e.g. Barber 1996). But in the face of intellectual incoherence and an inability to withstand attack from well-placed political opponents, the focus has moved on to a consideration of the parameters of the National Curriculum and the primacy of literacy and numeracy.

Teaching and learning for global citizenship through history

Pike and Selby (1995, p. 6) defined four dimensions of global education: the temporal dimension; the inner dimension; the spatial dimension; the issues dimension. They also list ten different areas for global education (Pike and Selby 1995, p. 14), including development education, environmental education, human rights education and peace education. It is clear then that citizenship is only one of these ten 'key areas' and that the role for teaching and learning history is only very explicitly made in relation to one of the four dimensions (the temporal). However, it is possible to show how history teachers can make a real contribution to global education and perhaps to global citizenship. Bracey (1995) has some useful advice for those who are developing work on the history of particular areas in a global context. He argues that:

- the history of Britain should be seen in a world and European context
- Britain has always been a diverse society
- regional diversity should be understood
- different interpretations of Britain's history should be understood
- different versions of events should be considered

Global 'content'

The first and perhaps most obvious way to ensure that a contribution is made by history teachers is to consider the nature of the content that is employed and the messages that are being transmitted to pupils. But 'content' in any discussion of global citizenship may have at least three different aspects. Firstly, it is important to ensure an appropriately wide coverage so that global considerations are properly raised. Secondly, the content of a programme that aims to develop understanding of global citizenship is often related strongly to working with others. The benefits of working together (either face to face or electronically) with people from other countries can be immense. Even if a less ambitious programme is established in which the others one works with are from the same classroom or local community, the processes of that engagement are often seen as being particularly important. Learning to work with others is relevant to all citizenship education but is often emphasised most strongly when global perspectives are applied. Thirdly, content relates to the particular perspective that is developed for so-called mainstream topics. A narrow national perspective will not be relevant. Davies (1999, p. 3) notes that:

> At Blenheim only one sixth of the troops at Marlborough's disposal were English. At Waterloo, less than a quarter of the Allied force was British. In the first world war, British forces made up one fifth of the Allied total. In the second world war, 75% of all German casualties were inflicted by the Soviet Army, while the British contribution was necessarily much smaller than the Americans.

Positive contributions made by a range of individuals and groups across the globe should be studied in detail. A syllabus that chooses to include certain people as victims by, for example, including the slave trade and the 'glorious' emancipation by figures such as William Wilberforce misrepresents the past. UNESCO has suggested that topics are taught in a particular way:

> The history of the Industrial Revolution and the consequent labor movement could be introduced by a similar review of Economic, Social and Cultural Rights.

The Second World War could be introduced with the Universal Declaration of Human Rights emphasising the relationship between the rights that are violated by war, and whose violation often causes war.

(UNESCO 1997, p. 127)

In this way it will be possible to avoid a false global history in which the interrelationships between areas of the world and global and national issues are not recognised by students who are essentially involved in a study of national history in a global context. This possibility needs to be considered carefully, as a number of Council of Europe documents refer to a European citizenship project in a global context rather than developing a more explicit and intended global citizenship. The teacher needs to consider if global issues are 'merely' to be used as a context for a national history or as something more complete in itself.

The past must not be colonised by the people of the present in a way that is both inaccurate and harmful to the achievement of legitimate contemporary educational goals. In this sense it is important to be open about the links between action and education. It is not suggested by the supporters of global education that a narrow, perhaps party-political, agenda is to be developed. However, some of the attacks that have been made suggest that this is the message that has been read into the work of these supporters (e.g. Scruton 1985). There is, however, a sense that global education is a part of much more than academic education, and involvement in a local project with a global purpose or perhaps even participation in an internationally based organisation are opportunities which schools frequently offer their pupils.

Linking past, present and future

The second key strand in global education through history is a matter of ensuring appropriate links are made between past, present and future. Those who promote global education often quote some lines from Eliot (1974, p. 189) in which time in the present and past are seen to be linked and themselves connected to the future.

This link between the present, the past and the future, of course, need not be explored in all history classrooms. Heater (1980) argues that an unfortunate misunderstanding has sometimes led to the assumption that world or global also necessarily means 'contemporary'. Often an excessive concentration on the very recent past can lead to a failure to see the true nature of interdependence, and perhaps encourages students to believe that alternatives have never existed to current power elites. Kniep (1986, p. 444), in an influential article that explores the content of a global education, makes a strong case for grounding students in the knowledge that contact and exchange among civilisations have been more or less continuous for the last 2000 years. The future is also important in global education. Hicks (1994) shows a number of ways in which classroom-based activities can be developed in an exploration of the future. Pike and Selby (1995, p. 102) present an activity titled 'inventing the future backwards' in which students develop over a period of weeks ideas about possible and probable futures. They are asked to explore whether they feel those futures are optimistic or pessimistic and to explain clearly how these scenarios link to their perception of current and past events and trends. This juxtaposition of the past and its links with a – not necessarily 'the' – present could be developed by use of counterfactual history. This approach essentially asks 'what if' and has been developed in an academic context by such authors as Ferguson (1997) under the heading of 'virtual history'. These links between the past, present and future, therefore, are not intellectually lightweight. They are the stuff of 'proper' academic work. It is also important to note that there are already many published examples of activities and exercises appropriate for use in classrooms. It is particularly impressive that many of these activities are contextualised within an appreciation of the existence of different learning styles.

Emphasising affective approaches

One of the strongest distinguishing features of global education is the emphasis upon school or classroom ethos or climate. Whereas a traditionalist approach emphasises factual knowledge and a more didactic style, a reformist approach focuses on issues that are to do with 'real life', and a 'radical' approach encourages critical understanding to develop an appreciation of the dynamic nature of society (Mellor and Elliott 1996). Within this critical approach is a sense of holism that relies heavily upon affective matters. This does not mean that skills are neglected but, rather, that emotion is recognised as important. An understanding of chronology, for example, might be developed by teachers who issue 'green history' cards on which are written statements about the killing of the last great auk (a bird), the establishment of a green belt around London, or the explosion within the Chernobyl nuclear plant (Pike and Selby 1995). As pupils organise themselves into a timeline they are also presented with opportunities to reflect on the meaning and likely implications of these issues for individuals and the planet. In an even more personal exercise students are asked to experience 'guided fantasies' (Pike and Selby 1988) and to reflect using their inner voices.

A history project for global education

The three areas explored above can be integrated in particular projects (see Davies and Rey 1998). The use of genuinely global history, the interrelationship between past, present and future and, to some extent, an affective approach can be integrated by focusing on the opportunities for exploring interpretations of history. There are three threads that can help teachers plan work about interpretations:

- interpretations combine fact and fiction, imagination and points of view
- interpretations are dependent, if they are of historical worth, on evidence
- differences between interpretations can be explained by reference, among other things, to purpose and intended audience, and to the background of the author of any interpretation (NCC 1993, p. 50)

Further guidance suggested five key questions that teachers could use:

- which parts of the interpretation are factual and which parts are views or imagination?
- how plausible is the interpretation?
- how far are these views supported by evidence? How selective has the use of evidence been?
- what was the purpose and intended audience of the interpretation?
- how far was the interpretation affected by the background of the author? (adapted from NCC 1993)

Using the above guidelines, pupils could be directed towards a statement such as that made by John Major in the 1997 British general election when he referred to a thousand years of British history, or that of Norman Tebbit who apparently believed that there have been a thousand years of British parliamentary history. Such statements were obviously designed for political purposes. They could be set against other versions of the past showing dates of invasions by various groups, developing contacts with countries overseas, the dates and origins of monarchs such as William III and the links between the present royal family and Greece, Germany and Russia. Following this introduction, pupils could be encouraged to compare and contrast national and global symbols. The former would perhaps include special days such as St George's Day, flags (the origins of the Union Jack), music such as 'Land of hope and glory', and place names including Waterloo and Trafalgar Square. The global symbols could include the flags, buildings and special commemorative days promoted by the United Nations. It would be useful to include the symbols of organisations such as UNICEF, UNESCO, the International Labour Organisation and the World Health Authority. The prime purpose of such an analysis would be to encourage pupils to examine the tradition that is being 'invented' before their eyes (Hobsbawm and Ranger 1987). For example, a school could be represented in a variety of ways, with choices over the use of local and/or international symbols. Heater's (1997) vague and precise formulations of global citizenship (see Figure 9.2) would then become explicit. By focusing on this sort of work, pupils would have an opportunity to explore the way in which tradition is invented, apply some of that thinking to their own country and then to the world, and so be able to develop their own understanding of the range of opportunities possible in the development of global citizenship.

Conclusion

Teaching and learning about and for global citizenship through history is not straightforward. There are many tensions between world history, global education and global citizenship. These fields are not the same and attempts to paper over the cracks by a well-intentioned determination to make the world a better place may not ultimately be successful. It is to be hoped that some coherence can be developed in this area and that links can be established between conceptual and pedagogical understanding. Currently there is some evidence to suggest that teachers' conceptions of citizenship can be cast uncomfortably narrowly (Davies et al. 1999). For some, a local and somehow moral outlook is preferable to anything more comprehensive. However, it is also clear that global education, however imprecise it may be, has attracted the most gifted of curriculum developers. There has been impressive in-service work. There are charismatic and inspirational pedagogical leaders in various centres around the globe. The work strikes a chord among many teachers and many young people. Many examples of classroom activities are enjoyable and worthwhile. Arguing for what could be a more coherent form of education for global citizenship means taking a risk. It remains to be seen whether attempt to achieve greater coherence will produce better results.

Key questions

1   Radical educational work that stressed global interconnectedness seems to have become less significant while debates about globalisation have assumed more prominence. Do you agree that this change has occurred? If so, can you explain it?

2   Derek Heater has said that global citizenship is merely a metaphor. Do you agree? What does your reaction to this question tell you about the way you think about citizenship?

3   If you established an e-mail project with a school in the USA to discuss the causes and consequences of the American War of Independence, would you necessarily have developed global citizenship education? How would you justify your answer?

Recommended reading

A. Green (1997) *Education, Globalisation and the Nation State.* Basingstoke, Macmillan.
An intelligently written account of the nature of globalisation and how education relates to it. Green is rather sceptical about the claims made by some about globalisation. His historical account will be of interest to readers of this book.

G. Pike and D. Selby (1988) *Global Teacher, Global Learner.* London, Hodder and Stoughton.
A fascinating and extremely practical book which contains many examples of classroom activities. It remains one of the best statements about a particular form of global education.

Chapter 10

Slave, subject and citizen

Her Britannic Majesty's Secretary of State Requests and requires in the Name of Her Majesty all those who it may concern to allow the bearer to pass freely without let or hindrance and to afford the bearer such assistance and protection as may be necessary.

(Preface to current UK passport)

As a young teacher in the 1980s I took a holiday in Ireland. I remember sitting in a Gaelic pub near Killarney. Republican posters dominated the walls and irritating Irish jig music rang in my ears. The only good thing about it at the time seemed to be the privilege of drinking real Guinness which just doesn't taste the same anywhere else. My table was shared by a local Irish tourist guide and a female American tourist.

The American was expounding her Irish ancestry with great enthusiasm but also felt obliged to apologise for polluting English blood of which she felt ashamed. Although I didn't betray this at the time, my feelings were outraged. How dare she denigrate her English ancestry? Yet my attitude was also tempered by personal knowledge of the dubious historical record of English intervention in Ireland. The two feelings jostled inside me, a sense of injured indignation juxtaposed with images of the Famine and 800 years of occupation. (In my mind I automatically thought of myself as English first and British second.) Surely the American was right to be proud of her Irish ancestry, identifying with a suffering culture? Wasn't it also understandable that she wished to jettison the unwanted blood of the English oppressor? Yet, in my mind, it wasn't that simple, for my mental baggage, as well as carrying a record of English–Irish relations, was also aware of English national achievements of which I was secretly proud. How was it possible to square those conflicting feelings in one person's head while also balancing the perceptions of two very different individuals? First, I myself, a young Englishman, of confused emotions, proud yet simultaneously ashamed of my identity in that setting. Second, a flag-waving American, identifying with that part of her ancestry linked to the oppressed victims of one culture while disowning the part of her ancestry she deemed shameful. Also a wry and pragmatic Irishman, who confided afterwards that he despised plastic Irishmen from the Mid West. On the other hand, he said, their money was useful.

Issues of identity are intimately bound up with citizenship. However desirable it might be to define the term within legally established and manageable rights and responsibilities, the way people think of 'citizen' as a term (if they think of it at all) is frequently related to the state, and the state helps to shape identity.

The passport preface cited at the beginning of this chapter smacks of Pax Britannica and Palmerston's willingness to send a gunboat to protect any British subject threatened by 'Johnny Foreigner'. However much has changed in British society, the Victorian wording of the passport invokes the pride in being a 'subject' of the British Crown which, despite the submission to authority the word emphasises, carries rights and freedoms equal and often superior to many a republic. As the Crick Report (QCA 1998) said, 'the very concept of "British subject" and "British citizen" seem much the same to most people'. Concepts of citizenship therefore overlap with those of identity. At any one time an individual might simultaneously possess a number of types of citizenship and therefore identity (see Figure 10.1).

Figure 10.1 Multiple citizenship
Source: Heater (1998).

As Dr Nicholas Tate commented in his address to the Historical Association Education Conference in 1997, many identities jostle within the term 'British subject' or 'citizen'. We may identify ourselves through our families and particular local communities within which there may be religious, ethnic or class differences. Those living in Scotland might choose to be Scottish before British. An Ulster Protestant might claim to be British first and hardly Irish at all. A nationalist living in the north of Ireland might claim to be Irish and deny British identity though carrying a British passport. These complexities within British society are reflected in the Citizenship Orders: 'Pupils should be taught about . . . the diversity of national, regional, religious and ethnic identities in the United Kingdom and the need for mutual respect and understanding' (DfEE/QCA 1999b). This overlaps with requirements in the History Orders: 'Pupils should be taught about the social, cultural, religious and ethnic diversity of the societies studied, both in Britain and the wider world' (QCA/DfEE 1999a).

Chesterton Community College in Cambridge is a comprehensive school for 11–16-year-olds with a broad intake from a diversity of ethnic and social backgrounds. The college's history department were keen to pilot a unit of work which experimented with delivering an element of citizenship within Year 9 history lessons. The historical 'content' was centred on the British slave trade and its abolition, which falls within the national curriculum area of study 'Britain 1750–1900'. The teachers within the department followed a scheme of work where blocks of content were organised for teaching around an overarching key question or 'big question'. This was then broken down into 'little questions' around which a lesson or sequence of lessons could be taught (see Table 10.1).

The big question in this case was 'Who are the British?', the little question being 'What does it mean to be British?' Stemming from the little question, the second and fourth columns state the teaching and learning objectives at the outset of the lesson and their outcomes as a result of the activity. The term 'Hook' in the column marked 'Activities' assumes as a part of good practice that the teacher will introduce the lesson with an activity that helps to bridge the gap between the subject matter and the students' own experience.

The big question 'Who are the British?' is a timely one as many historians (Colley, 1992; N. Davies 1999a) maintain that both 'Britain' and 'Britishness' are historical constructs, now currently breaking down or facing rapid change. The activities around 'What does it mean to be British?' were designed to expose the students' current thinking about the term and to provoke discussion. In multi-ethnic classes sensitivity has to be shown in referring to the descent and background of any individual students. So to avoid undesirable focus on individuals, the scheme of work activities made use of Figure 10.2. This shows the family tree of a Chesterton student from a very multi-ethnic background. However, the information is fictional so that while there might be similarities to the descent of other students, questions of identity could be debated on neutral ground.

The lesson was planned to match the requirements of the Key Stage 3 citizenship programme of study by considering 'the diversity of national, regional, religious and ethnic identities in the United Kingdom'.

The activities fitted the 'skills of enquiry and communication': 'think about topical political, spiritual, moral, social and cultural issues, problems and events; justify orally a personal opinion about such issues, problems or events; contribute to group and exploratory class discussions, and take part in debates'. The lesson can be justified as a combination of citizenship and history because the family tree of the fictional Sayi McDermott stretches back several generations. To explain her ancestry, reference has to be made to the changing status over time of territories formerly part of the British and Portuguese empires.

The culminating task of transferring the countries from which her ancestors came onto a world map illustrates the complexity of her descent. It can only be properly understood in the context of historical immigration and emigration patterns into and out of the United Kingdom. It puts historical flesh on the bones of the requirement in the Citizenship Orders that 'pupils should be taught about . . . the world as a global community and the political, economic, environmental and social implications of this'. It brings into historical focus the concept of multiple forms of citizenship and identity shifting in the experience of an individual British citizen.

Table 10.1 Big question: Who are the British?

Title of Unit: Big question: Who are the British?

Little questions	Teaching/learning objectives	Activities	Teaching/learning outcomes
What does it mean to be British?	To discuss possible definitions of Britishness and to link these definitions to the record of immigration and emigration in and out of Britain up to the present time	*Hook* Play a recording of the national anthem. Get the class to list words they each associate with it. Share in pairs, then draw upon a collective class list of words. Discuss. *Main activities* Repeat the above activity for associations with the word 'British'. Get the class to list any words they would use to label themselves e.g. 'lazy', 'attractive', 'intelligent', Muslim, male, etc. In separate circles on the board, place the categories of common terms pupils use about themselves e.g. 'personal', 'religious', 'gender', 'national', etc. Discuss any overlaps between their personal identities and what has already been listed a characteristic of British identity. Discuss what a definition of Britishness might be. Discuss the family tree of Sayi McDermont (see Figure 10.2). Is she British? Is she English? Both? Transfer onto a world map showing the places her ancestors came from.	To develop and discuss definitions of British identity. To begin to develop an understanding of how these definitions may have been shaped by the past.

These classroom activities provided a rich vein of debate for Chesterton's ethnic mix of students. A Year 9 girl originally from Aberdeen asserted that she was Scottish and that Britishness did not exist. A white boy, described by his teacher as English and lower middle-class, defended traditional notions of Britishness. He wrote 'I am proud to be British because we won both world wars, we have a famous royal family and the best Army and RAF'. Then again, a girl of Saudi Arabian parentage carefully distinguished between her own Britishness, which she was happy to acknowledge, and Englishness which she felt was alien to her.

The non-statutory exemplification for the area of study 'Britain 1750–1900' in the National Curriculum History Orders (DfEE/QCA 1999a) lists 'the abolition of slaves and the slave trade in the British Empire, and the work of reformers such as William Wilberforce and Olaudah Equiano'. The Chesterton scheme of work for this content chose to centre on Olaudah Equiano, the black abolitionist and former slave who married a local white English woman. A memorial of Equiano's daughter is inscribed on a stone tablet in the churchyard of St Andrew's, Chesterton. The coincidence of Equiano's presence in the Cambridge area met part of the requirement in the programme of study for Key Stage 3 that content for 'Britain 1750–1900' should cover 'how expansion of trade and colonisation, industrialisation and political changes affected the United Kingdom, including the local area'.

Figures such as Equiano occupy a controversial role in the historiography of the slave trade and its abolition. Recent debate about the causes of abolition have tended to veer between polarised positions.

1   A white Eurocentric emphasis on black slaves as helpless victims owing the abolition of the slave trade to the white abolitionists in Britain. The suppression of the Atlantic trade after 1807 is attributed to the actions of the Royal Navy. This and abolition gave a moral superiority to the British during the days of empire. However, it also perpetuated the view of Africans as inferiors who needed the benevolence of British rule from the Victorian period onwards. Many white abolitionists, while appalled by the cruelty of the trade, would have shared what we now see as this racist and patronising view of Africans. The effect on historical writing was to minimise or totally exclude the role of blacks themselves in the process of abolition.

2   A black Afrocentric emphasis on the dignity and achievements of African civilisations prior to the iniquity of the slave trade. This is particularly well developed in the United States. The Eurocentric interpretation came under fierce attack in the 1940s by a Trinidadian historian, Eric Williams. He claimed that the economic decline of the Caribbean islands by the nineteenth century inevitably led to British capitalism abolishing an unprofitable trade in slaves. The role of black resistance in undermining the trade and slavery itself has also been emphasised. This takes away much of the glory of the white abolitionists and seeks to find or rediscover heroes of black resistance such as Olaudah Equiano in Britain.

Between these positions the debate has twisted and turned on different problems at different times. These include:

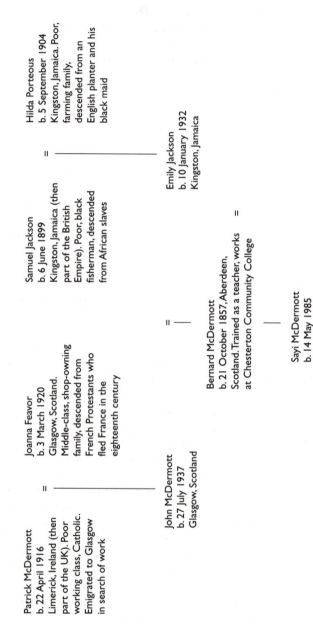

Patrick McDermott
b. 22 April 1916
Limerick, Ireland (then
part of the UK). Poor
working class, Catholic.
Emigrated to Glasgow
in search of work

=

Joanna Feavor
b. 3 March 1920
Glasgow, Scotland.
Middle-class, shop-owning
family, descended from
French Protestants who
fled France in the
eighteenth century

Samuel Jackson
b. 6 June 1899
Kingston, Jamaica (then
part of the British
Empire). Poor, black
fisherman, descended
from African slaves

=

Hilda Porteous
b. 5 September 1904
Kingston, Jamaica. Poor,
farming family,
descended from an
English planter and his
black maid

John McDermott
b. 27 July 1937
Glasgow, Scotland

Bernard McDermott
b. 21 October 1857, Aberdeen,
Scotland. Trained as a teacher, works
at Chesterton Community College

=

Emily Jackson
b. 10 January 1932
Kingston, Jamaica

Sayi McDermott
b. 14 May 1985
pupil at Chesterton

Figure 10.2 The family tree of Sayi McDermott (father's side)

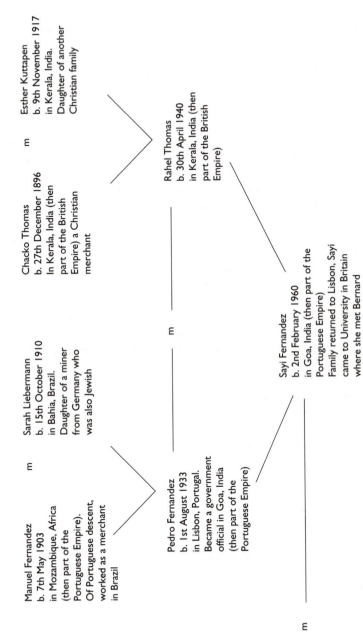

Manuel Fernandez
b. 7th May 1903
in Mozambique, Africa
(then part of the
Portuguese Empire).
Of Portuguese descent,
worked as a merchant
in Brazil

m

Sarah Liebermann
b. 15th October 1910
in Bahia, Brazil.
Daughter of a miner
from Germany who
was also Jewish

Chacko Thomas
b. 27th December 1896
In Kerala, India (then
part of the British
Empire) a Christian
merchant

m

Esther Kuttapen
b. 9th November 1917
in Kerala, India.
Daughter of another
Christian family

Pedro Fernandez
b. 1st August 1933
in Lisbon, Portugal.
Became a government
official in Goa, India
(then part of the
Portuguese Empire)

m

Rahel Thomas
b. 30th April 1940
in Kerala, India (then
part of the British
Empire)

Sayi Fernandez
b. 2nd February 1960
in Goa, India (then part of the
Portuguese Empire)
Family returned to Lisbon, Sayi
came to University in Britain
where she met Bernard

m

The family tree of Sayi McDermott (mother's side)

- the extent to which white abolitionists were themselves racist
- the number of black victims who were carried across the Atlantic and how many died
- the validity of Williams's economic assertion that the Caribbean islands and the slave trade itself were actually in decline by 1807
- the role of blacks in the slave trade itself, particularly as slave traders
- the extent of kidnapping of black captives by white traders
- the impact of the trade on the West African hinterland in provoking wars and economic collapse

The schemes of work are designed to introduce some of these issues and debates in relation to Equiano. The significance of a figure like Equiano in the historiographical debate should be clear at an adult level. In a nineteenth-century, late Victorian interpretation of the causes of slave trade abolition, Equiano and other black figures like him would probably not even warrant a mention. All credit would go automatically to Wilberforce, Clarkson and their white colleagues. The late twentieth-century, Afro-centric attempt to right this bias of omission seeks to rediscover neglected black figures such as Equiano and give them the recognition they deserve. However, in the attempt to 'rescue' these figures from relative obscurity, a current-day, politically motivated influence on historical interpretation needs to be recognised. A society or culture typically seeks to ignore its heroes' blemishes in the struggle to assert their rightful place in the historical pantheon and set up role models for students in the present. The same factors that airbrushed blacks from the imperialist history of the past, other than as victims, can also influence the way their contribution to slave trade abolition is perceived and the behaviour and motivation of heroic figures exonerated. Students were able to share in the issues raised, by considering the big question 'Olaudah Equiano: African hero?' Looking in some detail at Equiano and interpretations of him, the students would be able to debate the extent to which he actually deserves to be treated as a hero of Africa, either then or in the present.

The main text for use was Equiano's classic autobiography produced in later life and titled *The Interesting Narrative of the life of Olaudah Equiano, or Gustavus Vassa, the African. Written by himself*. Prior to the work on Equiano, students had been given a series of images illustrating the experience of Africans from capture to sale. They then arranged the images in chronological order along the horizontal axis of a living graph marked from capture to sale (see Figure 10.3). The vertical axis invited students to decide what the feelings of the Africans in the images might have been in each image and move an individual image up or down against this axis. The graph (adapted from thinking skills methodology (Fisher 1999)) was itself an interpretation in which students consciously reflected on the past (McAleavey 1993) drawing conclusions about the suffering of Africans from capture to sale.

Students were then given extracts from Equiano's narrative describing his childhood experience of the slave trade from his capture in the hinterland of West Africa to later sale in the Caribbean. Students had to decide from the extracts how Equiano's feelings and experience changed from capture to sale by cutting the extracts from the *Interesting Narrative* into cards (Box 10.1) and plotting them onto a second living graph (Figure 10.4).

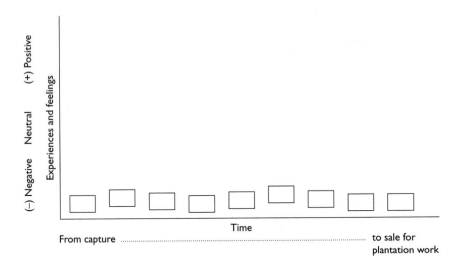

Figure 10.3 Living graph of most slaves' experiences and feelings

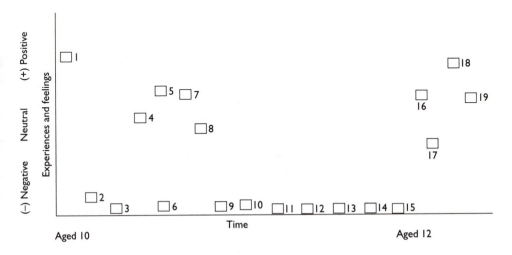

Figure 10.4 Living graph of Olaudah Equiano's experiences and feelings from age 10 to 12

Box 10.1 Statements from the life of Equiano

1   As I was the youngest of the sons, I became of course, the greatest favourite with my mother and was always with her.

2   Two men and a woman . . . seized us both . . . stopped our mouths, tied our hands and ran with us into the nearest wood.

3   My sister and I were then separated . . . She was torn from me . . . While I was left . . . I cried and cried continually.

4   I got into the hands of a chieftain. This man had two wives and some children and they all used me extremely well and did all they could to comfort me.

5   'I was again sold . . . I had been travelling for a considerable time, when . . . to my great surprise, whom should I see brought to the house where I was but my sister . . . she gave a loud shriek and ran into my arms.

6   Even this small comfort was soon to have an end. For scarcely had the morning appeared when she was torn from me for ever.

7   I came to a town called Tinmah . . . I was bought of [by] the merchant . . . all their treatment of me, made me forget I was a slave.

8   One morning early . . . I was awakened to fresh sorrow, and hurried away . . . it would be tedious and uninteresting to relate. . . all this journey.

9   a slave ship . . . filled me with astonishment . . . I was immediately tossed up to see if I were sound . . . and I was now persuaded . . . they were bad spirits . . . and were going to kill me.

10   'I asked if we were not to be eaten by those white men with horrible looks, red faces and long hair?

11   I was soon put under decks. . . with the loathsomeness of the stench, I became so sick and low I was not able to eat . . . one of them held me fast . . . while the other flogged me severely.

12   The whole ship's cargo . . . together . . . air became unfit . . . sickness . . . chains . . . filth of the tubs, into which the children fell – shrieks of the woman . . . groans of the dying.

13   Two who were chained together . . . jumped into the sea.

14   We came in sight of the island of Barbados . . . we were all pent up together like so many sheep in a fold . . . we were sold.

15   I . . . shipped off to North America . . . I was miserable . . . I had no person to speak to that I could understand.

16   'Michael Henry Pascal . . . a Lieutenant in the Royal Navy gave thirty or forty pounds to me . . . I could smatter a little imperfect English . . . told me they were going to carry me back . . . this made me very happy.

17   While I was on board, my master named me Gustavus Vassa . . . when I refused to answer to my new name it gained me many a cuff . . . so . . . I submitted.

18   On board. . . a young lad about four or five years older than myself . . . Richard Baker . . . my constant companion and instructor.

19   Falmouth . . . twelve years of age . . . snow . . . never seen anything of the kind before, I thought it was salt.

This idea again borrowed from a similar exercise using extracts from Anne Frank's diary (Fisher 1999). The students could then compare the two graphs to answer the little question 'How typical is Equiano's *Interesting Narrative* of the feelings and experiences of slaves taken from Africa to the West Indies?' While Equiano's *Interesting Narrative* could clearly be categorised as a 'primary' source it also falls within the definition of a historical interpretation since it is a 'conscious reflection on the past' (McAleavy, 1993). (Equiano wrote his *Interesting Narrative* from an adult perspective on his experience as a child with specific purposes in mind.) Using interactive questioning and explanations from teachers, students used a worksheet (Figure 10.5) to debate possible answers to the little question 'How close to the truth is Equiano's *Interesting Narrative*?' The worksheet's concluding interpretations frame makes explicit to students McAleavy's criteria for analysing the historic worth of any interpretation. It asks the students to plot onto the triangle their own judgement of Equiano's *Interesting Narrative*, given that it will consist of a combination of 'fact and fiction, imagination and point of view' (NCC 1993).

Readers may balk at the little question beginning 'How close to the truth is Equiano's *Interesting Narrative*?' Does the question ask how close the narrative is to Equiano's own memory of his experiences or to some notion of absolute truth? It could be either, and the wording of the question is designed to provoke debate about this philosophical point, particularly among higher attainers.

To complete the evaluation of Equiano's text as an interpretation, the students were given a chart outlining Equiano's life (Table 10.2) and asked in pairs to highlight events they would include for a BBC documentary on his life.

They then had to discuss their conclusions and the criteria they had used for selecting details. Chesterton history department already possessed a recording of a recent BBC television programme on Equiano's life, part of a series called 'Hidden empire'. The video commentary was interspersed with interviews from historians and dramatised excerpts from the *Interesting Narrative*. While viewing the video, students highlighted in a different coloured pen on the chart of Equiano's life details the BBC had selected or left out. In addition, they compared a script of one of the dramatised episodes of the programme with the equivalent extract of the 'Narrative' on which it was based. The students then considered some related questions, comparing the two (Box 10.2). Finally classes considered the overall nature of the programme as an interpretation, using a frame identical to the one used previously for evaluating the *Interesting Narrative*. This helped them to address the third little question: 'How close to the truth is "Hidden empire"?'

The implications of this question cast possible doubt on the historic worth of this programme as an interpretation of Equiano's life. Not only had the film makers taken liberties with their dramatisation based on the 'Narrative' (itself a partial view of Equiano's life experience); they seemed to be motivated by an attempt to turn him into a hero. He may well deserve to be treated thus, but the process of turning him into one should not go unquestioned. Are we left with an unbalanced view of Equiano's life from the programme? It chooses to leave out his controversial role as a purchaser of slaves before his final conversion to the cause of abolition and his involvement in the failed attempt to repatriate blacks to Sierra Leone. Students can consider the motivation of the film makers in leaving these details out.

Step One

Read the following statements carefully.

'This is a superb first hand account.'
Dr Ian Duffield, Edinburgh University

He was about 47 in 1789 when he wrote the *Interesting Narrative*. He was partly writing about events when he was only 10.

Equiano saw himself as an African but was also proud to call himself British.

'Equiano's own ... fairly objective descriptions of places remote from both Europe and Africa suggest that his descriptions and evaluations of Africa, America, the West Indies and England are reliable'.
Professor Vincent Carretta, University of Maryland, USA

'He was a mobiliser. He mobilised around it (i.e. the book). He read extracts from it. He took it around anti-slavery meetings for mobilising opinion.'
Professor Stuart Hall, Open University

At his death, Equiano left nearly £950 (worth nearly £80,000 today), earned partly from the sales of his autobiography.

'The name "Gustavus Vassa" appears on the muster book of the ship Roebuck as of 1 January 1756, about a year earlier than recounted in the *Narrative*'.
Professor Vincent Carretta, University of Maryland, USA

Figure 10.5 How close to the truth is Equiano's *Interesting Narrative?*

Figure 10.5 continued

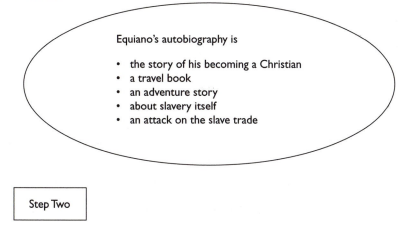

Equiano's autobiography is

• the story of his becoming a Christian
• a travel book
• an adventure story
• about slavery itself
• an attack on the slave trade

Step Two

On a 1 to 5 scale decide where Equiano's '*Interesting Narrative*' belongs.

Not
very
true

Very
true

1   2   3   4   5

Step Three

Interpretations of history are made up of fact, fiction, imagination and point of view. Put a cross on the diagram, where you think Equiano's *Interesting Narrative* belongs.

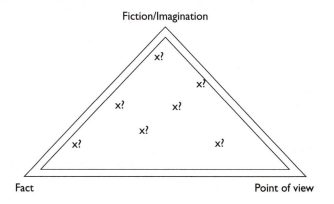

Fiction/Imagination

Fact   Point of view

Table 10.2 The life of Olaudah Equiano

Age of Equiano	Date	Event
	1745	Born. Son of a chief of the Ibo people in West Africa.
10–12	1755–6	Kidnapped with his sister by Africans from another tribe. Sold several times, eventually to white traders. Crossed the Atlantic and put up for sale in Barbados. Unsold, he was shipped to Virginia and sold to a plantation owner as a domestic slave. Equiano was purchased by a Royal Naval officer, Michael Henry Pascal, and taken to sea on board the *Roebuck*.
12–18	1756–62	Equiano served his master in the Royal Navy. He witnessed sea battles against the French. He was also befriended by an American boy, Richard Baker. He was sold to an American merchant, Robert King.
18–21	1762–66	Equiano worked as a clerk and administrator for his master, partly in the West Indies. After careful private trading he bought his own freedom.
22–28	1767–73	He spent most of his time working as a sailor at sea, including a voyage of exploration to the Arctic.
29–33	1773–7	Equiano became a Methodist (a type of enthusiastic Christian). He joined a previous employer, Dr Charles Irving to help set up a plantation in Central America. He purchased slaves for the plantation and acted as an overseer. Eventually he returned to London.
33–40	1777–84	Equiano was mostly employed as a servant in England. He offered to become a missionary in Africa, but was turned down. In 1774 he tried to save a fellow black John Annis from being kidnapped from London into slavery. In 1783 Equiano brought the case of the slave ship *Zong* (whose captain threw 133 slaves overboard to claim the insurance) to the attention of the white abolitionist, Granville Sharp.
40–43	1784–7	Travelled to America. Back in Britain, in 1786 joined a government expedition to move black people who had been living in London to Sierra Leone, West Africa. Equiano was accused of corruption but cleared. The expedition was a complete failure.
43–45	1787–88	Equiano wrote and published his autobiography, 'The interesting narrative . . .'
45–53	1789–97	In 1792 he married Susanna Cullen, a white woman, at Soham in Cambridgeshire. Two daughters were born – Ann Mary, 16 October 1793, and Joanna, 11 April 1795. Equiano died in 1797.

Box 10.2   Equiano's life as portrayed on film

Watch the clip where Equiano buys his freedom. The script is given below.

Robert King and Captain Farmer sit at a table. A clock ticks heavily.

ROBERT KING: Well?

(*Equiano places bag of money on desk*)

EQUIANO: Forty pounds sterling.

ROBERT KING: You deserve freedom? I treat you well Gustavus. Isn't life sweet?

EQUIANO: A life without liberty is no life, sir. Besides which, I have always known you to be a man of your word, and did you not say forty pounds would buy my freedom?

[*Video commentary*]

ROBERT KING: Draw up the manumission [freedom] papers.

[*Video commentary*]

ROBERT KING: There's gratitude for you. He'll be back. He'll soon find freedom a heavy load.

(*Equiano glances at Farmer during the dialogue. Farmer says nothing at all*)

Now read this extract from Equiano's 'Interesting Narrative'.

We set sail once more for Montserrat and arrived there safe; but much out of humour with our friend, the silversmith. When we had unladen the vessel and I had sold my venture finding myself master of about forty-seven pounds, I consulted my true friend, the captain, how I should proceed in offering my master the money for my freedom. He told me to come on a certain morning, when he and my master would be at breakfast together. Accordingly, on that morning I went and met the captain there, as he had appointed. When I went in I made my obeisance to my master and with my money in my hand and many fears in my heart, I prayed him to be as good as his offer to me, when he was pleased to promise me my freedom as soon as I could purchase it.

This speech seemed to confound him; he began to recoil, and my heart that instant sank within me. 'What', said he, 'give you your freedom? Why, where did you get the money? Have you got forty pounds sterling?' 'Yes Sir,' I answered. 'How did you get it?' replied he. I told him, 'very honestly'. The captain then said he knew I got the money very honestly and with much industry and that I was particularly careful. On which my master replied, I got money much faster than he did and said he would not have made me the promise which he did, had he thought I should have got the money so soon. 'Come, come,' said my worthy captain, clapping my master on the back, 'Come, Robert, I think you must let him have his freedom. You have laid your money out very well, you have received good interest for it all this time and here is now the principal at last. I know Gustavus has earned you more than a hundred a year and he will still save you money, as he will not leave you. Come, Robert, take the money'.

continued

My master then said, he would not be worse than his promise and, taking the money, told me to go to the Secretary at the Register Office and get my manumission drawn up.

These words of my master were like a voice from heaven to me. In an instant all my trepidation was turned into unutterable bliss and I most reverently bowed myself with gratitude, unable to express my feelings, but by the overflowing of my eyes and a heart replete with thanks to God; while my true and worthy friend, the captain, congratulated us both with a peculiar degree of heartfelt pleasure.

As soon as the first transports of my joy were over and that I had expressed my thanks to these my worthy friends in the best manner I was able, I rose with a heart full of affection and reverence and left the room in order to obey my master's joyful mandate of going to the Register Office. As I was leaving the house I called to mind the words of the Psalmist, in the 126th Psalm and like him, I glorified God in my heart, in whom I trusted. These words had been impressed on my mind from the very day I was forced from Deptford to the present hour and I now saw them as I thought, fulfilled and verified.

Question 1.

a) Underline the parts of the extract the film makers used.

b) Now write proper sentences to give answers to the following:
    i) what did they put in the film?
    ii) what did they leave out?
    iii) what did they change?
    iv) what did they make up?
    v) why did the film makers make these decisions?

Question 2.

a) From all that you have heard and read what impression do you get of Equiano?

b) What do the historians say about him?

c) Now decide where 'Hidden empire' belongs on the scale shown below.

Not very true   Very true

          1   2   3   4   5

The use of Equiano's *Interesting Narrative* as a focus of study served a maximal combination of history and citizenship aims. The sequence of questions set the study of the text (the *Interesting Narrative*) and the 'Hidden empire' programme within the context of National Curriculum knowledge, skills and understanding: 'Pupils should be taught to . . . use a range of appropriate sources of information . . . as a basis for independent historical enquiries, (b) evaluate the sources used . . . and read conclusions.' However, while Equiano's *Interesting Narrative* is clearly a source of information, it is also an interpretation by Equiano, 'a conscious reflection' on his past, shaped by the passage of time and other motives. The same can be said of the 'Hidden empire' programme. So when students considered National Curriculum knowledge, skills and understanding 'Historical interpretation', they were evaluating two interpretations of the same life produced in very different circumstances. The evaluation of both interpretations gives students as much insight into the way subsequent views of history are constructed as it does into the detail of Equiano's boyhood experiences and feelings.

The well-developed processes of historical interpretation within school history also strengthen the skills of 'enquiry and communication' set out in the Citizenship Orders: 'Pupils should be taught to think about topical political, spiritual, moral, social and cultural issues, problems and events by analysing information and its sources.'

An objection might be raised here that Equiano is not topical or contemporary. However, consider two questions the students were asked to discuss at the conclusion of the schemes of work: 'Why was Equiano (originally) chosen as a statue for the faith zone in the Millennium Dome?' 'Was Equiano's identity: (a) African; (b) English; (c) British; (d) Afro-British; (e) Black British; (f) Black English? Why does this question matter?'

Students' opinions split when considering these issues alongside the big question 'Olaudah Equiano – African Hero?' In discussion the majority considered that Equiano was a suitable candidate for African hero status, though with reservations about possible embellishments to the *Interesting Narrative*. A minority, particularly shocked by the barbarity of the trade, defended Equiano, maintaining that it was not possible to exaggerate these horrors. A small group of sceptics remained extremely cautious about Equiano's record, because of the context in which the *Interesting Narrative* was written. Debate about Equiano's identity picked up issues raised in discussions on Sayi McDermott's family tree. Students were comfortable with Heater's (1998) concept of multiple identities in relation to Equiano but considered him more African than anything else. The students concluded their study of differing interpretations of the slave trade and its abolition by analysing responses from members of the public to an exhibition about the Bristol slave trade. This was particularly controversial since Bristol was one of Britain's principal slaving ports and reactions to the exhibition brought into focus issues at a city level, which British society as a whole is still struggling with.

Equiano was born in Africa but died a wealthy gentleman in England. He was happy to be known by both his African name and, perhaps as an ironic badge of pride, his slave name 'Gustavus Vassa'. Yet he tempered this last name by calling himself 'Gustavus Vassa the African'. There was no contradiction in this devoutly Christian convert reviling the slave trade of the country which had enslaved him while simultaneously adopting it as his home. Rich stories like his need to be analysed in the light of the shifting definitions of citizenship and identity in the present. However, the many contradictions of the present can only be fully understood by exploration of the past. This is why school history and citizenship education pushed to their maximal extent are natural allies.

Key questions

1   To what extent is the overlap of definitions between citizenship and identity valid?

2   What implications does this treatment of Equiano have for multicultural approaches in both citizenship and history?

3   Does the role of interpretations of history in this sequence of teaching support the claim that citizenship need not become a vehicle for any present political viewpoint?

Recommended reading

W. Kymlicka (1995) *Multicultural Citizenship*. Oxford, Oxford University Press.

D. Lowenthal (1998) *The Heritage Crusade and the Spoils of History*. Cambridge, Cambridge University Press.

Part III

Conclusions

Conclusions

The past is the fabric that throws citizenship into relief; it is the springboard from which citizens learn to think and act. As an academic discipline, history is closely allied with the issues of citizenship, and the aims and methods of teaching and learning history in schools coincide neatly with the principal concerns of the characterisation of citizenship developed by the authors of the National Curriculum. The current situation is a positive one in which the purpose and place of history in the secondary school curriculum are more assured. This is both in spite of the largely unhelpful, negative, angst-ridden outbursts (occurring on an almost annual basis), that describe history as being forever in danger, and because of the boost that can be provided by citizenship. History has always been potentially important and useful for adolescents. The opportunity is now more readily available for teachers and others to help school students learn and act as citizens.

These positive developments may alarm some people. If one considers the full range of purposes of the school curriculum, some may feel that teachers are being asked to do too much or to do what can be done elsewhere. Some of these ideas have been rebutted earlier in this book. It is worth emphasising, however, that if one sees the curriculum as offering opportunities for academic pursuit, personal growth or some sort of professionally based utilitarian method of developing individuals and democratic society in particular ways, then citizenship education can help the history teacher. The issues of citizenship are intellectually demanding, they are intimately bound up with intensely personal notions such as identity and the goal is for education to make a positive contribution. Citizenship education offers teachers the opportunity to develop their own particular emphasis within a coherent but flexible framework.

It is hoped that this book will assist teachers to develop clearer insights into citizenship. The proliferation of models of citizenship has led to what, at times, have been confused and confusing debates, often conducted between separate and somewhat closed groups of political scientists, philosophers and sociologists rather than with and between teachers. The need to clarify the debates associated with rights, responsibilities, identity and action for a pluralistic modern democracy is still pressing and will not be achieved in a simple and straightforward manner. There is not only the challenge of characterising citizenship theoretically but also, and very importantly, considering how key ideas can be seen to relate in the real world of citizenship as practised. Furthermore, there is a need to deliberately identify the links between theory and practice by focusing on the perspectives that are used to interpret applications, expressions or developments of citizenship. This can only be done in a way that includes teachers. The purpose of this book is to discuss and explore issues and to try to encourage responses from teachers, not to pretend that the one way forward has been found.

This rather recessive approach is important. We wish to make it clear that while all aspects of citizenship education cannot be covered in a single book, an attempt has been made to allow the reader to make certain links. The authors want to encourage readers to develop a variety of pathways through the book. Two brief examples will be given of work that is necessary but not covered in any great detail in this book.

Local history and initial teacher education do not have their own chapters in this book but both are very important. In the Foreword to the subject Orders it is stated that the rationale behind the National Curriculum is to allows schools 'to develop a distinctive character and ethos rooted in their local communities' (DfEE/QCA 1999b: p. 4). We do, of course, recognise that there is a great value in the contribution of local history to historical education. Perhaps history education has the potential to help build local communities, an intention expressed in the new National Curriculum. We support the claim made explicitly in the History Order that we should seek a balance between global, national and local history. However, we suggest that there is potential in seeing historical work as contributing both to developing understanding of these particular contexts (e.g. local history) and in developing a more integrated perspective on the nature of historical knowledge. Our chapters, we hope, illuminate the meaning of citizenship, provide clarity about policy making undertaken by a national committee, and show case studies bounded by both geographical frameworks and by historical/citizenship topics. Local history, while not given exhaustive treatment in this book, is nevertheless, we would argue, considered explicitly. Local history is a matter that relates generally to citizenship, it is of obvious relevance to communitarianism, it is affected by the policy statements of national government agencies and it is linked with historical topics that have international resonance. We see citizenship education as emerging from an analysis of the development of contemporary society and as a way of equipping learners with the knowledge, skills and understanding to contribute to a democratic global community, but in various ways and at a number of different levels.

Teacher education is similarly not covered exhaustively and yet the links are there if the content, concepts and processes discussed in this book are explored. The general issues about the meaning of citizenship and its place within history education are of course relevant. All of the authors are involved in initial and continuing education for teachers that relates directly to citizenship education, and some of the discussions and issues that are covered in this book have been tested with student teachers and more experienced colleagues. The new PGCE courses (graduate initial teacher education) in history and citizenship are welcomed. But the focus of this book is on what should and could happen in schools. The focal point of education systems is young people: how well they understand difficult issues and how they approach their assignments.

Given the positive opportunity that now exists, what needs to be done? In very general terms two difficult questions need to be answered. Firstly, what do school students need to demonstrate for us to be convinced that they have achieved a good standard? Secondly, how should school students relate to their peers and others when achieving professionally based goals? Both questions require careful thought and action. Whereas we do have at least a developing research-based notion of the types and levels of thinking normally achieved in history by students, we are seemingly still in a rhetorical phase of citizenship education, in which assertion is met with counter-assertion without supporting evidence. Democratic goals are not the same as intended learning outcomes. We need to know a good deal more about, for example, students' understandings (whether justified or not) of citizenship. The question of student action is also important but very challenging. Perhaps one of the key defining features of citizenship is concerned with the way in which we interact with others. The task of uncovering and promoting the processes that provide meaningful democratic discourse is very demanding. This is not to suggest some simple and inappropriate point about the supposed necessity, for example, for classrooms to reflect the ideal of a participative democracy. If our wider democratic society cannot achieve this it would be unfair and inappropriate to exhort schools to do so. However, there is currently a lack of understanding about what works best, in educational terms, for engaging students with a variety of people. Citizenship education cannot take place in a vacuum; it will never exist if we imagine that we are making plans for a utopian desert island; but some progress may be made if we celebrate those who have achieved successful outcomes with students through responsible and appropriate pedagogy. Personal experience suggests that these and other difficult matters may be at least partially resolved if teachers are invited to join curriculum projects. This would not mean handing more work to already hard-pressed people but rather forging partnerships between a variety of individuals and institutions (universities, local education authorities, schools, community groups) so that new methods can be developed. At the end of a long period in which teachers were ignored or used only as technicians to be dictated to, more collaborative approaches may now be possible. The justification for and elaboration of the nature of these projects cannot be given here but the fact that the DfES is currently funding a range of initiatives that involve teachers gives some cause for hope.

It is our hope that all those involved in the teaching and learning of history will find this book is of some use in their search for clearer understanding and better practice.

References

Abrams, F. (1993) 'Rights, duties and the greater scheme', *Times Educational Supplement*, 4020, 16 July, p. 10.

Acton, E. (2000) 'The great history debate', symposium, University of East Anglia, Norwich, 23 May.

Adey, K. (2000) 'Factors influencing pupils' decision to take history at Key Stage 4', paper presented at History Teacher Education Network (HTEN) Conference, Homerton College Cambridge, July.

Ahrendt, D. (1998) *Young People's Attitudes to the European Union: a typology of public opinion among young Europeans (Eurobarometer 47.1)*, Brussels, European Commission, DG X.

Albala-Bertrand, L. (1995) 'The need to reinforce citizenship education worldwide: a conceptual framework for research', *Educational Innovation and Information*, 82, March.

Aldrich, R. (1997) *The End of History and the Beginning of Education*, London, Institute of Education.

Anderson, B. (1991) *Imagined Communities*, London, Verso.

Andrews, G. (ed.) (1991) *Citizenship*, London, Lawrence and Wishart.

Angell, A.V. and Hahn, C.L. (1996) 'Global perspectives', in W.C. Parker *Educating the Democratic Mind*, New York, SUNY.

Annette, J. (1997) 'Citizenship studies and higher education', paper presented at Values and the Curriculum Conference, Institute of Education, London, 10–11 April.

Appiah, L. (1999) 'Reflections or transformations: representations of Britishness in the Citizenship Curriculum', paper presented at the University of London Institute of Education Conference on Citizenship, July.

Appleby, J., Hunt, L. and Jacob, M. (1994) *Telling the Truth About History*, New York, W.W. Norton.

Arnold, J. (2000) *History: a very short introduction*, Oxford, Oxford University Press.

Arnot, M., Araújo, H., Deliyanni-Kouimtzi, K., Rowe, G. and Tomé, A. (1996) 'Teachers, gender and discourses of citizenship', *International Studies in the Sociology of Education*, 6(1) pp. 3–35.

Arthur, J. (1998) 'Communitarianism: what are the implications for education?', *Educational Studies*, 24(3) pp. 353–68.

Arthur, J. (2000) *Schools and Community: the communitarian agenda in education*, London, Falmer Press.

Arthur, J. and Davison, J. (2000) 'Social, literacy and citizenship education in the school curriculum', *The Curriculum Journal*, 11(1) pp. 9–23.

Audigier, F. (1998) *Basic Concepts and Core Competences of Education for Democratic Citizenship: an initial consolidated report*, Strasbourg, Council of Europe.

Bage, G. (1999) *Narrative Matters*, London, Falmer Press.

Baker, K. (1988) 'A pattern of timeless moments', *Daily Telegraph*, 14 April.

Baker, C., Cohn, T. and McLaughlin, M. (1999) 'Inspecting subject knowledge', in J. Arthur and R. Phillips (eds) *Issues in History Teaching*, London, Routledge.

Baldwin, G. (1994) 'A Dearing opportunity: history teaching and moral education', *Teaching History*, June, 76 pp. 29–32.

Banham, D. (1998) 'Getting ready for the Grand Prix: learning how to build a substantiated argument in year 7', *Teaching History*, 92 pp. 6–15.

Banham, D. (2000) *King John*, London, John Murray.

Barber, M. (1996) *The Learning Game: arguments for an education revolution*, London, Indigo.

Batho, G. (1990) 'The history of the teaching of civics and citizenship in English schools', *The Curriculum Journal*, 1(1) pp. 91–100.

Beck, J. (1998) *Morality and Citizenship in Education*, London, Cassell.

Beck, U. (2000) *What is Globalisation?*, London, Polity Press.

Bell, D. (1993) *Communitarianism and its Critics*, Oxford, Clarendon Press.

Bellah R.N., Madsen, R., Sulliva, W.M., Swidler, A. and Tipton, S.M. (1985) *Habits of the Heart: individualism and commitment in American life*, Berkeley, University of California Press.

Bentley, T. (1999) 'Will we blow apart society?', *New Statesman*, 27 September, pp. xviii–xix.

Bloom, A. (1987) *The Closing of the American Mind*, New York, Simon and Schuster.

Blunkett, D. (1999) Address, University of London Institute of Education Conference on Citizenship, 7 July.

Blunkett, D. (2000) Quoted in 'Tomorrow's citizens', *Times Educational Supplement*, 1 December.

Boult, M. (1980) 'A recent research project into children's historical thinking, and its implications for history teaching', *Developments in History Teaching*, University of Exeter Perspectives, 4 pp. 3–15.

Bourne, H. (1905) *The Teaching of History and Civics in the Elementary and the Secondary School*, London, Longmans/Green.

Bousted, M. and Davies, I. (1996) 'Teachers' perceptions of models of political learning', *Curriculum*, 17(1) pp. 12–23.

Bracey, P. (1995) 'Ensuring continuity and understanding through the teaching of British history', in R. Watts and I. Grosvenor (eds) *Crossing the Key Stages of History: effective history teaching 5–16 and beyond*, London, David Fulton.

British Youth Council (BYC) (1997) *Lobby Queue: a young person's guide to lobbying*, London, British Youth Council.

Brittan, L. (1996) 'European citizenship', unpublished speech to the annual conference of the Politics Association, University of York, September.

Brown, C. (1991) 'Education for citizenship – old wine in new bottles?', *Citizenship*, 1(2) pp. 6–9.

Brown, L. (1994) *State of the World*, New York, W.W. Norton.

Bryant, C.G.A. (1997) 'Citizenship, national identity and the accommodation of difference: reflections on the German, French, Dutch and British cases', *New Community*, 23(2) pp. 157–72.

Bryson, V. (1993) 'Feminism', in R. Eatwell and A. Wright (eds) *Contemporary Political Ideologies*, London, Pinter Publishers.

Burston, W.H. and Green, C.W. (1972) *Handbook for History Teachers*, London, Methuen.

Butterfield, H. (1951) *History and Human Relations: moral judgement in history*, London, Collins.

Callan, E. (1997) *Creating Citizens: political education in a liberal democracy*, Oxford, Oxford University Press.

Cannon, D. (1994) *Generation X and the New Work Ethic*, The Seven Million Project Working Paper 1, London, DEMOS.

Carr, E.H. (1961) *What is History?*, London, Pelican.

Cassidy, S. (1999) 'School day to be made longer', *Times Educational Supplement*, 14 May, pp. 1–2.

Claire, H. (1996) *Reclaiming Our Pasts: equality and diversity in the primary history curriculum*, Stoke on Trent, Trentham Books.

Cloonan, M. and Davies, I. (1998) 'Improving the possibility of better teaching by investigating the nature of student learning: with reference to procedural understanding in politics in higher education', *Teaching in Higher Education*, 3(2) pp. 173–83.

Cogan, J.J. (1998) 'Citizenship education for the 21st century: setting the context', in J.J. Cogan and R. Derricott (1998) *Citizenship for the 21st Century*, London, Kogan Page.

Cogan, J.J. and R. Derricott (1998) *Citizenship for the 21st Century*, London, Kogan Page.

Colley, L. (1992) *Britons: forging the nation 1707–1837*, London, Pimlico.

Coman, P. (1999) 'Mentioning the war: does studying World War II make any difference to pupils' sense of British achievement and identity?', *Teaching History*, 96, October.

Commission for Racial Equality (CRE) (1996) *Roots of the Future: ethnic diversity in the making of Britain*, London, CRE.

Commission on Citizenship (1990) *Encouraging Citizenship: report of the Commission on Citizenship*, London, HMSO.

Convery, A., Evans, M., Green, S., Macaro, E. and Mellor, J. (1997) *Pupils' Perceptions of Europe: identity and education*, London, Cassell.

Council for Environmental Education/Development Education Association (CEE/DEA) (1998) *Education for Sustainable Development in the Schools Sector: a report to DFEE/QCA from the Panel for Education for Sustainable Development*, Reading, CEE.

Counsell, C. (1997) *The Twentieth Century World*, London, The Historical Association.

Crawford, K. (1995) 'A history of the Right: the battle for control of National Curriculum History 1989–1994', *British Journal of Educational Studies*, 43(4) pp. 433–456.

Crewe, I., Searing, D. and Conover, P. (1996) *Aspects of Citizenship in Britain and the United States: a comparative study*, Brentwood, University of Essex.

Crick, B. (1978) 'Basic concepts for political education', in B. Crick and A. Porter *Political Education and Political Literacy*, London, Longman.

Crick, B. (1998) *Education for Citizenship and the Teaching of Democracy in Schools*: part one, *Advisory group initial report*, London, QCA.

Crick, B. (2000) *Essays on Citizenship*, London, Continuum.

Crick, B. and Lister, I. (1978) 'Political literacy', in B. Crick and A. Porter *Political Education and Political Literacy*, London, Longman.

Crick, B. and Porter, A. (eds) (1978) *Political Education and Political Literacy*, London, Longman.

Davies, I. (1994a) 'Whatever happened to political literacy?', *Educational Review*, 46(1) pp. 15–27.

Davies, I. (1994b) 'Teaching and learning about interpretations of the recent European past for the purposes of developing European citizenship in secondary schools', *Discoveries: a journal for history teachers*, 4 pp. 22–5.

Davies, I. (1995a) 'Teaching and learning about the recent European past – one contribution to the development of European citizenship', *Teaching History*, 81 pp. 26–31.

Davies, I. (1995b) 'Education for European citizenship and the teaching and learning of history', in A. Osler, H.-F. Rathenow and H. Starkey (eds) *Teaching for Citizenship in Europe*, Stoke on Trent, Trentham Books.

Davies, I. (1996) 'Values and the teaching and learning of European history', *Children's Social and Economics Education*, 1(1) pp. 51–60.

Davies, I. (1997) 'Education for European citizenship: issues in history education', *Evaluation and Research in Education*, 11(3) pp. 119–128.

Davies, I. (1999) 'What has happened in the teaching of politics in schools in England in the last three decades and why?', *Oxford Review of Education*, 25 (1 and 2) pp. 125–40.

Davies, I. and John, P. (1995) 'History and citizenship', *Teaching History*, 78 pp. 5–7.

Davies, I. and Rey, M. (1998) 'Questioning identities: issues for teachers and children', in C. Holden and N. Clough (eds) *Children as Citizens: education for participation*, London, Jessica Kingsley Publishers.

Davies, I. and Sobisch, A. (eds) (1997) *Developing European Citizens*, Sheffield, SHU Press.

Davies, I., Gray, G. and Stephens, P. (1998) 'Education for citizenship: a case study of "Democracy Day" at a comprehensive school', *Educational Review*, 50(1), pp. 15–27.

Davies, I., Gregory, I. and Riley, S. (1997) 'Concepts of citizenship: results of research on teacher perceptions in England', paper for British Education Research Association, 1997, Conference at University of York.

Davies, I., Gregory, I. and Riley, S. (1999) *Good Citizenship and Educational Provision*, London, Falmer Press.

Davies, N. (1999a) *The Isles: a history*, London, Macmillan.

Davies, N. (1999b) 'But we never did stand quite alone', *The Guardian*, 13 November, review section p. 3.

De Tocqueville, A. [1835] (1945) *Democracy in America*, ed. P. Bradley, New York, Vintage.

Dekker, H. and Portengen, R. (1996) 'European citizenship: policies and effects', in W. Friebel (ed.) *Education for European Citizenship: theoretical and practical approaches*, Freibourg, RIF 1, pp. 176–86.

Demaine, J. and Entwistle, N. (1996) *Beyond Communitarianism: citizenship, politics and education*, Basingstoke: Macmillan.

Department for Education and Employment (DfEE) (1995) *History*, London, DfEE.

Department for Education and Employment (1998a) 'Blunkett welcomes initial report of advisory group on citizenship education in schools', *DfEE Press Release 155/98*, London, DfEE.

Department for Education and Employment (1998b) 'New report points the way to citizenship education for all pupils', *DfEE Press Release 433/98*, London, DfEE.

Department for Education and Employment (1999) *Preparing Young People for Adult Life: a report by the National Advisory Group on Personal, Social and Health Education*, London, DfEE.

Department for Education and Employment/QCA (1999a) *History: the National Curriculum for England*, London, DfEE/QCA.

Department for Education and Employment /QCA (DfEE/QCA) (1999b) *Citizenship: the National Curriculum for England*, London, DfEE/QCA.

Department for Education and Employment/Qualifications and Curriculum Authority (1999c) *Citizenship: Key Stages 3–4*, London, DfEE/QCA.

Department for Education and Employment/Qualifications and Curriculum Authority (1999d) *Framework for Personal Social and Health Education and Citizenship at Key Stages 1 and 2*, London, DFEE/QCA.

Department for Education and Science (DES) (1985) *History in the Primary and Secondary Years: an HMI view*, London, HMSO.

Department for Education and Science (DES) (1990) *History in the National Curriculum*, London, HMSO.

Department for Education and Science (DES) (1991) *History in the National Curriculum* (England), London, HMSO.

Dewey, J. (1966) *Democracy and Education*, London, Free Press/Macmillan.

Di Gennaro, A.M. (1998) *Teacher Training Courses 1992–1997: an overview*, Education for Democratic Citizenship, CDCC In-Service Teacher Training Programme, Strasbourg: Council of Europe.

Dreyden, J. (1989) 'Multiculturalism and the structure of knowledge', paper given to the National Foundation for Educational Research.

Edgington, D. (1982) 'The role of history in multi-cultural education', *Teaching History*, 32, pp. 4–6.

Eliot, T.S. (1974) *Collected Poems*, London, Faber.

Equiano, O. (1995) *The Interesting Narrative and Other Writings*, London, Penguin.

Etzioni, A. (1997) *The New Golden Rule: community and morality in a democratic society*, New York, Basic Books.

European Commission (1997a) *1997: European Year Against Racism: the survey*, Brussels, European Commission, DG X.

European Commission (1997b) *Towards a Europe of Knowledge*, Brussels, European Commission.

European Commission (1997c) *Accomplishing Europe through Education and Training*, Study Group on Education and Training report, Brussels, European Commission.

European Commission (1998) *Education and Active Citizenship in the European Union*, Brussels, European Commission.

Evans, A. (1999) 'Citizenship and identity: European dimensions', paper given at the University of London Institute of Education Conference on Citizenship, July.

Evans, R. (1997) *In Defence of History*, London, Granta Books.

Ferguson, N. (ed.) (1997) *Virtual History: alternatives and counterfactuals*, London, Picador.

Ferro, M. (1981) *The Use and Abuse of History*, London, Routledge and Kegan Paul.

Finberg, H.P.L. and Skipp, V.H.T. (1973) *Local History: objective and pursuit*, Newton Abbott, David and Charles.

Firth, C.B. (1929) *The Learning of History in Elementary Schools*, London, Kegan Paul, Trench, Trubner.

Fisher, P. (1999) 'Analysing Anne Frank: a case study in the teaching of thinking skills', *Teaching History*, 95.

Fontaine, P. (1991) *A Citizen's Europe*, Brussels, Commission of the European Communities.

Fowler, R.B. (1995) 'Definitions of community', in A. Etzioni (ed.) *The New Communitarian Thinking*, Richmond, University of Virginia Press.

Fullan, M. (1991) *The New Meaning of Educational Change*, London, Cassell.

Gardner, J. (ed.) (1995) *The History Debate*, London, Calliers and Brown.

Giddens, A. (1998) *The Third Way: the renewal of social democracy*, London, Polity Press.

Giddens, A. (1999) 'Social change in Britain', 10th ESRC Annual Lecture.

Giroux, H.A. *et al.* (1996) *Counter Narratives*, New York, Routledge.

Goalen, P. (1999) 'Pupils' perspectives on the history curriculum', in R. Phillips and G. Easdown (eds) *History Education: Subject Knowledge, Pedagogy and Practice*, Standing Conference of History Teacher Educators in the United Kingdom.

Goalen, P. (1988) 'Multiculturalism and the lower school history syllabus', *Teaching History*, 53 pp. 8–16.

Gold, K. (2000) 'Stick with Blunkett's belief in social glue', *Times Educational Supplement*, 28 December, p. 8.

Goldby, M. (1997) 'Communitarianism and education', *Curriculum Studies*, 5(2) pp. 125–38.

Gooch, G.P. (1936) *Citizenship and History*, London, Association for Citizenship in Education.

Goodson, I. (1997) 'The educational researcher as public intellectual: modernist dinosaur or postmodernist prospect?', The Stenhouse Lecture, British Educational Research Association Annual Conference, University of York, September.

Green, A. (1997) *Education, Globalization and the Nation State*, Basingstoke: Macmillan.

Gutman, A. (1985) 'Communitarian critics of liberalism', *Philosophical and Public Affairs*, 14(3).

Hahn, C.L. (1998) *Becoming Political: comparative perspectives on citizenship education*, New York, State University of New York Press.

Happold, F.C. (1935) *Citizens in the Making*, London, Christophers.

Harber, C. (1991) 'International contexts for political education', *Educational Review*, 43(3) pp. 245–55.

Haydn, T. (1992) 'History for ordinary children', *Teaching History*, 67 pp. 8–11.

Haydn, T. (1999) 'Citizenship and school history: in defence of or as a protection against the state?', *School Field: theorising citizenship education II*, X(3) pp. 33–46.

Haydn, T. (2000) 'Teaching the Holocaust through history', in I. Davies (ed.) *Teaching the Holocaust: educational dimensions, principles and practice*, London, Continuum.

Heater, D. (1974) *History Teaching and Political Education*, London, Politics Association, Occasional Pamphlet, 1.

Heater, D. (1978) 'History and political literacy', in B. Crick and A. Porter, *Political Education and Political Literacy*, London, Longman.

Heater, D. (1980) *World Studies: education for international understanding in Britain*, London, Harrap.

Heater, D. (1984) *Peace through Education: the contribution of the Council for Education in World Citizenship*, London, Falmer Press.

Heater, D. (1990) *Citizenship: the civic ideal in world history, Politics and Education*, Harlow, Longman.

Heater, D. (1991) 'Citizenship: a remarkable case of sudden interest', *Parliamentary Affairs*, 44(2).

Heater, D. (1997) 'The reality of multiple citizenship', in I. Davies and A. Sobisch (eds) *Developing European Citizens*, Sheffield, Sheffield Hallam University Press.

Heater, D. (1998) *The Elements of Citizenship*, London, The Citizenship Foundation.

Heater, D. (1999) *What is Citizenship?*, Cambridge, Polity Press.

Held, D. (1995) *Democracy and the Global Order: from the modern state to cosmopolitan governance*, Cambridge, Polity Press.

Hertz, N. (2001) *The Silent Takeover: global capitalism and the death of democracy*, London, Heinemann.

Hicks, D. (ed.) (1988) *Education for Peace: issues, principles and practice in the classroom*, London, Routledge.

Hicks, D. (1994) *Educating for the Future*, Godalming, WWF.

Hicks, D.W. and Holden, C. (1995) *Visions of the Future: why we need to teach for tomorrow*, Stoke on Trent, Trentham Books.

Hield, M. (1888) *Living Pages from Many Ages*, London, Cassell.

Hill, B., Pike, G. and Selby, D. (1998) *Perspectives on Childhood: an approach to citizenship education*, London, Cassell.

Hill, C. (1953) *Suggestions on the Teaching of History*, Paris: UNESCO.

Hobsbawm, E. (1997) *Hobsbawm on History*, London, Weidenfeld and Nicolson.

Hobsbawm, E. and Ranger, T. (eds) (1987) *The Invention of Tradition*, Cambridge, Cambridge University Press.

Holden, C. (1996) 'Enhancing history teaching through a human rights perspective', *Evaluation and Research in Education*, 10(2–3) pp. 113–27.

Horton, J. (1984) 'Political philosophy and politics', in A. Leftwich (ed.) *What Is Politics?*, Oxford, Blackwell.

Hoskin, W.G. (1972) *Local History in England*, London, Longmans.

House of Commons (1997) *Excellence in Schools* (Cm. 3681), London, HMSO.

Hurd, D. (1988) 'Citizenship in the Tory democracy', *New Statesman*, 29 April, p. 14.

Husbands, C. (1996) *What is History Teaching?*, Buckingham, Open University Press.

Ichilov, O. (ed.) (1998) *Citizenship and Citizenship Education in a Changing World*, London, Woburn Press.

Ignatieff, M. (1996) 'Belonging in the past', *Prospect*, November, pp. 22–8.

International Bureau of Education (IBE) (1997) 'What education for what citizenship?', *Educational Innovation and Information*, Geneva, International Bureau of Education.

Janoski, T. (1998) *Citizenship and Civil Society: a framework of rights and obligations in liberal, traditional and social democratic regimes*, Cambridge, Cambridge University Press.

Jenkins, K. (1991) *Rethinking History*, London, Routledge.

Jenkins, K. (1995) *On 'What is History': from Carr and Elton to Rorty and White*, London, Routledge.

Jenks, J. (1998) *Passport: a framework for personal and social education*, London, Gulbenkian Association.

Johnson, M.N. (1995) 'Nineteenth century agrarian populism and twentieth century communitarianism: points of contact', *Peabody Journal of Education*, 70(4) pp. 86–104.

Johnson, P. (1994) *Daily Mail*, 30 April.

Jonathan, R. (1993) 'Education, philosophy of education and the fragmentation of value', *Journal of Philosophy of Education*, 27(2) pp. 171–8.

Jones, B. (ed.) (1973) *Practical Approaches to the New History*, London, Hutchinson Educational.

Joseph, K. (1984) 'History's unique contribution', *Times Educational Supplement*, 17 February.

Jowell, R. and Park, A. (1998) *Young People, Politics and Citizenship: a disengaged generation?*, London, Citizenship Foundation.

Kennedy, K.J. (ed.) (1997) *Citizenship Education and the Modern State*, London, Falmer Press.

Kennedy, P.M. (1993) *Preparing for the Twenty-first Century*, New York, Random House.

Kerr, D. (1999) *Re-examining Citizenship Education: the case of England*, Slough, NFER.

Kerr, D. (1999a) 'Re-examining citizenship education in England', in J. Torney-Purta, J. Schwille and J.-A. Amadeo (eds) *Civic Education Across Countries: twenty-four case studies from the Civic Education Project*, Amsterdam, Eburon Publishers for the International Association for the Evaluation of Educational Achievement (IEA).

Kerr, D. (1999b) *Citizenship Education: an international comparison*, International Review of Curriculum and Assessment Frameworks Paper 4, London, QCA.

Kincheloe, J.L. and Steinberg, S.R. (1997) *Changing Multiculturalism*, Buckingham, Open University Press.

Kniep, W.M. (1986) 'Defining a global education by its content', *Social Education*, October, pp. 437–46.

Knight, P. (1987) 'Historical values', *Journal of Moral Education*, 16(1) pp. 46–53.

Kragh, G. (1995) 'Education for democracy, social justice, respect for human rights and global responsibility: a psychological perspective', in A. Osler and H. Starkey (eds) *Teaching for Citizenship in Europe*, Stoke on Trent, Trentham Books.

Kymlicka, W. (1993) 'Community', in R.E. Goodwin and P. Pettit (eds) *A Companion to Political Philosophy*, Oxford, Blackwell.

Kymlicka, W. (1995) *Multicultural Citizenship*, Oxford, Clarendon.

Lang, S. (1999) 'Democracy is not boring', *Teaching History*, 96.

Lasch, C. (1991) *The True and Only Heaven: progress and its critics*, New York, W.W. Norton.

Lee, P. (1992) 'History in school: aims, purposes and approaches. A reply to John White', in P. Lee, J. Slater, P. Walsh and J. White, *The Aims of School History: the National Curriculum and beyond*, London, Tufnell Press.

Lister, I. (1984) 'The problem with peace studies', paper available from the Department of Educational Studies, University of York.

Lowenthal, D. (1998) *The Heritage Crusade and the Spoils of History*, Cambridge, Cambridge University Press.

Lynch, J. (1992) *Education for Citizenship in a Multicultural Society*, London, Cassell.

McAleavy, T. (1993) 'Using the attainment targets in Key Stage 3: AT 2 Interpretations of History', *Teaching History*, 72 pp. 14–17.

McAleavy, T. (2000) 'Teaching about interpretations', in J. Arthur and R. Phillips (eds) *Issues in History Teaching*, London, Routledge.

McCormick, J. (1996) *The European Union: politics and policies*, Boulder, Colo., Westview Press.

Macdonald, I. (1989) *Murder in the Playground: the report of the Macdonald Enquiry into racism and racial violence in Manchester schools*, London, Longsight.

MacGregor, J. (1990) 'Helping today's children become tomorrow's citizens', speech at the Consultative Conference on Citizenship, Northampton, 16 February.

MacIntyre, A. (1981) *After Virtue: a study in moral theory*, London, Duckworth.

McKienan, D. (1993) 'History in a National Curriculum: imagining the nation at the end of the 20th Century', *Curriculum Studies*, 25(1) pp. 33–51.

McLaughlin, T.H. (1992) 'Citizenship, diversity and education: a philosophical perspective', *Journal of Moral Education*, 21(3) pp. 235–50.

Madeley, H.M. (1920) *History as a School of Citizenship*, Oxford, Oxford University Press.

Major, J. (1993) Correspondence with F. Jarvis, General Secretary to the National Union of Teachers, quoted in C. Chitty and B. Simon (eds) *Education Answers Back*, London, Lawrence and Wishart.

Marsden, W.E. (1989) '"All in a good cause": geography, history and the politicization of the curriculum in the 19th and 20th century England', *Journal of Curriculum Studies* 21(6) p. 510.

Marshall, T.H. (1963) 'Citizenship and social class', in T.H. Marshall, *Sociology at the Crossroads and Other Essays*, London, Heinemann.

Marwick, A. (1981) *The Nature of History*, London, Macmillan.

Mellor, S. and Elliott, M. (1996) *School Ethos and Citizenship*, Melbourne, Australian Council for Educational Research.

Micklewright, J. and Stewart, K. (1999) *Is Child Welfare Converging in the European Union?*, Innocenti Occasional Papers, ESP 69, Florence, UNICEF International Child Development Centre.

Ministry of Education (1952) *Teaching History*, Pamphlet 23, London, HMSO.

Mulhall, S. and Swift, A. (1996) *Liberals and Communitarians*, Oxford, Blackwell.

Murray, M. (1999) 'Three lessons about a funeral: Second World War cemeteries and twenty years of curriculum change', *Teaching History*, 94.

Musgrave, P.H. (1983) 'Some social influences on moral education', in L.O. Ward (ed.) *The Ethical Dimension of the School Curriculum*, Swansea, Pineridge Press.

Naismith, D. (1988) 'My country right or wrong', *Daily Telegraph*, 17 July.

Nash, R. (1998) *Answering the 'Virtuecrats': a moral conversation on character education*, New York, Columbia University, Teachers College Press.

National Advisory Committee on Creative and Cultural Education (NACCCE) (1999) *All Our Futures: creativity, culture and education*, Warwick, NACCCE.

National Center for History in the Schools (1994) *National Standards for History*, Los Angeles, UCLA.

National Commission on Education (1993) *Learning to Succeed: a radical look at education today and a strategy for the future*, report of the Paul Hamlyn Foundation, London, Heinemann.

National Curriculum Council (NCC) (1990) *Education for Citizenship*, Curriculum Guidance 8, York, NCC.

National Curriculum Council (NCC) (1993) *Teaching History at Key Stage 3*, York, NCC.

National Curriculum Council (NCC) (April 1993) *Spiritual and Moral Development: a discussion paper*, York, NCC.

National Forum for Values in Education and the Community (1996) *Values in Education and the Community: final report and recommendations*, London, SCAA.

Oakshott, M. (1956) 'Political education', in P. Laslett (ed.) *Philosophy, Politics and Society*, Oxford, Basil Blackwell, pp. 1–21.

OfSTED (February 1994) *Spiritual, Moral, Social and Cultural Development: an OfSTED discussion paper*, London, OfSTED.

OfSTED (May 1994) *Framework for the Inspection of Schools* (revised edition), London, OfSTED.

Oliver, D. (1991) 'Active citizenship in the 1990s', *Parliamentary Affairs*, 44(2) pp. 157–71.

Oliver, D. and Heater, D. (1994) *The Foundations of Citizenship*, London, Harvester Wheatsheaf.

Oommen, T.K. (1997) *Citizenship, Nationality and Ethnicity*, Cambridge, Polity Press.

Osler, A. and Starkey, H. (1999) 'Rights, identities and inclusion: European action programmes as political education', *Oxford Review of Education* 25 (1&2), pp. 199–215.

Osler, A., Rathenow, H.-F. and Starkey, H. (1996) *Teaching for Citizenship in the New Europe*, Stoke on Trent, Trentham.

Pankania, J. (1994) *Liberating the National Curriculum*, London, Falmer Press.

Park, A. (1995) 'Teenagers and their politics', in R. Jowell, J. Curtice, A. Park, L. Brook and D. Ahrendt with K. Thomson (eds) *British Social Attitudes: the 12th Report*, Aldershot, Dartmouth.

Paul, R. (1998) Quoted in J. MacBeath, 'Turning the tables', *Observer*, 22 February.

Pearce, N. and Hallgarten, J. (2000) *Tomorrow's Citizens: critical debates in citizenship and education*, London, IPPR.

Phillips, D.L. (1993) *Looking Backward: a critical appraisal of communitarian thought*, Princeton, NJ., Princeton University Press.

Phillips, M. (1997) 'The national debt', *New Statesman*, 9 May, pp. 30–1.

Phillips, M. (1999) 'The indoctrination of Citizen Smith jr.', *The Sunday Times*, 7 March, p. 17.

Phillips, R. (1996) 'History teaching, cultural restorationism and national identity in England and Wales', *Curriculum Studies*, 4(3): pp. 385–99.

Phillips, R. (1998a) *History Teaching, Nationhood and the State: a study in educational politics*, London, Cassell.

Phillips, R. (1998b) 'Contesting the past, constructing the future: politics, policy and identity in schools', *British Journal of Educational Studies*, 46 pp. 40–53.

Phillips, R. (1999) 'Government policies, the state and the teaching of history', in J. Arthur and R. Phillips (eds) *Issues in the Teaching of History*, London, Routledge.

Piaget, J. (1932) *The Moral Judgement of Children*, London, Routledge and Kegan Paul.

Pike, G. and Selby, D. (1988) *Global Teacher, Global Learner*, London, Hodder and Stoughton.

Pike, G. and Selby, D. (1995) *Reconnecting: from National to Global Curriculum*, Godalming, WWF.

Popenoe, D. (1994) 'The roots of declining social virtues: family, community and the need for a "natural communities policy"', in D. Popenoe, A. Norton and B. Maley, *Shaping Social Virtues*, St Leonards, NSW, Australia, Centre for Independent Studies.

Porter, A. (1983) *Teaching Political Literacy*, London, Bedford Way.

Postman, N. (1996) 'School's out, forever', *The Guardian*, 20 December.

Postman, N. and Weingartner, C. (1998) Quoted in J. MacBeath, 'Turning the tables', *Observer*, 22 February.

Power, F.C., Higgins, A. and Kohlberg, L. (1989) *Lawrence Kohlberg's Approach to Moral Education*, New York, Columbia University Press.

Price, M. (1968) 'History in danger', *History*, 53 pp. 342–7.

Pring, R. (1999) 'Political education: relevance of the humanities', *Oxford Review of Education*, 25(1&2) pp. 71–87.

Purkis, S. (1980) 'The unacceptable face of history', *Teaching History*, 26, February, pp. 34–5.

Putnam, R. (2000) *Bowling Alone: civic disengagement in America*, New York, Simon and Schuster.

Qualifications and Curriculum Authority (QCA) (1998) *Education for Citizenship and the Teaching of Democracy in Schools*, The Crick Report, London, Qualifications and Curriculum Authority.

Qualifications and Curriculum Authority (1999a) *History: the National Curriculum for England*, London, QCA.

Qualifications and Curriculum Authority (1999b) *Rationale for the School Curriculum and Functions of the National Curriculum*, London, QCA.

Qualifications and Curriculum Authority (1999c) *Revision of the National Curriculum Documents*, London, QCA.

Qualifications and Curriculum Authority (1999d) *The Distinctive Contribution of History to the School Curriculum*, London, QCA.

Qualifications and Curriculum Authority/Department for Education and Employment (QCA/DfEE) (2000a) *Citizenship at Key Stages 3 and 4: initial guidance for schools*, London: QCA/DfEE.

Qualifications and Curriculum Authority/Department for Education and Employment (QCA/DfEE) (2000b) *Personal Social and Health Education and Citizenship at Key Stages 1 and 2: initial guidance for schools*, London: QCA/DfEE.

Rafferty, F. (1999) 'Supporters Rally to Keep Socrates Alive', *Times Educational Supplement*, 29 October, p. 7.

Rauner, M. (1997) 'Citizenship in the curriculum: the globalization of civics education in anglophone Africa: 1955–1995,' in C. McNeely (ed.) *Public Rights, Public Rules: constituting citizens in the world polity and national policy*, New York, Garland Publishing.

Rauner, M. (1999) 'UNESCO as an organizational carrier of civic education information', *International Journal of Educational Development*, 19 pp. 91–100.

Ravitch, D. (1991) 'Pluralism v particularism in American education', *The Responsive Community*, 1(2) pp. 32–45.

Roberts, H. and Sachdev, D. (eds) (1996) *Young People's Social Attitudes – Having their Say: the views of 12–19 year olds*, Ilford, Barnardos.

Roche, M. (1992) *Rethinking Citizenship: welfare, ideology and change in modern society*, Cambridge, Polity Press.

Rogers, A. (1972) *This Was Their World: approaches to local history*, London, BBC Publications.

Rowe, D. (1997) 'Value pluralism, democracy and education for citizenship', in M. Leicester, C. Modgil and F. Modgil (eds) *Values, Culture and Education: political and citizenship education*, London, Cassell.

Rowe, D. (1998) 'Moral and civic education: the search for a robust entitlement model', *Curriculum*, 19(2) pp. 74–83.

Runnymede Trust (2000) *Commission on the Future of Multi-Ethnic Britain*, London, Runnymede Trust.

Said, E. (1993) *Culture and Imperialism*, London, Chatto and Windus.

Samuel, R. (1996) '"Heritage" and the school curriculum', paper delivered to the SCAA Conference on Curriculum, Culture and Society, London, 7 February.

Saunders, L., MacDonald, A., Hewitt, D. and Schagen, S. (1995) *Education for Life: the cross-curricular themes in primary and secondary schools*, Slough, NFER.

Scottish Education Department (1907) *Memorandum on the Study of History in Schools*, Cd 3843, Edinburgh, HMSO.

Scruton, R. (1985) *World Studies: education as indoctrination*, London, Institute for European Defence and Strategic Studies.

Sears, A. (1996) 'Something different to everyone: conceptions of citizenship and citizenship education', *Canadian and International Education*, 25(2) pp. 1–16.

Shemilt, D. (1980) *History 13–16: evaluation study*, Edinburgh, Holmes McDougall.

Sherwood, M. (1988) 'Sins of omission and commission: history in English schools and struggles for change', *Multicultural Teaching*, 16(2) pp. 14–20.

Showman, P.B. (1923) *Citizenship and the School*, Cambridge University Press, – pt II 'a scheme of civic instruction based on history', pp. 39–141.

Singh, B. (1988) 'The teaching of controversial issues: the problems of the neutral-chair approach', in B. Carrington and B. Troyna (eds) *Children and Controversial Issues: strategies for the early and middle years of schooling*, London, Falmer Press.

Slater, J. (1989) *The Politics of History Teaching: a humanity dehumanised?*, London, Institute of Education.

Slater, J. (1995) *Teaching History in the New Europe*, London, Cassell.

Slater, J. and Hennessey, R. (1978) 'Political competence', in B. Crick and A. Porter (eds) *Political Education and Political Literacy*, London, Longman.

Smith, A. (1991) *National Identity*, Harmondsworth, Penguin.

Smith, R.I. (1986) 'Values in history and social studies', in P. Tomlinson and M. Quinton (eds) *Values across the Curriculum*, London, Falmer Press.

Sobisch, A. and Immerfall, S. (1997) 'The social basis of European citizenship', in I. Davies and A. Sobisch (eds) *Developing European Citizens*, Sheffield, Sheffield Hallam University Press.

Steiner, M. (ed.) (1996) *Developing the Global Teacher: theory and practice in initial teacher education*, Stoke on Trent, Trentham Books.

Stenhouse, L. (1970) *The Humanities Curriculum Project*, London, Heinemann.

Stenhouse, L. and Verma, G.K. (1981) 'Educational procedures and attitudinal objectives: a paradox', *Journal of Curriculum Studies*, 13 pp. 329–37.

Stokes, J. (1990) Speech in the House of Commons, quoted in *Sunday Telegraph*, 1 April.

Storry, M. and Childs, P. (eds) (1997) *British Cultural Identities*, London, Routledge.

Stradling, R. (1987) 'Political education and politicization in Britain: a ten year retrospective', paper presented at the International Round Table Conference of the Research Committee on Political Education of the International Political Science Association, Ostkolleg der Bundeszentrale fur Politische Bildung, Cologne, March, pp. 9–13.

Stradling, R. (1995) *The European Content of the School History Curriculum*, Strasbourg, Council for Cultural Co-operation, Council of Europe.

Stradling, R., Noctor, M. and Baines, B. (1984) *Teaching Controversial Issues*, London, Edward Arnold.

Sylvester, D. (1994) 'Change and continuity in history teaching', in H. Bourdillon (ed.) *History Teaching*, London, Routledge.

Supple, C. (1994) 'Teaching about the Holocaust', *Citizenship*, 3(2): pp. 27–8.

Tam, H. (1998) Communitarianism: *a new agenda for politics and citizenship*, London, Macmillan.

Tate, N. (1995a) 'The role of history in the formation of national identity', speech to the Council of Europe Conference, York, 18 September.

Tate, N. (1995b) 'Why we must teach our children to be British', *The Sun*, 19 July.

Tate, N. (1996a) 'Citizenship and lifetime learning,' in Association of Teachers and Lecturers, *Why Learn? Report of an ATL Education Conference*, London, Association of Teachers and Lecturers.

Tate, N. (1996b) Introductory speech at the SCAA Invitation Conference on 'Curriculum, Culture and Society', London, 7–9 February.

Tate, N. (1996c) article in *The Independent*, 27 October.

Teacher Training Agency (1999) *Teaching Standards*, London, TTA.

Thatcher, M. (1993) *The Downing Street Years*, London, HarperCollins.

Thomas, H. (1997) *The Slave Trade: the History of the Atlantic slave trade 1440–1870*, New York: Simon and Schuster.

Torney-Purta, J. (1996) 'The connections of values education and civic education: the IEA civic education study in twenty countries', paper presented at the conference 'Morals for the Millennium: educational challenges in a changing world', Lancaster, July 1996.

Torney-Purta, J., Schwille, J. and Amadeo, J.-A. (eds) (1999) *Civic Education across Countries: 24 case studies from the IEA Civic Education Project*, Amsterdam: Eburon Publishers for the International Association for the Evaluation of Educational Achievement.

Torres, C.A. (1998) *Democracy, Education and Multiculturalism: dilemmas of citizenship in a global world*, Oxford, Rowman and Littlefield.

Travis, A. (1999) 'Britons: the optimists of Europe', *The Guardian*, 1 June.

Turner, B. (ed.) (1993) *Citizenship and Social Theory*, London, Sage.

Turner, B.S. (1990) 'Outline of a theory of citizenship', *Sociology*, 24 pp. 189–217.

UNESCO (1997) *UNESCO for Human Rights Education*, Paris: UNESCO.

Walsh, B. (1999) 'Practical classroom approaches to the iconography of Irish history in the classroom or: how far back do we really go?', *Teaching History*, 97 pp. 16–19.

Walsh, B. (2000) *The Struggle for Peace in Northern Ireland*, London, John Murray.

Walsh, P. (1992) *Education and Meaning*, London, Cassell.

Ward, L.O. (1975) 'History and humanity's teacher', *Journal of Moral Education*, 4 (2) pp. 101–4.

Watts, R. (2000) 'History in Europe: the benefits and challenges of co-operation', in J. Arthur and R. Phillips (eds) *Issues in History Teaching*, London, Routledge.

Westminster Catholic Federation (WCF) (1927) *Historical Textbooks and Readers*, London.

Wexler, P. (1990). 'Citizenship in the semiotic society', in B. Turner (ed.) *Theories of Modernity and Postmodernity*, London: Sage.

White, J. (1996) 'Education and nationality', *Journal of Philosophy of Education*, 30(3) pp. 327–43.

White, P. (1994) 'Citizenship and "spiritual and moral education"', *Citizenship*, 3(2) pp. 7–8.

Whitty, G., Rowe, G. and Appleton, P. (1994) 'Subjects and themes in the secondary school curriculum', *Research Papers in Education*, 9(2) pp. 159–81.

Wilkinson, H. and Mulgan, G. (1995) *Freedom's Children*, London, Demos.

Williams, A.W. (1996) *Researching Local History: a human journey*, London, Longman.

Williams, E. (1964) *Capitalism and Slavery*, London, Collins.

Willow, C. (1997) *Hear! Hear! Promoting Children and Young People's Democratic Participation in Local Government*, London: Local Government Information Unit.

Wort, F.R. (1935) *The Teaching of History in Schools: a new approach*, London, Heinemann.

Wrenn, A. (1998) 'History without the flag-waving', *Times Educational Supplement*, 12 June.

Wrenn, A. (1999) 'Build it in, don't bolt it on: history's opportunity to support critical citizenship', *Teaching History*, 96, pp. 6–12.

Wringe, C. (1999) 'Issues in education for citizenship at national, local and global levels', *The Development Education Journal*, 6(1) pp. 4–6.

Index